The Collaboratory
A co-creative stakeholder engagement process
for solving complex problems

The Collaboratory

A co-creative stakeholder engagement process for solving complex problems

Edited by Katrin Muff

With contributions from

Aaron Williamson, Adam Kahane, Anders Aspling, Anthony Buono, Bill Burck, Caroline Rennie, Claire Maxwell, Eddie Blass, Gregoire Serikoff, Jackie Bagnall, Janette Blainey, John North, Jonas Haertle, Katrin Muff, Louie Gardiner, Mark Drewell, Otto Scharmer, Patrick Frick, Paul Shrivastava, Peter Hayward, Philip Mirvis, Ronald Fry, Stephen Hickman, Svenja Rüger, Thomas Dyllick, Zaid Hassan.

Routledge
Taylor & Francis Group

LONDON AND NEW YORK

First published 2014 by Greenleaf Publishing Limited

Published 2017 by Routledge
2 Park Square, Milton Park, Abingdon, Oxon OX14 4RN
711 Third Avenue, New York, NY 10017, USA

Routledge is an imprint of the Taylor & Francis Group, an informa business

Cover design and illustrations in Introduction: The Value Web www.thevalueweb.org

British Library Cataloguing in Publication Data:
   A catalogue record for this book is available from the British Library.
     ISBN-13: 978-1-78353-143-1 [pbk]
     ISBN-13: 978-1-78353-227-8 [hbk]

This book is dedicated to everybody engaged in making this world a better place—Thank you!

Contents

Foreword by Paul Polman, Chief Executive Officer, Unilever xiii

Introduction 1

Part 1: The collaboratory idea 9

  1 Defining the collaboratory 11
    Katrin Muff

  2 The 50+20 origin of the collaboratory 16
    Katrin Muff, Thomas Dyllick, Mark Drewell, John North,
    Paul Shrivastava, and Jonas Haertle

  3 The social lab revolution 26
    Zaid Hassan

  4 The collaboratory methodology at the Rio+20 conference 31
    Katrin Muff

Part 2: The many dimensions of the collaboratory 39

  5 Enabling the transformative journey: the DesignShop 41
    Bill Burck

  6 Facilitating a collaborative space 47
    Bill Burck, Svenja Rüger, Patrick Frick, Aaron Williamson,
    and Grégoire Serikoff

7 Creating collaboratories in society 58
Zaid Hassan

8 Inviting stakeholders to engage 69
Caroline Rennie

9 Creating and holding a space: learning circles 76
Janette Blainey

10 Whole person learning 85
Claire Maxwell

11 Building cooperative capacity for
generative action: Appreciative Inquiry 92
Ronald Fry

12 Stepping into the emerging future:
principles of Theory U 101
Otto Scharmer

13 Transformative scenario planning: a new way
to work with the future 112
Adam Kahane

Part 3: Examples of the collaboratory 125

14 The collaboratory in the classroom:
Bentley University 127
Anthony Buono

15 Students leading collaboratories:
University of St. Gallen 134
Thomas Dyllick and Katrin Muff

16 Creating connection, conversations,
and courage: the Exeter collaboratory 150
Jackie Bagnall and Stephen Hickman

17 Transforming an organization: participatory
leadership and the Art of Hosting 162
Caroline Rennie

18 Regional organizational change:
community-building in action 171
Philip Mirvis

19 Transforming collaborative institutions:
Australian business schools 186
Eddie Blass and Peter Hayward

20 Long-term stakeholder engagement:
Initiatives of Change in Caux 193
Louie Gardiner

21 A meta-collaboratory: the Globally Responsible
Leadership Initiative 211
John North and Anders Aspling

Part 4: How to get started 227

22 Designing a collaboratory: a narrative roadmap 229
Katrin Muff

23 Differences from other facilitation approaches 246
Eddie Blass and Peter Hayward

24 Concluding summary 252
Katrin Muff

Bibliography 271

About the authors 276

Figures, tables, and boxes

Figures

1 Mind map of authors 4

2 Mind map of contributions 6

2.1 The vision for management education for the world 19

2.2 Benches define the circular space of our collaboratory 21

2.3 Participants in a collaboratory 25

5.1 The model to trigger storytelling about the future 46

12.1 The blind spot of leadership 103

12.2 How the structure of attention (Fields 1–4)
determines the path of social emergence 105

12.3 The U: one process, five movements 107

13.1 The five steps of transformative scenario planning 120

16.1 Collaboratory: a sense-making forestructure 151

18.1 Stages of development in groups, dialogue,
and communities 174

20.1 Initiatives of Change: a theory of change in action 207

22.1 The proposed skeleton agenda one week before the event 231

22.2 Day One check-in on "what wants to move now?" 235

22.3 Collaboratory setting with inner circle (fishbowl) 237

22.4 Attempt to see shifts from check-in to visioning harvesting 240

22.5 Harvesting result from visioning of Day Two 241

22.6 The challenge of combining emerging
      brainstorming prototypes and open space
      projects from the previous day 243

Tables

20.1 Quiet time and adaptive action 199

20.2 Seeding the practice and spirit of Caux and IofC 204

Boxes

4.1 Script to invite selected thought leaders who form
     the inner circle of the discussion 37

13.1 Overview of resources for transformative
      scenario planning processes 122

15.1 Students' learning outcomes 146

18.1 Key FCE principles of community-building 175

18.2 Facilitating community-building: key practices 182

21.1 Fishbowl sessions 213

21.2 Open Space (also known as Open Space
      Technology or OST) 214

21.3 The GRLI Guiding Principles 216

22.1 Storyline developed for the visioning process 238

Foreword

Paul Polman
Chief Executive Officer, Unilever

> If you want to go fast, go alone; if you want to go far, go together.
>
> African Proverb

It is a truism to say the world is changing at a faster pace than any of us can remember—or could ever have imagined. Yet the challenges we face today stem not only from the pace of change but also from its sheer unpredictability. The fact is we are living in a world that is increasingly—and accurately—characterized as Volatile, Uncertain, Complex, and Ambiguous (VUCA).

Wherever we look, old assumptions are giving way to new realities. Natural resources, for example, we are discovering, are not finite. Economic growth is not guaranteed. The world order is not immutable. Planetary boundaries are not inviolable. Navigating these new realities is made more difficult by the increasingly interdependent and highly connected nature of today's society. An issue in one part of the world soon magnifies as it ripples and spreads throughout the globe.

Many of these new realities derive from advances in science and technology. If anything, therefore, we can expect the pace of change to quicken even further, because what we have learned over time is that each new technology simply becomes a tool with which to invent other new technologies. That is why, for example, science has advanced more in the last five years than in the previous five thousand! Change is exponential.

Whatever the uncertainties inherent in all of this, one thing is clear: the scale and magnitude of the changes we face are too big for any one organization, or even one nation, to deal with alone. Real progress can only be made on the basis of genuinely collaborative efforts.

That is the concept that sits at the heart of this book. It is also the thinking that underpins the new model we have developed at Unilever. Under the Unilever Sustainable Living Plan we have made a commitment to double the size of the company, generating much needed growth and prosperity, but in a way that has never been done before: by reducing our overall environmental footprint and by increasing our positive social impact on the communities in which we operate. It is a model based on a total value chain approach. In short, we are only as strong as our weakest link.

The Unilever Sustainable Living Plan represents an audacious goal. More remarkably still, it represents a new approach. From the outset we have made clear that we cannot deliver our objectives alone. We have to learn from—and partner with—others. And the reasons are clear. When you pledge, for example, to source all of your agricultural raw materials from sustainable supplies, it is not enough merely to change your own practices; you have to change the whole context in which you operate. Change has to be systemic, not incremental. This can only be done on an industry-wide basis and with the active participation of other stakeholders, including governments and NGOs. We see this particularly on an issue such as sustainable palm oil and the collective attempts now being made—by governments, retailers, producers, and suppliers—to put an end to illegal deforestation, a major contributor to climate change.

The stakes are high but there is a huge prize if we can get it right. As Klaus Schwab, founder of the World Economic Forum, has shrewdly observed: "The greater the complexity of the system, the greater the risk of systemic breakdown—yet also the greater the opportunities for transformation."

New approaches of the kind we are pioneering at Unilever require leaders with a different mind-set and with a new set of capabilities— men and increasingly women comfortable working in collaborative networks and in partnership with others. That is the only way to address issues as pervasive and deep-seated as, for example, food security, climate change, water scarcity or access to basic sanitation.

Yet, as we know, many business leaders have grown up in traditional hierarchical structures and with a relatively narrow focus on serving the interests of shareholders. Leaders of the future will need to have an intrinsic understanding instead of how networks operate and how to collaborate and build coalitions of the willing. They will need to be as comfortable and as well versed in dealing with NGOs and policy-makers as with customers and suppliers.

For all these leaders—current or potential—this book provides an invaluable roadmap. It demystifies the process of collaboration and shows how, through a structured approach, it can become firmly embedded in any organization. Refreshingly, however, it also recognizes that this is an art not a science. Experimentation is encouraged.

In commending this book, I do so on the basis of proven experience. A year after we launched the Unilever Sustainable Living Plan we initiated our first "Sustainable Living Lab"—an open but structured online forum in which to collect ideas, share good practice, discuss possible partnerships and ultimately co-create solutions to the many challenges we face. The response, in terms of both quality and quantity, was extraordinary. It is an exercise that we have repeated—and will repeat. Guided by the ideas and suggestions in *Collaboratory*, we can now take it to another level.

Paul Polman, April 2014

Introduction

In February 2010, a facilitator by the name of Dan Newman had just received disturbing news.

He was standing in the middle of a ramshackle, cluttered restaurant atop the Harmony Hotel in Addis Ababa, Ethiopia. It was morning, and the restaurant was filling with a group of more than 60 government officials, NGO representatives, herdsmen, farmers, and village elders. Some were dressed in suits, some in uniforms and others in traditional robes. Many of the tribal representatives had never been to a city before. At eight stories, the hotel was one of the tallest buildings in Addis Ababa, and they stood gazing at the views overlooking the city in all four directions.

This group had been assembled for one purpose: to design an equitable, ten-year water-rights program in three water-stressed provinces of Ethiopia. Dan Newman already knew that most of them simply wanted to stake their claim on a diminishing piece of a finite pie. Many had prepared scripts and PowerPoint decks, expecting to address the gathering, formally state their case and await a government decree.

They were in for a big surprise. This was not what worried Dan at the moment, however. He was used to that sort of thing.

What worried him was that he had just been told, ten minutes before the two-day session was about to kick off, that there was no common language across the group. The expectation coming in was that all of them spoke English, meaning Dan would be able to communicate directly with them. But he had just learned this was not the case; most of them did not speak English. Instead, they would have to facilitate the session in

Amharic, which Dan and some of the participants did not speak. There would need to be translations throughout. This complicated things enormously, but it was too late to do anything but plunge ahead.

With no formal introductions or explanation about the process, Dan simply welcomed them and put them right to work.

Within the first hour, there was general annoyance and discomfort across the group that only deepened in the second hour. When would they be able to present their cases? Why were they split into teams drawing diagrams of stakeholder relationships?

Even though Dan did not speak any of the three native languages, he could tell from people's energy and body language that they were very upset. This was okay. He wanted to challenge and break down their usual patterns and expectations.

And it worked. Less than an hour later, the energy in the room was just as high, but it had shifted dramatically. Teams were hard at work, full of excitement as they told stories about a shared future. They were no longer defending what they saw as their right; they were collaboratively designing that future. They had let go of their constituency agendas and were focused on finding answers to the bigger questions. They were no longer visibly frustrated with the challenge of communicating to other language speakers. They were doing everything in their power and good humor to make themselves understood.

By the end of the next day, they had created a shared story about the future. And that future had come alive as they collaborated, not as a brainstorming technique or an abstract idea, but as something real they had created together and believed in. During the debrief at the end of the two-day session, one of the farmers compared the design session to how she makes butter, saying you have to agitate the milk forcefully, but then, with patience, it becomes sweet, rich butter.

This story was written and contributed by Bill Burck.

Finding out how this transformation happened is just one of the reasons you should read this book.

This book is about the kind of transformation that emerged in that group of 62 Ethiopians and that is increasingly emerging in groups around the world thanks to collaboratory practices. This book is about empowering ordinary people to make a difference in the world. It is about providing them with ways to collaboratively make sweet, rich butter out of breathtakingly complex problems.

Buckle up. It will be an exciting journey, full of bumps and hard turns and mysteries, some of which we hope you will solve and all of which we hope you will enjoy.

For some of you, this book will be full of magnificent insight. For others, it may be nothing more than magnificent poppycock.

We do not claim to have all of the answers. We make no claims or guarantees at all. We simply wish to share our approaches to collaborative co-creation and design.

We have seen the value of the approaches described in this book. People we work with tell us they have experienced that value. We hope to show you the many aspects of that value as you turn the pages. We hope to empower you to discover that value for yourself. Or even better, to realize that value in ways we have not even imagined and share them with us in return.

This book is a result of an engaged conversation on comfortable long chairs while on vacation in Sardinia. Thomas was sharing his insights of the reflection papers of his recently completed 12-week collaboratory master's-level course at the University of St. Gallen: the breadth and depth of learning surprised us both and we started sharing stories of our 50+20 community friends who had been experimenting with the "collaboratory" idea we had introduced so colorfully at the United Nations Rio+20 conference in June 2012. We also reflected on the many emails we had been getting asking for help in how to successfully conduct collaboratories. I realized how curious I was to learn more about the ins and outs of the magic around the collaboratory, to understand the larger context of social labs emerging over the past decades and how these enabled the societal transformation so many of us are working for. Claire at Greenleaf was very supportive of the idea to bring together these stories and for better understanding the magic of the collaboratory and off we went.

The landscape of the authors: a mind map of social contributions

It is astonishing to realize how different groups of people spread around the world are working on very similar issues, mostly in total ignorance of each other, until they discover amazing synchronicities and start learning from each other and collaborating, while cross-pollenating their fascinating insights.

The views of the group of authors presented in this book are to some degree a reflection of my own journey of discovering facilitation, my passion for transformative learning and enabling change, and my eternal curiosity of how to create powerful group dynamics and how to work with so many unrelated people on complex issues. I am immensely grateful to every single co-author of this book—many thanks to all of you for having contributed to this work.

The mind map at Figure 1 is a visual attempt to highlight the interconnections among the contributing authors and the related thought leadership.

Figure 1 Mind map of authors

Illustration by The Value Web

How to navigate this book: a mind map of chapter contributions

This book was designed as a practical handbook for those active in transformation change, irrespective of their fields of action: in society, in organizations of all kinds and in the field of education.

- Part 1 of the book sets the stage by explaining what a collaboratory is, where it emerges from, how it is defined and how it fits into the larger context of the social lab revolution that is happening all over the world

- Part 2 unpacks the many dimensions and considerations that contribute to the magic of a collaboratory experience. We offer nine unique insights and perspectives that need to be considered and form an integral part of a successful collaboratory. Certainly there are more dimensions that contribute to a collaboratory. Some of these are covered in the examples of Part 3

- Part 3 offers ten inspiring examples of how a collaboratory could be applied. We look at applications in the educational field (three examples), within organizations (two examples), among institutions (one example), and as movements (four examples in two chapters)

- Part 4 offers a pragmatic outlook on how to get started if you want to use the collaboratory in your own field of work. We do this by providing a narrative roadmap using a real-life example of a co-designed and co-created collaboratory in Norway (Chapter 22), linking it to relevant chapters of Part 2 and Part 3. We also look at how collaboratories differ from other group facilitation approaches and how to best use the methodology in different situations

The mind map here (Figure 2) is a visual attempt to help you navigate this book by pointing out the interconnections between various chapters.

Figure 2 Mind map of contributions

Illustration by The Value Web.

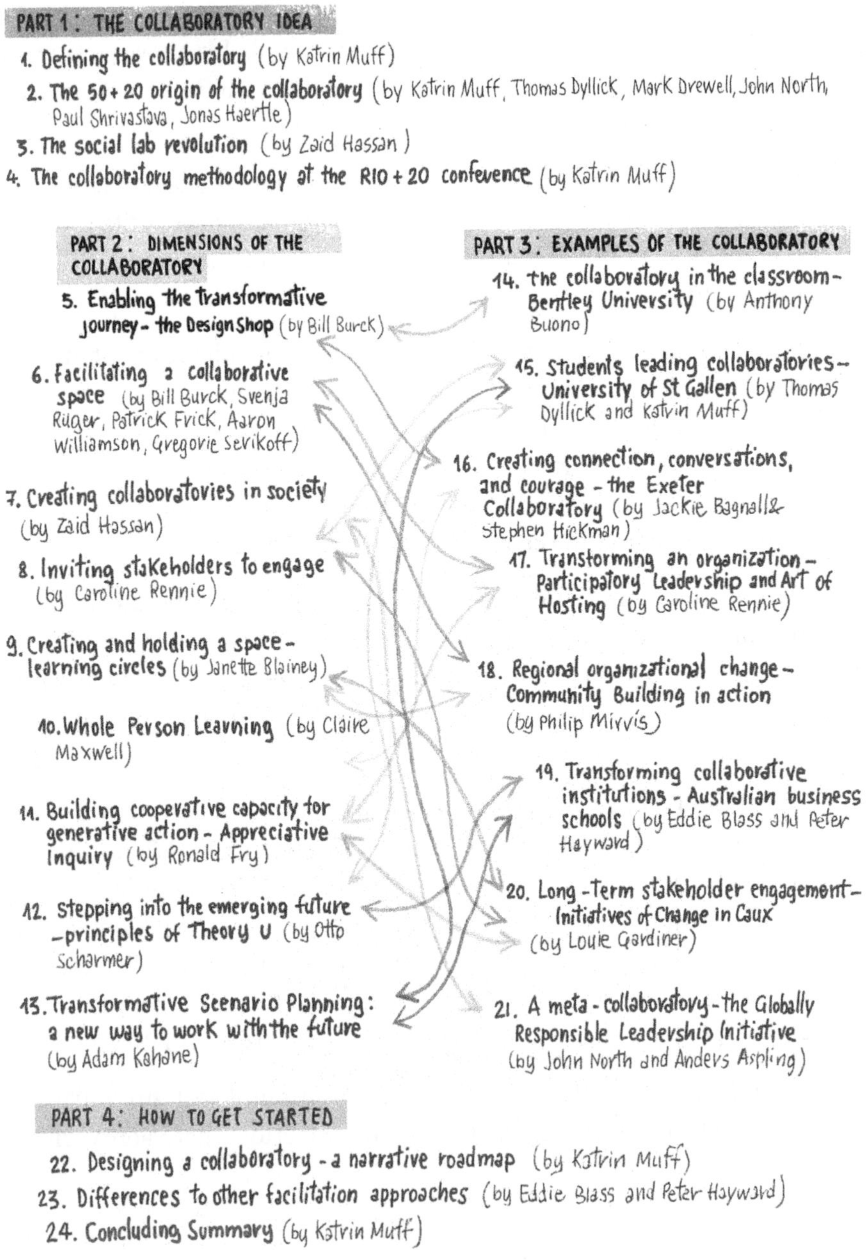

PART 1 : THE COLLABORATORY IDEA

1. Defining the collaboratory (by Katrin Muff)
2. The 50+20 origin of the collaboratory (by Katrin Muff, Thomas Dyllick, Mark Drewell, John North, Paul Shrivastava, Jonas Haertle)
3. The social lab revolution (by Zaid Hassan)
4. The collaboratory methodology at the RIO+20 conference (by Katrin Muff)

PART 2 : DIMENSIONS OF THE COLLABORATORY

5. Enabling the transformative journey - the Design Shop (by Bill Burck)

6. Facilitating a collaborative space (by Bill Burck, Svenja Rüger, Patrick Frick, Aaron Williamson, Gregoire Serikoff)

7. Creating collaboratories in society (by Zaid Hassan)

8. Inviting stakeholders to engage (by Caroline Rennie)

9. Creating and holding a space - learning circles (by Janette Blainey)

10. Whole Person Learning (by Claire Maxwell)

11. Building cooperative capacity for generative action - Appreciative Inquiry (by Ronald Fry)

12. Stepping into the emerging future - principles of Theory U (by Otto Scharmer)

13. Transformative Scenario Planning: a new way to work with the future (by Adam Kahane)

PART 3 : EXAMPLES OF THE COLLABORATORY

14. The collaboratory in the classroom - Bentley University (by Anthony Buono)

15. Students leading collaboratories - University of St Gallen (by Thomas Dyllick and Katrin Muff)

16. Creating connection, conversations, and courage - the Exeter Collaboratory (by Jackie Bagnall & Stephen Hickman)

17. Transforming an organization - Participatory Leadership and Art of Hosting (by Caroline Rennie)

18. Regional organizational change - Community Building in action (by Philip Mirvis)

19. Transforming collaborative institutions - Australian business schools (by Eddie Blass and Peter Hayward)

20. Long -Term stakeholder engagement - Initiatives of Change in Caux (by Louie Gardiner)

21. A meta -collaboratory -the Globally Responsible Leadership Initiative (by John North and Anders Aspling)

PART 4 : HOW TO GET STARTED

22. Designing a collaboratory - a narrative roadmap (by Katrin Muff)
23. Differences to other facilitation approaches (by Eddie Blass and Peter Hayward)
24. Concluding Summary (by Katrin Muff)

As a closing comment, I feel it is important to be very much aware of the fact that there is no need to search for perfection when trying to design or co-create a collaboratory event. "Clumsy solutions for wicked problems"[1] are more than good enough as an ambition and outcome when attempting to resolve complex challenges of a systemic nature. The collaboratory is one way to design a co-creative space for stakeholders to engage in solving our current wicked problems. Please take this as an invitation and an encouragement to simply dive into the experience.

We are all here to help you if you need us.

Katrin Muff, Lausanne, March 2014

---

1 Thanks to Jonathan Reams for this expression.

Part 1

The collaboratory idea

In order to contextualize the many contributions in this book, Part 1 starts with a retrospective reflection on how the collaboratory came about. In many ways, the "collaboratory" is the heart and soul of the vision of management education that the 50+20 initiative developed in an 18-month period leading up to the United Nation Rio+20 Conference in June 2012.[1]

To set the stage, Chapter 1 presents a definition of the collaboratory. Chapter 2 offers insights into the central role the collaboratory plays in the 50+20 movement and develops the intellectual foundation of the collaboratory. 50+20 proposes a radically new vision for management education in the hope of inspiring business schools to embrace their societal responsibilities and to develop responsible leaders. It proposes to support companies in becoming sustainable with relevant research and to

---

1 There is some interesting visual material to look at for those interested to see what we are talking about first:
   - The collaboratory experience we brought to Rio+20: www.50plus20.org/documentary
   - A TED Talk on the collaboratory as part of the 50+20 vision: Muff, K. (2013) '50+20: Rethinking Management Education for the World', http://youtu.be/jvipxPqS_38
   - The 50+20 vision: www.50plus20.org/film

play an important role in transforming business, the economy, and society. The collaboratory serves as the heart and the metaphor of the vision. It is the place where education research and societal engagement meet. Zaid Hassan shows in Chapter 3 that other, very similar forms of collaborative co-creation have existed for many decades and form what he calls "the social lab revolution"—an entirely new way of approaching and resolving societal challenges. Finally, Chapter 4 offers a concrete approach as an example (and only one of an unlimited number of examples) of how a collaboratory can work. To illustrate a particular setting we describe how we organized three parallel collaboratory sessions at the UN Rio+20 Conference.

1

Defining the collaboratory

Katrin Muff
Business School Lausanne, Switzerland

This chapter sets the stage for the book by providing the context. We uncover where the term emerged for us, what it means to us and what ambitions we connect to it. We also look at the magic space of the circle and its importance in collaborative work.

The collaboratory idea stems from the visioning work of a large group initiative including scholars, artists, consultants, students, activists, and other professionals who worked together on the 50+20 vision (www.50plus20.org), of which I had the privilege to be a part. The 50+20 Initiative set out to develop a radically new vision for how business schools can transform to become custodians of society. While a deep sense of the vision emerged during our own deep dive visioning process in a dance studio in New York in 2011, it took us about nine months (!) to find the words, metaphors, and images to describe what we had felt, sensed, and seen with our inner eyes. In hindsight, we realized that the 18-month process was what we ended up calling a "collaboratory."

The "collaboratory"—a blended word that emerged in our very first visioning session in New York—emerged as the centerpiece of the very vision we sought to create. The word fuses two elements: "collaboration" and "laboratory," suggesting that we are building a space where we explore collaborative innovations. The laboratory also nicely implies a notion of exploration and experimentation, thus staying clear of the notion of perfection or standardization.

The philosophy of the collaboratory involves a facilitated circular space that is open to stakeholders to meet and discuss burning societal issues. It is an open space for all stakeholders where action learning and action research join forces, and students, educators, and researchers work with members of all facets of society to address current dilemmas. A collaboratory focuses on visceral real-life issues and provides solutions that are driven by issues, *not* by theory. Participants in a collaboratory employ problem-solving tools and processes that are iterative and emergent. Emerging solutions are directly tested and amended while supporting both knowledge production and diffusion, which occur in parallel.

In the 50+20 vision we talk about the business school itself becoming a role model. Imagine an open space accessible to everybody—no more silos, no more elitism, no separation between research and practice, and issue-centered learning—where students work side by side with researchers and societal stakeholders. We talk about a facilitated space that could be created anywhere. Hence our idea of the "pop-up business school" in developing countries. To us, business schools should serve the people and the world as "custodians of society."

Our understanding of the term "collaboratory"

A collaboratory is a facilitated space open to everybody, and in particular to concerned stakeholders, to meet on an equal basis to co-create new solutions for societal, environmental or economic issues by drawing on the emergent future. It is a place where people can think, work, and learn together to invent their common futures.

The philosophy of the collaboratory revolves around an inclusive learning environment where action learning and action research meet and where the formal separation of knowledge production and knowledge transfer dissolves.

In our dreams, the collaboratory becomes the preferred meeting place for citizens to jointly question, discuss, and construct new ideas and approaches to resolving sustainability challenges on a local, regional, and global level.

Each collaboratory is different and needs to be carefully designed to fit the context, ambition, and purpose, the stakeholders, culture, setting, and anticipated duration of the space given to address an issue. Ideally, collaboratories are ongoing and evolving processes of a defined duration. They may, however, also be used as single sessions in settings where stakeholders want to consider future-inspired solutions that are both deeper and more collaborative than a normal debate or discussion.

For creating and holding such a space facilitation is of critical importance. The term "holding a space" is deeply grounded in our human heritage. It is, for example, considered an important duty of the elders in many indigenous peoples (see Chapter 9 for more on this). A much ignored and little discussed aspect of the collaboratory is the magic of the circle.

The magic of the circle

A group sitting in a circle is able to hold entirely different discussions from a group sitting around a conference table, behind tables, in a square or rectangle or in different rows in a classroom. Even the semi-circular amphitheatre arrangement used in teaching and executive training settings featuring consecutive rows oriented towards a lower central stage that features a screen and the faculty falls into this category of suboptimal solutions.

Circular talks are age-old traditions in many if not all indigenous traditions around the world. A circle ensures that all members are considered as equals. Everybody has the same position and everybody sees everybody else. In many traditions, circles had centers—and the center held the intention of the circle. In some traditions this center is a fire, which holds a specific symbolism. Today, the centers of circles are often decorated in order to create an energetic foundation for the conversation to take place. Kay Pranis (2005) has highlighted six structural elements indigenous people put in place to ensure that circular talks can be used as peacemaking instruments: ceremony, talking piece, guidelines, storytelling, keeper/facilitator, and consensus decision-making. She reminds us of the importance of using ceremony in opening and closing a circle to hold the intention that always reaches beyond the issue at hand to honor the connection to a deeper value of a circle for the benefit of humanity. Indigenous people have felt and honored this connection as an integral part of their understanding of themselves as a part of nature.

In their Earth Wisdom Teachings, the elders of the Native Americans talk of the Children's Fire. This fire is a reminder of the promise: "No law, no action of any kind, shall be taken that will harm the children" (Tim "Mac" Macartney, "The Children's Fire").[2]

In my engagement in an emerging political party and societal movement[3] in Switzerland, I have learned that every single discussion at any level of the organization has great benefits when held in a circle. From the smallest sessions of three to five persons to our annual meeting of several hundreds, we always sit in circles. And there is always one specific person responsible for "taking care of the center," by bringing flowers, a candle, or some other symbol and laying it out prior to a session. In that movement, this is one of many very deliberately chosen symbolic traditions to mark a different space. I have personally hesitated to apply this to my various professional settings, but I am sure one day I will have the courage to experiment with this. It is, after all, visually and emotionally pleasing to have a beautiful arrangement to look at when sitting in a circle. Feng Shui, considered as one of the Chinese metaphysics, looks at space in metaphoric terms and considers invisible forces, known as "chi," that exist between an individual, the planet Earth, and the universe. In its practices, the centre of any space is considered sacred and is deliberately left unconstructed.

It took us a while to realize how central the circle had become to our visionary work in the 50+20 project. The few of us engaged with facilitation of the various events had, naturally, always insisted on using the

---

2 http://thechildrensfiremovement.com/2012/07/childrens-fire-tim-macartney/, accessed 13 April 2014.

3 Integrale Politik: http://www.integrale-politik.ch.

circle as the basic setting of any discussion. As a group, however, we did not consciously reflect on this until about halfway into the proc-ess. During our 50+20 visionary work, the importance of the circle and the wisdom related to creating and holding a space emerged only over time to us. The circle represented the foundation of all of our creative work and of the many tools connected to such work including Open Space Technology, Appreciative Inquiry, Theory U and whole person learning. We applied a variety of existing methods and tools to our own co-creative process and realized only slowly that the true innovation of a new kind of management education lies in the very fact of how differ-ently such conversations are held and to what different results these can lead. If we had not aspired to achieve the impossible and to co-create a radically new vision for business schools, we certainly would not have relied on such exotic methods and tools to get there.

The circle has become an implicit element of many modern group processes and co-creative innovation. Good examples for this are World Café, community-building, Open Space, Art of Hosting, whole person learning and "quiet time" in Caux, as demonstrated in many examples throughout this book. As Christina Baldwin (Baldwin and Linnea 2010) in *The Circle Way* says, "Meetings in the round have become the pre-ferred tool for moving individual commitment into group action." It is, by the way, an excellent source for more insight and inspiration on how to effectively structure a circle discussion and to develop new collabora-tive solutions. The collaboratory is also one of many emerging forms in the "social labs" as defined by Zaid Hassan in Chapter 3 of this book. And, without doubt, there are many other equally important approaches that we are not aware of and we hope that many more will emerge as we move forward.

References

Baldwin, C., and A. Linnea (2010) *The Circle Way: A Leader in Every Chair* (San Francisco: Berrett-Koehler).

Pranis, K. (2005) The Little Book of Circle Processes: A New/Old Approach to Peacemaking (Intercourse, PA: Good Books).

2

The 50+20 origin of the collaboratory[1]

Katrin Muff
Business School Lausanne, Switzerland

Thomas Dyllick
Institute for Economy and the Environment, University of St. Gallen, Switzerland

Mark Drewell
The Foresight Group, Sweden

John North
GRLI Africa, South Africa

Paul Shrivastava
David O'Brien Centre for Sustainable Enterprise, Concordia University, Canada

Jonas Haertle
PRME, UN Global Compact, USA

This chapter looks at the central space the collaboratory takes in the 50+20 vision, which redefined management education for the Rio+20 conference. It explains the symbolism of benches and looks at the roots of the word "collaboratory," all the way from its origins in the 1980s in the ITC world to the way we now define, understand, and use the term.

1   Extract from Chapter 5 of Muff, Dyllick, Drewell, North, Shrivastava, and Haertle (2013) *Management Education for the World: A Vision for Business Schools Serving People and Planet*, reproduced with kind permission of Edgar Elgar Publishing.

The 50+20 vision is founded on the insight that providing responsible leadership for a sustainable world is first and foremost about creating and holding a **space** for the incarnation of the three roles of educating, enabling, and engaging. The various visioning exercises conducted in the creation process of the vision revealed a profound and multi-dimensional connectedness with a larger field—from the single individual human being to organizations, societies, animals, plants, and the natural world in general. This larger field is directly related to the philosophy of creating a space.

The central feature of our vision is expressed in the **collaboratory** (the inner circle in Figure 2.1)—a powerful space of co-creation in service of resolving issues relevant to local, regional, and global societies. The collaboratory represents the core mission of management educators adopting the role of transient gatekeepers who hold a space for responsible leadership for a sustainable world. Holding such a space enables an individual to connect to their full potential, while also reconnecting with all parts of society and the world. We found the circle of the collaboratory to be an appropriate symbol, representing a universal meeting place for discussing communal matters. It is rooted in many cultural traditions, such as gatherings around a large tree (the German *Dorflinde*), a fire (a Native American symbol for honoring future generations) and countless other examples in indigenous cultures around the world.

Educating, enabling, and engaging

Rather than train managers for organizations that operate within 20th-century logic, management educators need to answer the call of service to become custodians that provide a service to society. The 50+20 project is searching for ways to tackle the challenge.

The management school of the future understands that transforming business, the economy, and society begins with its own internal transformation. A school that embraces the vision will make the leap in a transparent and inclusive manner, leading by example by *being the change* it wishes to progress. More concretely, we envision three fundamental roles in management education that refine and enlarge the current purpose of education and research:

- **Educating** and developing globally responsible leaders

- **Enabling** business organizations to serve the common good

- **Engaging** in the transformation of business and the economy

We also refer to the vision as the **Triple E vision**: educating, enabling, and engaging.

Implementing each of these new roles represents a challenge in its own right. While not every player in the landscape needs to embrace all the roles, management educators may want to use this vision to reflect on their strategic choices for the coming decades.

The realization of this vision requires individuals with a certain mind-set, typified by a deep awareness and understanding of the global challenges we face, a sense of urgency to bring about change, and an unwavering belief that all of us "own" the responsibility to create change and contribute to making the world a better place.

Our vision consists of the three roles for management education (educating, enabling, and engaging), each of which is supported by three underlying enablers. These elements represent not only the essential roles of management education for the world but also point to three different levels of engagement:

- **The individual level.** Educating and developing globally responsible leaders

- **The organizational level.** Enabling business organizations to serve the common good

- **The societal level.** Engaging in the transformation of business and society

The philosophy of the collaboratory involves a circular space that is open to concerned stakeholders for any given issue. Action learning and research join forces in collaboratory—where students, educators, and researchers work with members of all facets of society to address current dilemmas. The collaboratory is a key feature of the 50+20 vision, a new philosophy in promoting management education for the world.

Figure 2.1 The vision for management education for the world

Educating
and developing globally
responsible leaders

COLLABORATORY

Engaging
in the transformation
of business and the
economy

Enabling
business organizations
to serve the
common good

Educating	Enabling	Engaging
• Transformative learning	• Research in service of society	• Open access between academia and practice
• Issue-centered learning	• Supporting companies towards stewardship	• Faculty as public intellectuals
• Reflective practice and Fieldwork	• Accompanying leaders in their transformation	• Institutions as role models

COLLABORATORY
• As the preferred place for stakeholders to meet
• Where all three domains overlap and where the vision truly comes alive
• Collaborative acion learning and research platforms organized around regional & global issues

The collaboratory represents an open-source metaspace: a facilitated
platform based on open space and consciousness-building technologies. Once understood, a collaboratory can be established anywhere, virtual or real, within companies, communities—or within a management
school. Its primary strengths lie in enabling issue-centered learning,
conducting research for a sustainable world, and providing open access
between academia and practice. The collaboratory also offers a powerful alternative for public debate and problem-solving, inclusive of views
from business and management faculty, citizens, politicians, entrepreneurs, people from various cultures and religions, the young, and the
old. Everybody must have a voice, hence the need for a transdisciplinary
approach.

A collaboratory is conducted without formal separation between knowledge production and knowledge transfer, while focusing on visceral real-life issues and providing solutions that are driven by issues, *not* theory. Participants in a collaboratory employ problem-solving tools and processes that are iterative and emergent. Proposed solutions are directly tested, contested, and modified while supporting both knowledge production and diffusion, which occur in parallel.

The co-creation of meaning

Of course, the idea of open and equal collaboration is nothing new. Sometimes it works, sometimes not. One may easily mistake the philosophy of the collaboratory as a free-for-all gathering of affable individuals who automatically become friends and miraculously agree on credible resolutions without encountering any significant obstacles. We know all too well that without the proper systemic approach a gathering of this kind may disintegrate following (for example) a prolonged argument over the minutiae of an issue under discussion. Skilled facilitation and a robust methodology are therefore required to address the complexities of vested interests, group dynamics, and problem resolution. To us, the collaboratory is a living experiment whereby we co-create its meaning, its power and strength during each session held around the world.

Paradigm-shifting innovations do not usually occur in well-established institutions, but tend to emerge among the outliers: the smaller, hidden, and often ignored pockets of creativity that are also part of the colorful landscape of management education. We refer to these innovative initiatives as **emerging benchmarks:** an initial set of examples related to the three proposed roles of responsible leadership. Collecting emerging benchmarks runs parallel to the 50+20 vision development, and will continue as the initiative grows.

We consider benches a useful visualization for a new paradigm of joint learning and research. The term "benchmark" was derived from cobblers who measured their customers' shoe sizes by placing their feet on a bench and marking an outline, or rather a *measure*. We may progress the metaphor further: sitting on a bench involves sharing one's own space with another individual in a public space. The proximity of an adjacent stranger sharing the same view provides a different kind of exchange when compared to individuals sitting oppositely in single chairs. A series of benches can further be used to create a circle of learning (see Fig. 2.2).

Figure 2.2 Benches define the circular space of our collaboratory

Finally, benches are often perceived as a temporary place for rest, reflection, and brief reunions—reminding us of the transient nature of our activities and existence while stressing both the common origin and purpose we share as global citizens.

The evolution of the collaboratory

The term "collaboratory" was first introduced in the late 1980s (Wulf 1993) to address problems of geographic separation in large research projects related to travel time and cost, difficulties in keeping contact with other scientists, control of experimental apparatus, distribution of information, and the large number of participants. In their first decade of use, collaboratories were seen as complex and expensive information and communications technology (ICT) solutions supporting 15 to 200 users per project, with budgets ranging from US$0.5 to 10 million (Sonnenwald, Whitton, and Maglaughlin 2003). At that time, collaboratories were designed from an ICT perspective to serve the interests of the scientific community with tool-oriented computing requirements, creating an environment that enabled systems design and participation in collaborative science and experiments.

The introduction of a user-centered approach provided a first evolutionary step in the design philosophy of the collaboratory, allowing rapid prototyping and development circles. Over the past decade the concept of the collaboratory expanded beyond that of an elaborate ICT solution, evolving into a "new networked organizational form that also includes social processes, collaboration techniques, formal and informal communication, and agreement on norms, principles, values, and rules" (Cogburn 2003: 86). The collaboratory shifted from being a *tool*-centric approach to a *data*-centric approach, enabling data sharing beyond a common repository for storing and retrieving shared data sets (Chin and Lansing 2004). These developments have led to the evolution of the collaboratory towards a globally distributed knowledge work that produces intangible goods and services capable of being both developed and distributed around the world using traditional ICT networks.

Initially, the collaboratory was used in scientific research projects with variable degrees of success. In recent years, collaboratory models have been applied to areas beyond scientific research and the national context. The wide acceptance of collaborative technologies in many parts of the world opens promising opportunities for international cooperation in critical areas where societal stakeholders are unable to work out solutions in isolation, providing a platform for large multidisciplinary teams to work on complex global challenges.

The emergence of open-source technology transformed the collaboratory into its next evolution. The term "open source" was adopted by a group of people in the free software movement in Palo Alto in 1998 in reaction to the source code release of the Netscape Navigator browser. Beyond providing a pragmatic methodology for free distribution and access to an end-product's design and implementation details, open-source represents a paradigm shift in the philosophy of collaboration. The collaboratory has proven to be a viable solution for the creation of a virtual organization. Increasingly, however, there is a need to expand this virtual space into the real world. We propose another paradigm shift, moving the collaboratory beyond its existing ICT framework to a methodology of collaboration beyond the tool- and data-centric approaches, and towards an *issue*-centered approach that is transdisciplinary in nature.

Hold that space

Translating the concept of the collaboratory from the virtual space into a real environment demands a number of significant adjustments, leading us to yet another evolution. While the virtual collaboratory could count on ICT solutions to create and maintain an environment of collaboration, real-life interactions require facilitation experts to create and hold a space for members of the community, jointly developing transdisciplinary solutions around issues of concern. The ability to hold a space is central to the vision of management education.

The technology involved with holding a space implies the ability to create and maintain a powerful and safe learning platform. Such a space invites the whole person (mind, heart, soul, and hands) into a place where the potential of a situation is fully realized. Holding a space is deeply grounded in our human heritage, and is still considered an important duty of the elders among many indigenous peoples. In Western society, good coaches fulfill a similar role, including the ability to be present in the moment, listening with all senses, being attuned to the invisible *potential* about to be expressed. As a result, what needs to happen, *will* happen. Facilitation and coaching experts understand the specific challenges involved in setting up an environment in which a great number of people can meet to discuss solutions that none of them could develop individually. Coaching and facilitation solutions already exist to create and hold such spaces, but are nevertheless distinctly different in a felt sense from the ICT-driven virtual collaboratories we have seen over the past two decades.

The evolution from the virtual collaboratory bears its own challenges and opportunities. In the co-creative process of the 50+20 vision, we learned to appreciate the power of the collaboratory both in real-life retreats as well as interactions between our gatherings. We propose that the next evolutionary step of the collaboratory will include both the broader community of researchers engaged in collaboratories around the world and stakeholders in management education who seek to transform themselves by providing responsible leadership.

In our new definition, **a collaboratory is an inclusive learning environment where action learning and action research meet**. It involves the active collaboration of a diversified group of participants that bring in different perspectives on a given issue or topic. In such a space, learning and research is organized around issues rather than disciplines or theory. Such issues include: hunger, energy, water, climate change, migration, democracy, capitalism, terrorism, disease, the financial crisis, new economic models, management education that serves the world and similarly pressing matters. These issues are usually complex, messy, and hard to resolve, demanding creative, systemic, and divergent approaches. The collaboratory's primary aim is to foster collective creativity.

The collaboratory is a place where people can think, work, learn together, and invent their respective futures. Its facilitators are highly experienced coaches who act as lead learners and guardians of the collaboratory space. They see themselves as transient gatekeepers of a world in need of new solutions. Subject experts are responsible for providing relevant knowledge and contributing it to the discussion in a relevant and pertinent matter. Students will continue to acquire subject knowledge outside the collaboratories—both through traditional and developing channels (such as online or blended learning).

As such, the faculty [of a business school] is challenged to develop their capacities as facilitators and coaches in order to effectively guide these collaborative learning and research processes. To do this, they must step back from their role as experts and rather serve as *facilitators* in an open, participative, and creative process. Faculty training and development needs to include not only a broad understanding of global issues, but also the development of facilitation and coaching skills.

The circular space of the collaboratory can become the preferred meeting place for citizens to jointly question, discuss, and construct new ideas and approaches to resolve environmental, societal, and economic challenges on both a regional and a global level. Collaboratories should always reflect a rich combination of stakeholders: coaches, business and management faculty, citizens, politicians, entrepreneurs, people from different regions and cultures, youth, and elders (see Fig. 2.3). Together they assemble differences in perspective, expertise, and personal backgrounds, thereby adding a vital creative edge to every encounter, negotiation or problem-solving session.

Figure 2.3 Participants in a collaboratory

Source: Fernando D'Alessio.

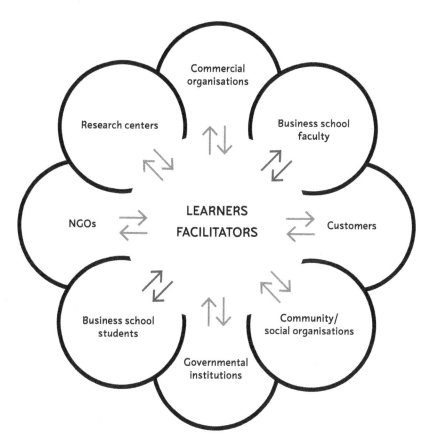

References

Chin, G., Jr, and C.S. Lansing (2004) "Capturing and Supporting Contexts for Scientific Data Sharing via the Biological Sciences Collaboratory," in P*roceedings of the 2004 ACM Conference on Computer Supported Cooperative Work* (New York: ACM Press): 409-18.

Cogburn, D.L. (2003) "Human–Computer Interaction in the So-called Developing World," *Interactions*, March–April 2003: 80-87.

Sonnenwald, D.H., M.C. Whitton, and K.L. Maglaughlin (2003) "Scientific Collaboratories: Evaluating Their Potential," *Interactions* 10.4: 9-10.

Wulf, W. (1993) "The Collaboratory Opportunity," *Science* 261: 854-55.

3

The social lab revolution[1]

Zaid Hassan
Reos Partners, USA

This chapter expands the idea of the collaboratory into its wider global context of similar initiatives that have developed over the past decades. We expand the 50+20 perspective with the reflection of what defines such collaborative co-creative processes around societal issues.

Social labs have been quietly brewing for almost 20 years. Hundreds of people around the world have been and are developing social labs. Thousands more have participated in them. There are labs focused on eliminating poverty, on water sustainability, on transforming media, on government, on climate, on social innovation, and on many more issues. A growing number of people are focusing their heads, hearts, and hands on addressing complex social challenges.

The people running these labs represent a new breed—they are not simply scientists or academics, and neither are they activists or entrepreneurs. They are all of these things and a few things we do not have good names for yet. They are making the case for and launching social labs around the world, trying to address some of our most difficult challenges.

1 Summarized extract from the introductory chapter of Hassan (2014) *The Social Labs Revolution: A New Approach to Solving our Most Complex Challenges*, reproduced with kind permission of Berrett-Koehler Publishers.

Social labs are platforms for addressing complex social challenges that have three core characteristics.

1. **They are social.** Social labs start by bringing together diverse participants to work in a team that acts collectively. They are ideally drawn from different sectors of society, such as government, civil society, and the business community. The participation of diverse stakeholders *beyond* consultation, as opposed to teams of experts or technocrats, represents the social nature of social labs

2. **They are experimental.** Social labs are not one-off experiences. They are ongoing and sustained efforts. The team doing the work takes an iterative approach to the challenges it wants to address, prototyping interventions and managing a portfolio of promising solutions. This reflects the experimental nature of social labs, as opposed to the project-based nature of many social interventions

3. **They are systemic.** The ideas and initiatives developing in social labs, released as prototypes, aspire to be systemic in nature. This means trying to come up with solutions that go beyond dealing with a part of the whole or symptoms and address the root cause of why things are not working in the first place

While none of these characteristics is convenient, each is necessary, deeply so. Each characteristic represents hard-won conclusions wrestled at great cost from many thousands upon thousands of hours of trial and error. Each represents countless workshops where many stakeholders shared their most agonizing and difficult challenges. And perhaps more than anything else, together they represent integrity and honesty—they are not what we want solutions to look like, but what we have found they actually look like when effective.

Everywhere I go, I meet people who want to change things. The first thing that usually strikes me about these encounters is the nobility of the intention. The second thing that strikes me is the lack of realism that all too often accompanies such intentions and desires. I often hear from people who do not seem to entirely grasp the nature of the challenges they seek to address.

Corporate attitudes were either defensive or, at best, focused on minimal compliance, as opposed to seeing sustainability as a competitive advantage or as being part of their broader civic role (Zadek 2001). A key example of this shift is Unilever's sustainability policies, which were heavily influenced by their long-standing participation in the lab. In 2012 Unilever announced it would "endeavor to decouple growth from its environmental impact. By 2020, Unilever aims to halve the environmental footprint of its products and to improve the lives of a substantial number of smallholder farmers" (Vis, Hamilton, and Lowitt 2013).

The Sustainable Food Lab was the first social lab I was involved in that embodied these three criteria. Its focus was how to make the global food system more sustainable. The global nature of the challenge meant that participants came from around the world, as well as from different sectors. The Food Lab initially brought together approximately 30 participants, drawn from corporate food companies, such as Unilever and General Mills; civil society organizations, such as World Wildlife Fund and The Nature Conservancy; and government officials, including representatives from Brazil and the Netherlands. These participants formed the lab team, who committed to physically working together for approximately 20 days over two years. They were supported by a secretariat, of which I was a part. The role of the secretariat was to design, facilitate, document, and organize the overall lab, building what could be thought of as its *container*. Over two years, we met together five times: in the Netherlands, Brazil, the United States, Austria, and Costa Rica. Since then, the team has grown and met many times in many other countries. The Director of the Center for Organizational Learning at MIT, Peter Senge, said, "The Sustainable Food Lab is the largest and most promising systemic change initiative I know of."

The decision of scale is, in many ways, the first decision that needs to be made about what sort of social lab to run. Instead of seeing social interventions as always needing to take scaling up into account, the social realm is scale-free by nature. A social lab can be designed to operate at any scale, depending on the intentions of the people in it. It will grow in whatever direction and way is needed and does not necessarily require central planning. There is one caveat in creating purely local labs. When we start examining purely local challenges, we discover that the source of our problems lies far outside the boundaries of our communities—be that the death of manufacturing or adverse environmental effects brought about by climate change. In other words, while a social lab can be run at any scale, we soon discover that we are not cleanly separate from the big, bad world.

The contrast between how we approach scientific and technical challenges and how we treat social challenges is stark. Whereas the natural sciences have moved on from a Newtonian world-view, it sometimes feels in the social spheres that we are still trapped in mechanical, linear ways of thinking. Instead of supporting talented and committed teams to seek permanent solutions to our most serious challenges as we do in the sciences or in the technology sector, we fund tightly controlled five-year plans. This leaves little space for learning, innovation, and change. The success of any lab—scientific, technical, or social—must be measured through multiple indicators, as opposed to relying on a binary logic of did it work or not. Particularly when concerned with either basic science or long-term challenges, such as cures for cancer, for example, progress is sometimes hard to measure in the short term.

If successful, a social lab will produce direct results addressing the challenge at the scale it is designed for, be that a community or a country. Labs can also, however, produce results beyond the scale they are designed to work in. It is not simply that we lack resources, time, or people willing to tackle our most complex social challenges. Rather, we lack a theory of action; we need some way of guiding our actions, a practical theory. How do we deploy our talents, our time, our money, and our resources as a society? Where do we find the will to tackle complex challenges?

The practice of social labs aspires to answer these questions. This practice offers anyone interested in addressing complex social challenges an option. In contrast to this option, however, is the dominant planning-based response. It is into this dominant response that most attention, energy, and resources go. If we understand complex social challenges better, then we will see that such investments are nothing short of disastrous—hence the dire need for a different approach.

Perhaps one of the most exciting developments in the last few years is the birth of many new social labs. There has been an explosion in the number of labs focused on addressing complex social challenges. SociaLab, based in Chile, focuses on new enterprises to alleviate poverty. Some of these labs, such as the Abdul Latif Jameel Poverty Action Lab (J-PAL) at MIT, are formally labs in the sense of being housed in a university and staffed by academic practitioners (Banerjee and Duflo 2012). Others are not formally known as labs but are, for all intents and purposes, because of their practices. For instance, my friend Bob Stilger has helped create ResilientJapan, which is focused on community responses to the 2011 earthquake and tsunami.[2] Labs are also springing up as a way for organizations to learn with their partners, such as Greenpeace's Mobilisation Lab, or MobLab. At Reos, my colleagues and I have been busy with several labs, including ones on climate change, community resilience, and state collapse.

Considering the development of an entire ecology of social labs and having uncovered the theoretical and practical gaps in first-generation social labs leads us to an exciting question: what would we have if we built on first-generation social labs, theoretically and practically, making the improvements we know we need to make? We would have a battle-tested, mature approach. We would have a theory of systemic action to help guide us in addressing complex social challenges. We would have a revolution in how we address humanity's most pressing challenges.

References

Banerjee, A., and E. Duflo (2012) Poor Economics: A Radical Rethinking of the Way to Fight Global Poverty (New York: Public Affairs).

Vis, J.K., H. Hamilton, and E. Lowitt, (2013) "Renewing the Global Food System," in E. Lowitt, The Collaboration Economy: How to Meet Business, Social, and Environmental Needs and Gain Competitive Advantage (San Francisco: Jossey-Bass).

Zadek, S. (2001) The Civil Corporation: The New Economy of Corporate Citizenship (London: Earthscan).

2 http://www.resilientjapan.org/.

4

The collaboratory methodology at the Rio+20 conference

Katrin Muff

Business School Lausanne, Switzerland

To complete Part 1 of this book we will look at a concrete example of a collaboratory to help the reader to get a better picture of what a collaboratory looks like in practice. A more detailed example is provided in Chapter 22.

This chapter offers insight into an example of how we briefed the facilitators of three parallel collaboratories for a three-hour session at the UN Rio+20 conference. We engaged with a variety of stakeholders during the business sessions organized by the UN Global Compact and created three collaboratories on the following big global issues: poverty, gender conflicts, and corruption. Roughly 30–40 people participated in each of the three collaboratories, which were facilitated individually according to the following guidelines.

A methodology and approach for short one-time sessions

The philosophy of the collaboratory forms the key feature of the 50+20 vision and involves a circular space that is open to concerned stakeholders to meet on equal terms for any given transdisciplinary issue. As such, it represents an open-source metaspace: a facilitated platform based on open space and consciousness-building technologies. A collaboratory is conducted without formal separation between knowledge production and knowledge transfer. It focuses on burning real-life issues and seeks to develop solutions in a process of engagement that is driven by challenges, not theory.

While such a process typically spans a series of collaborative sessions over a period of time, it is also possible to run a single one-off collaboratory session, here used as a real-life demonstration of our emerging philosophy. A simple script is provided for one type of collaborative session that can be used by experienced coaches and facilitators. Clearly, each moderator is invited and required to use his or her own open space and consciousness-building methods and tools. Each session is unique and demands skillful and adaptive facilitation, which is, after all, more of an art than a science. I would strongly recommend that each collaboratory be co-designed (see Chapter 22 for more details).

The **basic set-up** of any collaboratory is *always* circular, with an inner circle of 4–8 people (the number depends on the total time available; the less time, the smaller the number) representing the key stakeholder perspectives of the issue to be addressed. This inner circle is embedded within an outer circle of an active audience of stakeholders who are interested and ready to contribute to the discussion and reflection. While the inner circle should be seated (ideally on benches), the outer circle can be either seated or standing. The shorter the session, the better the standing option works.

This script is not meant to be shared with the stakeholders invited to form the inner circle. They may feel quite overwhelmed by this phased approach. In Box 4.1 you will find a brief description that can be sent around to them in order to invite them to your session.

Irrespective of the length of the session, we suggest splitting the time into the following **three phases**, each using approximately the same amount of time. Please pay particular attention to your time management—there is nothing worse than getting stuck in one of the phases or not being able to complete the entire process (as this is a real challenge you may want to assign a timekeeper to assist you).

Phase 1: Understanding the different perspectives of the experts involved

Step 1

Each stakeholder in the inner circle (a fishbowl) is invited to express his or her perspective and understanding of the issue including the concerns, challenges, forgotten issues, unforeseen risks, long-term consequences, and considerations that need particular attention given the complex and transdisciplinary nature of the issue at hand.

Suggested method. It is helpful to use the talking-stick approach to slow down and deepen the discussion. Place an object (a stick or a stone) in the centre of the inner circle and explain to all participants that the discussion is led by the wisdom of the stone, which holds the capacity to listen in silence. Somebody wishing to speak picks up the stone and holds it while speaking from his or her seat. Once finished, the stone is put back. *Nobody* is allowed to interrupt a speaker holding the stone—this avoids mental interferences and unreflected debates. Please also mention that the stone likes to lie still for a moment after being placed back in the centre to digest what has been said. The facilitator intervenes sharply if these rules are not respected. Usually, only a couple of such interventions are needed before the group settles and the process starts.

Step 2

Once all experts and stakeholders have expressed themselves, the facilitator opens the inner circle to invite other participants in the outer circle to join the inner circle to further expose the issue at hand. This is an important step and facilitators should encourage new voices to be heard to ensure inclusiveness with those present.

Suggested method. Depending on the set-up, there are different options to include participants from the outer circle to join the discussion. You can either place an empty chair in the inner circle that can be filled by anybody who has something important to add to the dialogue (the best option if time and set-up options are limited). It is most practical for the new person to touch the shoulder of an expert to make him or her vacate the seat for the new person. Alternatively, if you use two-seater benches, a person from the outer circle can sit next to a person in the inner circle they would like to replace. Original stakeholders leave the benches as soon as somebody sits down beside them. If they are speaking, they will first finish what they want to say. A last option is to place an empty chair behind each chair of the inner circle. A participant from the outer circle chooses which stakeholder to sit behind and asks to change seats by touching the stakeholder's shoulder. Experts from the inner circle may also choose to vacate their seats at their own choice.

Phase 2: Imagining a new common vision

Step 1

Here, the energy shifts from collecting different perspectives to understand the issue at hand from all its many transdisciplinary perspectives, to imagining a systemic and holistic understanding that reflects the common consciousness of all people present (irrespective of whether they have expressed themselves or not). It is important to announce that nobody should leave the room in the next 10–15 minutes and that everybody's active engagement is needed for this phase. The objective of this phase is to let a holistic solution or resolution of the issue emerge from the collective visioning process.

There are different ways to call on the group consciousness and this is the phase that will be most demanding for a facilitator or coach. A coach is trained in creating and holding a space for the highest potential of the moment to emerge. Please feel free to use your own method and approach—this must work for you. Allowing you to be authentic and whole is critical for the success of this phase. Have trust in yourself and in the power of the moment. Personally, I like to use an abbreviated version of Otto Scharmer's Theory U process (see Chapter 12).

Suggested method. Always begin with a moment of silence as a way to shift from Phase 1 to Phase 2. Invite all present to take a deep breath and to close their eyes if they are comfortable doing so. Bring them into their bodies (breathing is easiest) and talk them through their thoughts and emotions that have been stirred up in Phase 1. Have them feel these in their bodies by inviting them to observe what changes they notice in their bodies as they let go of their thoughts and emotions. Prepare a story line of what the world would look like if the issue at hand was resolved (e.g. "Imagine a day in your future life when …") Set the stage by inviting everybody to imagine that together the wisdom of the crowd holds the seeds of the solution, and that this can be expressed or experienced by seeing images, hearing sounds or getting other inspirations from their broader senses—beyond thought and emotions.

Step 2

With a quiet voice and attitude, collect the images and impressions that have emerged from the group. Start first with the inner circle before inviting the outer circle to make their contribution with additional relevant input. Draw attention to the fact that most often a common theme or picture emerges, almost as a story that is told by all those present. Have somebody record the images on a flipchart. To close this phase, summarize what has been shared by picturing the image or theme that emerges from the stories told. Take notes or make pictures. This is fascinating work; something profoundly new and visionary nearly always emerges. If nothing comes up, simply summarize the key points that seem intuitively important to you.

Suggested method. Your facilitation is needed to ensure that contributors do not get into their headspace or share intellectual pre-thought solutions. While this can hardly be avoided, you need to reframe the inputs carefully. You want their impressions, not their analyses. Depending on your energy and how you hold the space, you may no longer need the talking stick. Again, trust the moment.

Phase 3: Developing prototypes for immediate action

Step 1

Another energy shift occurs as we emerge from Phase 2. We move from the space of deep reflection (group consciousness, if you want) to concrete action. The critical difference in our approach is that actions that emerge are inspired from a deeper place, rather than being simple intellectual or emotional reflections. Having attempted to identify the common vision, the ideal state of the issue at hand being actually resolved, and having gained a first glimpse at a new image, theme or story, the emerging actions are often fundamentally new. These actions emerge from the future from the imagined ideal state and are fundamentally different in nature from current solutions that emerged from having analyzed the problem in all of its sub-elements. Acting from the emerging future is quite different from our usual practice of acting from the past. You may want to make this difference clear.

Suggested method. Depending on time and how you sense the group, you can use the inner circle as a creative space for anybody creative or innovative with ideas to share. The method here is creative brainstorming where you ask two people from the outer circle (who you have ideally informed in advance) to note down any emerging ideas of concrete action from the audience that can be initiated right *here and now*, or in the coming month at the latest (ideally such actions are initiated at the event). The rule of the game is that nobody is allowed to comment on or question an idea. After a quick round, have all the ideas read aloud and have a third person write down particularly strong ideas where you can sense the most energy of the group. Feel free to use any method that works for you to narrow down the list on a maximum of three to five items. Make sure you include items that have local relevance and also at least one item that seeks a global solution.

Step 2

There are many different ways to obtain concrete outcomes: (a) you may want each participant to identify one concrete action to be undertaken and report it back to the group in the last step; (b) you may want a subgroup to engage in a concrete step towards a joint project; or (c) you may want the majority or entire group to agree to a joint next step, meeting, etc. This largely depends on the total time you have at hand for the collaboratory session (individual action is ideal for short sessions). If time permits, you need to identify people (names and contact details) with energy to work on the three to five items identified. Ensure that there are at least three people per item. Have each of them express in one sentence (strictly due to time) why he or she wants to do it and do it *now*. Ensure that the three people have a working space to sit together immediately after the end of this session. Identify one person who will report back to you within four to six days with concrete next steps.

Suggested method. Whatever works for you. This is basic project management and facilitation. Close the session with something of significance before the circle dissolves: a poem, a citation, your impressions or the impressions of anybody else among the participants. Thank all participants for their trust and confidence.

Box 4.1 Script to invite selected thought leaders who form the inner circle of the discussion

Dear thought leader,

It is a pleasure to invite you to take part in a collaboratory session that takes .... hours and is divided into three phases:

- In Phase 1 you will share your perspective of the issue at hand and will listen to others express theirs. We will facilitate the process so that nobody interrupts another, ensuring an open and respectful atmosphere. It may happen that you will be asked to leave the inner circle once you have expressed yourself, giving another stakeholder an option to present his or her perspective.

- In Phase 2 we will jointly work toward a common perspective that is new and emerges from the group. All you will have to do is to let go of your preconceived notions and join our journey of discovery.

- In Phase 3 the group (including *all* participants) will work toward concrete actions that can be prototyped, tested, and potentially implemented immediately.

Come with an open mind and heart, and be prepared for a fun and deep session that hopefully sheds new light on how we can embrace this issue we all care so much about, *together*. I am at your disposal for further questions and very much look forward to working with you.

Part 2

The many dimensions of the collaboratory

The collaboratory consists of many dimensions and a series of aspects to be considered, respected and taken into account:

- Enabling a collaborative journey
- Facilitating a collaborative approach
- Creating collaboratories in society
- Inviting stakeholders to engage
- Creating and holding a space: learning circles
- Whole person learning
- Building cooperative capacity for generative action: Appreciate Inquiry
- Stepping into the emerging future: principles of Theory U
- Transformative scenario planning: a new way to work with the future

Part 2 attempts to cover a few of these by discussing the importance of first understanding the big picture of the collaborative journey (Chapter 5) and how to facilitate a collaborative approach (Chapter 6). The founders of The Value Web who facilitate thousands of co-creative sessions around the world in many languages and contexts describe important considerations. From there, we shift to understanding how to go about creating collaboratories in societies (Chapter 7). We owe these to decades of such work in the various initiatives around the Society for Organizational Learning (SOL). Experience has shown that the initial invitation is critical to the long-term success: for example, knowing who is the "caller" of the initiative and how to invite relevant stakeholders to engage with the process (Chapter 8). We owe these lessons to insights developed by the Art of Hosting movement. Once these dimensions are clarified and the setting is clear, it is time to prepare the event. Creating and holding a space (Chapter 9) is probably the most forgotten or ignored element of any such endeavors and is beautifully understood and lived in aboriginal cultures (the chapter features the 50,000-year-old tradition of the Gumbaynggirr people in Australia). Understanding that creating change is about involving the whole person beyond simply the intellect is addressed in Chapter 10. Appreciative Inquiry unveils how to build cooperative capacity for generative action (Chapter 11). Of particular importance is the way a true collaboratory session embraces group consciousness (as defined by the Foundation for Community Encouragement—see also Chapter 18, a telling example of community-building in practice) and through it invites the future to emerge. Otto Scharmer's Theory U (Chapter 12) is an outstanding process to enable a community to go beyond simple conversations to reach out together for solutions that no discussion could ever bring forth. Chapter 13 shares important insights of transformative scenario planning, closing the circle back to where we started in Chapter 5.

We have of course omitted some considerations, dimensions, and thoughts. Please enrich our thinking and help those interested in creating collaboratories by adding further elements to this at http://collaboratorybook.wordpress.com.

Enjoy diving into a co-creative space!

5

Enabling the transformative journey

The DesignShop

Bill Burck

The Value Web, USA

This chapter provides an overview of the conditions and require-ments for a collaboratory given the increasingly complex challenges in our society and the world. The authors use the DesignShop system as a way to frame the collaboratory and point out the importance of considering a collaboratory as a journey, rather than a one-off event.

If we want to change the world, we must undergo a transformation. We must let go of assumptions and confront paradigms that may no longer be relevant. We must establish new relationships, new values, new ways of thinking, new behaviors, and new approaches, unplug from the struc-tures constraining us and journey into uncharted territory—the white space beyond the edges of our map, a place where anything is possible and crazy ideas have a chance.

Which brings us to the form of collaboratory known as the DesignShop.

The role of transformation

Developed by Matt and Gail Taylor in the 1980s and refined in the decades since, the DesignShop system and method is now practiced by a number of facilitation operations around the world, including The Value Web.

A DesignShop is not a consensus-building mechanism. It is not a place where you convince people your idea is right with Jedi mind tricks. A DesignShop is a crucible for transformation. It is a place to gather people who have a key stake in the change you are trying to make. And not just a few of them; the more the merrier. You need to represent all of the variety present in the system you are trying to change—from the grassroots to the front lines to the kitchen tables to the boardrooms to the tribal councils—all of the key constituencies and vantage points, as well as anyone else critical to making change happen.

If you are developing a ten-year water-rights program for Ethiopia, for example, you propose bringing together representatives from federal ministries, three regional governments, several district governments, Oxfam, six partner non-governmental organizations (NGOs), research affiliates, industrial farm operations, and rural farming communities.

Then you get ready to be called crazy.

Ethiopia is a police state governed by an entrenched elite very resistant to change. The notion that poor smallholding farmers might become primary agents of development and, worse yet, engage in formal policy-making discussions? What? Are you crazy? All those farmers really want to do is get their hands on enough water to grow crops and water livestock.

But crazy ideas have a chance in DesignShops, and this one was just outrageous enough to possibly work. And it wasn't the only crazy idea the facilitation team had in mind.

How a collaboratory facilitates transformation

DesignShop collaboratories are different from traditional workshops in a number of important ways. First of all, they foster collaboration by engaging participants in design conversations focused on work the participants find meaningful. This work is done in a variety of settings including small teams working in parallel, so that everyone has a chance to share their perspectives.

Second, a DesignShop is an intense, focused, collaborative experience that can last anywhere from three hours to three days (or more) depending on the complexity of the challenge being confronted and the scale of the transformation needed.

Third, DesignShop collaboratories follow an iterative, non-linear process, enabling a group to explore the full complexity of the challenge they are there to address before making major decisions and designing final outcomes. Because the make-up of the group reflects the variety of the larger system in need of change, the participants are able to share, test, and challenge that broad set of vantage points, and thereby become much smarter about the change they want to create. This iterative approach seeks to cut through power relationships and defuses competing agendas. In a sense, the participants spend a good portion of the session "creating" the problem.

Creating the problem involves developing a collective vision of what the future change could be. The difference between that vision and current conditions is the problem that needs to be solved. The process of the DesignShop collaboratory provides the space and activities for the group to reach that common vision and achieve the level of understanding of current conditions necessary for the problem to stand out with clarity. The group is ready to solve that problem when it possesses the collective intent and insight needed for a robust solution to emerge.

Fourth, DesignShop collaboratories are social systems designed and facilitated in such a way that this emergence happens naturally. It is, in effect, unavoidable. We create the right conditions for that emergence by applying techniques rooted in systems theory. Complexity science tells us that emergence occurs in processes that promote self-organization, so we create a purposeful process wherein participants self-organize around work. Complexity science also tells us that the behavior of a system as a whole can feed back on its component parts, changing their behaviors, so our collaboratories involve massive feedback loops. We assemble the social system, launch it on an intense journey, and remain watchful for that point where the system reorders itself and becomes a whole that is not merely more than, but different from, the sum of its parts. The system becomes emergent.

Fifth, this emergence is a form of group transformation—the system shifting into a higher order and establishing new patterns of thought and action, a new working culture that models the transformation needed in the larger system.

Sixth, the future is brought to life in the DesignShop through the stories participants tell each other about what life will be like when they change the world. These stories evolve and integrate into a shared story as the DesignShop collaboratory unfolds. And, if modern neuroscience is to be believed, we are no more than the stories we tell ourselves about ourselves. This shared story about how the participants want to change the world becomes their collective identity. They own it as well as the solutions they design within the logical framework of that story.

This was the central premise and another of the crazy ideas of the DesignShop in Addis Ababa (see Introduction to this book). Dan Newman from The Value Web and Adinda Van Hemelrijck from Oxfam believed the success of the water-rights program should be grounded in stories.

Dan Newman had done a lot of work in the area of poverty and world hunger. He knew that a much more traditional and conventional way to measure the program's success would be to go out and ask how many wells were dug, how much water went through the pipes, how much each village was able to use on a per capita basis, and so on. That is how the UN agencies he worked with would do it. He also suspected many of those approaches were largely rubbish. How can you really know? Even in a thoroughly modern nation, such metrics are challenging to collect and track, let alone trust. In primitive regions of Ethiopia, where there are virtually no roads and they do not even know the size of the population, how can you possibly track a program's impact in that manner?

This idea of using stories was one Adinda had used before at Oxfam, and it hadn't taken much for her to convince Dan that it was a good idea. In fact, it was an approach perfectly designed for a collaboratory. They would get the affected populations to tell the stories they hoped would be told ten years later about having adequate access to water. This would provide a benchmark for tracking the program's effectiveness. It would not be measured in terms of water; it would be measured in terms of stories. They would track the stories, and the stories would be the measuring stick.

They also knew that each of the affected populations would walk into the room already prepared to tell a carefully crafted story arguing rights and staking claims. But these were not the sort of stories they were looking for—stories that stacked the deck and insisted on specific outcomes.

Dan Newman and Adinda Van Hemelrijck had designed iterative rounds of work that would lead the group away from their entrenched positions and toward a transformation—a radical mind-set shift—a process from which the stories they sought would emerge naturally as participants collaboratively designed a shared future.

In the early stages of the collaboratory, the participants focused on a visual model depicting a realistic but simplified scenario of water usage in the affected regions of Ethiopia.

As Dan described it for us,

> The point of this model was not to completely describe that scenario. The point of the model was to provoke a discussion about the scenario. We broke them into teams and gave each team a piece of the model. For example, one team had the piece that showed the water coming out of the mountains. Their assignment was to talk about the model. What's present? What's missing? What makes sense? What's right? What's wrong? What stories might we hear in ten years about this piece of the model?

For a few minutes, the groups did not know what to do. They stared at their pieces of the cartoon model (Fig. 5.1). Then they started talking, and before long the room was filled with energy and excitement. They suddenly had a way to abstract their discussion about water.

Dan continues,

> Through a picture and through the stories they now tried to tell each other, they were able to abstract from here's what I want—which is what they had come to Addis Ababa for—to here's the future as it might be. And you could see this total change in mind-set. Through modeling and storytelling, they changed from defending what they thought to be a right to collaboratively designing a shared future. I spoke with some of them about this afterward, and they confirmed the transformation that occurred during this exercise. The interesting aspect of using this model is that it was so superficial. It looks as if it could have been drawn by any talented artist in about an hour.

Figure 5.1 The model to trigger storytelling about the future

Illustration by Lucia Fabiani.

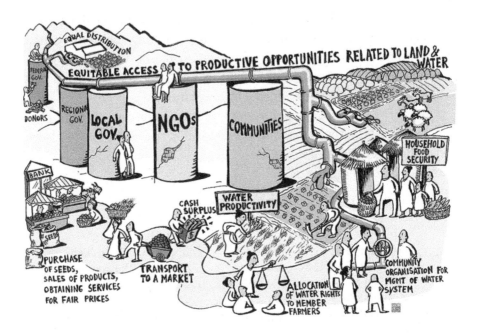

In actuality, the model had taken Dan, Adinda, and artist Lucia Fabiani several days to get right through a number of iterations and conference calls. Despite all of this work, Dan is certain that the model's usefulness came not from its accuracy but from its mistakes. Had the model been complete, it would have been useless. Its imperfections enabled them to focus on how to make it better.

"It provoked a depersonalized discussion," Dan observes.

> They could argue about it without having to argue with each other. Yet what they were doing was creating a story. And because it was a shared story, it created a powerful sense of alignment and shared destiny among people who see this through bitter experience as a zero-sum game. Meaning I gotta get my piece, and to hell with the rest of you, because the more you get the less I get. That was the attitude coming in, and the attitude leaving was let's build this together.

6

Facilitating a collaborative space

Bill Burck
The Value Web, USA

Svenja Rüger
The Value Web, Germany

Patrick Frick
The Value Web, Switzerland

Aaron Williamson
The Value Web, Canada

Grégoire Serikoff
The Value Web, France

Transformative change takes time and involves a complex set of interactions and interconnections among the various obvious and hidden stakeholders and issues. A collaborative approach lies in the heart of such deep change. The authors outline the role of a collaboratory to bring such a collaborative spirit to life and discuss key conditions that need to be assured for a collaboratory to be truly transformational.

Why a collaborative approach?

The true challenge when it comes to changing the world is not financial or organizational or political; it is cultural. Our habits, mind-sets, beliefs, assumptions, and norms—all of these sabotage our ability to respond to change rapidly or radically enough (let alone anticipate or get ahead of it).

It is a problem of imagination and creativity. To change the world, we have to become infected with crazy ideas. But the existing structures around us—our companies, institutions, and paradigms—are massive immune systems to the virus of crazy ideas, snuffing them out before they can cause so much as a sneeze.

The ways we try to effect change are ponderously slow relics of the Industrial Age. Hierarchical, linear, and incremental, they have no hope of keeping up. Worse yet, they tend to reinforce the very structures that meaningful change would threaten.

We can no longer depend on our leaders, our companies, our experts, or our NGOs to create the future. The changes we need to make will take the efforts of all of us.

The awesomely complex problems facing humanity call for approaches that unleash the group genius of people working together. We need approaches that empower and enable us to tap into our innately human capacities of creativity and collaboration. Approaches that trust these abilities and do not substitute mechanisms or shortcuts. Approaches that engage all of us—in all of our rich diversity of thinking and experience—in the important work of creating the future by design.

We need collaboratories.

Assembling complexity

The DesignShop is one example of the transformative power collaboratories have unleashed in recent years. And while the DesignShop collaboratory is a relatively new approach, it is one that has been evolving and maturing for several decades. All of which raises the question, "How do I go about creating one?"

The first thing to know is that you cannot plan the creative magic that will emerge at a collaboratory. What you can do is plan for and manage the conditions necessary for that emergence to occur.

We establish these conditions by treating the DesignShop as a system—a social system—and designing it accordingly. We have found that successful DesignShop collaboratories share six critical elements:

1. They have a clear and compelling purpose

2. They engage the right players

3. Their structures of time, environment, systems, and knowledge are planned and assembled

4. Their process features a series of interactions that enable self-organization and emergence

5. Their facilitation approach draws forth the best from individuals and the group

6. They depend on massive amounts of sharing and feedback

These six conditions do not assemble themselves by accident. The process we use for that assembly is called co-design. Key representatives from the facilitation and participant teams follow a rigorous process to design and implement the six conditions in the weeks leading up to the collaboratory. Before we explain any more about the six conditions, we should therefore explain a bit more about why co-design is so important and how the process works.

Co-design

In order to create a DesignShop collaboratory capable of changing the world, we fuse facilitation expertise with system expertise through a process called co-design. Key representatives of the facilitation team join key representatives from the system in need of change and together design the key elements of the collaboratory. [Editor's note: Most often, these are not the same people. We will describe incidents in this book, however, where the facilitators and initiators are one and the same group or person, for example, using the collaboratory in an educational setting.]

This conversation begins with an exploration of the landscape of change—its context, motivation, issues, and barriers—and then proceeds to create the initial articulation of the collaboratory's purpose, objectives, and givens. Although the purpose, objectives, and givens will inform design decisions regarding other aspects of the DesignShop, it is also true that they will be revisited and refined regularly throughout the co-design process in advance of the collaboratory.

With context established and a purpose in mind, the co-designers discuss and make decisions about all of the critical elements that will define and shape the DesignShop. This is a conversation across boundaries of time and space that will continue up to and through the collaboratory itself. In at least one early installment of this conversation, it is desirable for the co-designers to meet face to face. This yields benefits well worth the time and expense. The co-designers are a sample of the system to be created in the DesignShop. The value of the learning and insight that results when they are gathered and engaged in person is of a quantum order higher than can be gained virtually.

The co-design process, just like that in the DesignShop itself, is iterative. Many aspects of it evolve. For example, the purpose may evolve. This may require the engagement of additional or different stakeholders. Additional facts or inputs may need to be prepared.

The discipline embedded in this design conversation ensures that hidden or conflicting assumptions among the co-designers are surfaced and reconciled, that the right questions are asked, and that the various stakeholder perspectives represented have an opportunity to blend and mature.

The conversation among these key stakeholders provides valuable insight into the issues and conflicts that need to be resolved. It is, in many ways, a preview of the broader conversation to occur in the DesignShop. This is, of course, invaluable for the facilitators. But all of the co-designers benefit. Our understanding of the challenge matures as we share perspectives and design the collaboratory.

It is often the case that a change effort calls for multiple collaboratories. The co-design process becomes richer as each collaborative experience deepens our understanding of the change landscape and our fluency in the pattern language with which we can discuss it.

Condition 1: A clear and compelling purpose

Purpose orients us as designers and ultimately creates an orienting field for the DesignShop itself. It is the prerequisite for unleashing the Design-Shop collaboratory's full potential. That is why we always begin the co-design conversation with this important question: What is the purpose of the collaboratory?

It seems simple —of course the collaboratory has a purpose. But this cannot be assumed. All designers and participants of the collaboratory must be on the same page regarding what they have been brought together to achieve.

Because purpose is represented in words, it must be revisited and refined as the design conversation unfolds over time. Articulating the collaboratory's purpose enables the co-designers to confront it, live with it, and evolve it as their understanding deepens. We may understand the words one way early in this conversation and another way later as the co-designers develop a common language.

Putting the purpose into words also ensures that all the co-designers reconcile those words with their understanding of why they believe a collaboratory is needed. During this conversation, some of those understandings may come into conflict or create a tension that is then resolved by how the purpose is expressed.

In a way, the process that the co-designers go through as they discuss and refine the purpose is the true beginning of the collaboratory. Or perhaps more precisely, it is a prelude and a preview of tensions that may play out across the broader group of participants.

When the co-designers are satisfied they have expressed the collaboratory's purpose, it is ready to serve as "true north" for the collaborative journey of the participants. It will help keep them on course as they become passionate about conflicts, ideas, models, and new directions.

Purpose is ultimately an expression of intent. The participants will be presented with the purpose at the outset of the collaboratory journey. The goal of that journey is to help them reach the point where that expression of intent becomes their true intent —the point where they will make it theirs and take ownership of achieving it.

Once it becomes a passion for them, their collective creativity and genius of the group will be unleashed.

Objectives and givens complement purpose but should not be mistaken for it. Objectives are the expectations and outcomes associated with purpose. Givens are the collaboratory's operating assumptions and guardrails, things like scope statements and premises to be accepted.

Condition 2: Engaging the right players

(See also Chapter 8 on Inviting stakeholders to engage)
When it comes to changing the world, less is not more. One person alone cannot understand the change landscape in all its complexity or achieve the leverage necessary to effect change. Neither can a small group.

The players must represent the variety of the broader system if it is to become an emergent model of the change we hope to achieve. The collective memory, energy, and influence carried forth by the players from the DesignShop will be critical to achieving this desired impact.

Co-designers, participants and facilitators collectively form the players in the DesignShop collaboratory.

In a situation where there is a request to organize a collaboratory to address a certain complex issue, it is important that the co-design team consists of a handful of key players from the participant and facilitation teams, thereby bringing together two critical bodies of knowledge—of the system in need of change and of the collaboratory methodology. Principal stakeholder points of view should be represented on this team, especially when they are in conflict. Whether through authority, fame, connectedness or brand, the co-design team must be able to identify and gather the participants and facilitators required for a successful collaboratory. In a situation where the collaboratory is used to educate, to create awareness or where the initiators have facilitation experience, it may not be necessary to involve participants in the co-design phase.

The participant group is drawn from across the breadth and depth of the change landscape. It is important to identify the stakeholders that are concerned by the issue at hand and to include every single perspective of influence and concern. Assembling decision-makers, influencers, and implementers from key constituencies avoids blind spots, ensures the right conversations can happen and maximizes the potential for success.

The facilitation team is assembled based on the collaboratory's scale and facilitation approach. A collaboratory is social by nature. The facilitation team will profoundly influence and be influenced by the participant group. The collaboratory is a dance. The behaviors, capabilities, coordination, and flexibility of the facilitation team will serve as a model. They do not stand apart from the collaboratory system. They are part of it, and like the participant group will in all likelihood find themselves undergoing a transformation as the collaboratory unfolds.

Condition 3: Structural components

Structure defines all aspects of the DesignShop collaboratory's environment—from schedule to place to economy to the fact base required to support the work participants will do.

Designing and assembling this structure demands anticipation. It involves planning, securing, and scheduling. We give meaning to every single detail (because everything speaks) yet need to let go of certain things while we avoid accumulating too many compromises. It is a balancing act.

We limit constraints by securing in advance only what must be secured in advance. Not everything can be anticipated. Something will malfunction, break, disappear, or go wrong. So we build structure as an agile learning system.

Condition 4: The collaboratory journey

Process is the journey that unleashes the collaboratory experience. We believe that, if we properly assemble the players into a system, orient them toward a purpose, engage them in the right interactions, ask them the right questions, and allow them to self-organize, the system will reach a moment of truth. In the words of Nobel Prize winning chemist Ilya Prigogine, the system is "shifting into a higher order"—a true quantum leap—such that a new order emerges from the chaos of the old and produces the needed solution.

That is a mouthful. Simply put, it means we assemble the DesignShop in a way that facilitates emergence.

The shorter the journey, the more rigorously its entire course must be designed. There is less room for error. In longer journeys, the early stages are co-designed with great care. The system will begin to reveal itself as the journey advances. Subsequent stages can then be re-charted by the co-designers until that point when the DesignShop collaboratory charts its own course.

The design of the journey takes into account the mode and sequence of activities. Is there individual work, full group work, or small group work? Are participants considering the whole problem, a portion of it, or engaging it metaphorically? Are they working with their hands, their hearts, or their heads? Are they being playful, serious, wearing a mask? And does all this create a rhythm?

Condition 5: The right facilitation approach

The art of facilitation draws forth the best in individuals and groups by engaging their hearts, minds and spirits in a creative process.

Co-creation needs stewardship. When a group of people are gathered to make a difference, good facilitation makes it easy for them to work and play and together say what they must say, confront what they must confront, create what they must create and become who they must become in order to make that difference.

The facilitation approach should provide cues and establish an intuitive pattern language for when to move, what to do next, how to behave, and where best to discover order amid chaos.

Cadence and flow cannot be optimized unless the facilitation team has a rigorous capture and documentation process. This enables the participants to focus on knowledge creation then transition to what comes next with the confidence that their work, thoughts and conversations will be documented, curated, and available when needed.

Adaptation and flexibility are important. Up until the DesignShop begins, our design is a theory, our best guess at how the journey could play out. As that journey unfolds in reality, its true characteristics and needs will become manifest, and we must revisit and re-chart the journey accordingly. This may happen on a grand or minor scale, but it will happen. As the main story line unfolds, the facilitation team and co-designers must remain perceptive to subplots, subtexts, and weak signals. What are they trying to say? How should they be accommodated? Surfaced? Served? Dealt with? Ignored?

The facilitation team should model target behaviors for participants. The way each member of the team focuses, collaborates, listens, moves, responds, engages, and speaks will be apparent to the participants, especially because the team operates and moves and carries itself confidently and expertly in the same space they inhabit. It is an unfamiliar model, and one that will—more covertly than overtly—create a field that influences them.

Those who have facilitated where other languages are spoken know that you do not need to understand what people are saying to recognize their level of engagement. The energy is apparent. Over the course of a collaboratory, energy levels will wax, wane, and vary according to the nature of activities. This can be a diagnostic as well as something to design for and manage.

The facilitation approach is grounded in service, with a level of care and attention on a par with the finest restaurant. This does not mean saying yes to every request. The service bias is aimed at enabling the highest possible collaboratory performance and outcome, meaning that requests aligned with this bias are served to the utmost possible, while those that diverge are politely steered back on course.

The way the facilitation team organizes itself to bring all this to life has a profound influence on the DesignShop collaboratory. Likewise, each collaboratory will exert a unique influence on the facilitation team. Certain patterns in the operating model may be consistent from collaboratory to collaboratory, but each journey is different. The team's operating model must have flexibility and robust capacity for improvisation to meet the needs of the now.

Condition 6: The role of sharing: the virus of the collaboratory

A collaboratory is a social system that depends on sharing to unleash its full energy and potential. Social systems are extremely dynamic and challenging environments. The DesignShop collaboratory can be considered a highly designed and architected series of conversations that become increasingly effective as the journey unfolds. Their true power is in the outputs they produce and the way these are socialized, fed back into the system, and integrated in subsequent conversations. The extent to which this sharing process extends after the collaboratory into the broader change landscape will help determine the success of its impact.

The sharing that happens after a collaboratory is just as important as the sharing that happens within it. The collaboratory must not be thought of as an end. It is both a culmination and a beginning. It is a virus. To have any hope of becoming an epidemic, it must be shared. The most powerful and perhaps only true way to share it is through stories.

The stories that participants share about the collaboratory will spring from their memory of the collective experience. That is why it is so important to keep a complete and accurate record as the precipitate of that experience. The record is the knowledge base that shows the track, the attempts, and the achievements of the journey.

The facilitation team's practices ensure that sharing within and after the collaboratory can be as effective as possible. No iteration is complete without "shipping a product." These outputs must be captured, curated and made available. They can be used in subsequent work rounds. They can be used after the collaboratory.

The co-design team will specify the deliverables to be created as an output of the collaboratory. Making these available to the participants enables their memory to be rekindled and grounded as they tell the stories that attempt to make sense of their experience. The deliverables are Petri dishes for the collaboratory virus—vehicles to enable the post-collaboratory sharing process and advance the purpose of the event.

The notion of play

This is the approach that The Value Web and other practitioners of the MG Taylor methodology use in designing, assembling, and facilitating DesignShops. There is science to it, and there is art. But we take no aspect of it more seriously than the playfulness at its heart.

It is easy to take ourselves and the nature of our collaboratories too seriously. That tendency stems from an all-too-common belief that play and playfulness are the exclusive realm of children. This would be a mistake, because non-competitive, social play has a very important role in a collaboratory's success. Even competitive play can be of use at times.

Play is a constructive social behavior. It counteracts selfishness and promotes empathy and cooperation. Play is a state of mind. It opens us up to surprises and ideas we might normally perceive as threatening. Play is a process. Play is fulfilling in and of itself, which is why we so readily give ourselves over to it. Yet it can also lead us to valuable insights and designs.

Play is all of these things and more. It is by nature collaborative, involving the "players" in a joint exercise of pretend. As we play, we inhabit an imaginary reality existing in agreed-on form in all of our minds. Is that not what collaboratories are about?

If we ask a team to identify the changes Apple would make were it to come in and take over our medical clinic, we are not proposing a likely scenario. We are asking them to simply accept and "play out" an alternative reality that may, in fact, help them discover useful ideas.

By designing a journey that takes the participants into the realm of play, you loosen the current reality's hold on them and enhance their ability to entertain a future, quite different reality. Do not underestimate its importance.

7

Creating collaboratories in society[1]

Zaid Hassan

Reos Partners, USA

This chapter summarizes the experience and conclusions of many years of experience in building social labs and provides suggestions for how to go about designing social action.

Steps towards a theory of systemic action

While what is being outlined here is being called *theory,* this needs a little clarification. As previously explained, practical wisdom is best expressed through heuristics (rules of thumb, checklists) that are highly context-dependent, as opposed to universal principles, which are independent of context. A theory rooted in phronesis is therefore more akin to a recipe or a checklist than to a normal science theory or even a social science theory.

---

1 Summarized extract from chapters 7 and 8 of Hassan (2014) *The Social Labs Revolution: A New Approach to Solving our Most Complex Challenges,* reproduced with kind permission of Berrett-Koehler Publishers.

A recipe or a checklist is predictive in the sense that if one combines certain ingredients under particular conditions and uses the prescribed techniques, one gets the expected outcome.[2] However, it does not make sense to think of either being *falsifiable* in the way we would think of theory in the natural sciences. A recipe that fails in the hands of a bad cook does not mean the recipe does not work. But then how does one tell if a recipe is bad? Well, one simple answer is experience. When you cook it, it tastes bad. If a recipe corresponds to a set of instructions for producing a particular outcome, then the point of phronesis is that the only real way of learning how to cook is to cook.

1st requirement: constitute a diverse team

Given the opportunity to bring together a dream team to work on a systemic challenge, whom would you pick, and how would you pick them? On the first-generation social labs we ran, the rule of thumb for answering this question was "diverse and influential." There are two components to this rule of thumb that bear examination and explanation. *Diverse* was interpreted to mean *multi-sector*, which in turn was interpreted to mean that we constituted teams with representatives from government, civil society, and the business sectors.

The second half of the rule of thumb—*influential*—raises the question: who in the first half of the 21st century is influential? In the last ten years, the notion of who is influential and who is not has morphed several times. The rise of the networked society and increasing social complexity has prompted new research that has clarified our understanding of how highly connected societies function. In a *Nature* article, Duncan Watts and Steve Strogatz (1998) articulated a mathematical model for what they called "small-world networks."

Strogatz and Watts applied their model to a sociological explanation of how our world works. The basic idea is that small-world networks consist of clusters that are weakly linked through a small number of network agents. In social terms, this means that people are related to each other through relatively small, tight clusters, but a few members of these clusters are weakly connected to other clusters. It is through these weak links that information, viruses, and connections in general occur.

2   Paul Romer first came up with this idea (see Naam 2013: 119).

Commenting on Watts, Adams (2011) writes,

> The most important factor was not whether there were influential people but whether there was a critical mass of easily influenced people who were connected to other people who were easy to influence. When this critical mass of connected people didn't exist, not even the most influential people could get an idea to spread widely.

My colleague Mustafa Suleyman, in thinking about our convening strategy, had the breakthrough idea of simply broadcasting an invitation through our networks and seeing who turned up. After attempting our original strategy unsuccessfully while convening the Finance Innovation Lab (very few people from the finance sector we spoke to wanted to join an effort to change it), we eventually sent out an email invitation to 5,000 targeted people. This resulted in running three events where 300 people turned up. These people eventually coalesced into a network that formed the participants of the Finance Lab. It cost a fraction of what earlier convening strategy cost and took a month, compared to two years of searching high and low. This is what I refer to as *open convening*.

The question of how to constitute a dream team to respond to a complex social challenge therefore remains open. Developments such as the rise of the networked society, more sophisticated understandings of power, and the actual evidence base for who has influence in society means that people who would not be considered elite in Millsian terms are now able, more than in any other period in history, to determine the shape of their own lives. This shift in how power is approached represents one of the most significant differences between first-generation social labs and next-generation labs.

2nd requirement: design an iterative process

A good strategy in the context of complexity would include an iterative process. The simplest form of an iterative process is trial, error, observation, and reflection. You try something out, wait to see what happens, and then make another move based on what you have learned. The more complex the challenge, the more sophisticated a search strategy needs to be to find the way through the terrain, but the core essence of any iterative process is the same. Of course the ideal trial is one that is fail-safe—one that results in no lasting damage if it does not succeed.

3rd requirement: actively create systemic spaces

The work then of process is to create an environment—a container or a space—that lends itself to experiential learning. Social labs are space in the same sense. Process is used not in order to engineer a predetermined set of outcomes, but rather to create a container within which strategy can emerge from the friction of diverse participants working together as a team.

John le Carré once said, "The desk is a dangerous place from which to view the world." Yet, so many of our efforts to address complex challenges are born, live, and die at desks and boardroom tables.

Static spaces are designed to support static organizational structures where relationships are carved into org charts, facts are written in stone, access is controlled, and people come to work and do the same thing day in and day out. The furniture is bolted down, the doors are shut, and the world is a computer screen. Such spaces are designed for control, Soviet in spirit, and dominated by a set of unchanging dispositions.

In practice, unless you are an architect, urban planner, or interior designer, you probably work in an inherited space, that is, a space over which you exercise very little active control. The world, in static space, is not something we actively construct. Perhaps we can pin some postcards to a wall or put photos on our desks, but that is largely the extent to which modern working space is actively shaped by those within it.

Henri Lefebvre (1991) attempts to articulate a "unitary theory" of physical, mental, and social space, which serves to diagnose our current condition. For our purposes, Lefebvre makes three main claims. The first is "Social space is indistinguishable from mental space (as defined by philosophers and mathematicians) and physical space (as defined by practico-sensory activity)." The second is that social space is a social product. Third, "This act of creation is a process [and] ... every social space is the outcome of a process with many aspects and many contributing currents, signifying and non-signifying, perceived and directly experienced, practical and theoretical" (*ibid.*).

These three claims by Lefebvre can be used to understand how business-as-usual (BAU) habitus operates. BAU is the result of historical processes, which have produced a number of spaces. These BAU spaces—development, humanitarian, security and battle spaces—can all be thought of as examples of what Bourdieu calls "fields," or what

Lefebvre calls "dominated space," which are "invariably the realization of a master's project." All societies produce their spaces according to Lefebvre. BAU spaces are the products of a particular society—ours—that values episteme and techne over phronesis. Our spaces reflect this bias, and, hence, BAU spaces are hostile to the activities of phronesis.

We therefore require the production of a new, systemic space supportive of phronesis and of emergent strategy. Lefebvre comments, "new space cannot be born (produced) unless it accentuates differences" (*ibid.*). This space is in actuality a heterogeneous space, one that allows for the informal to exist with the formal. It is a space that is externally oriented but can also turn inward when the need arises, one that is supportive of diversity and difference.

Finally, it is clear from the countless examples of the kinds of spaces that engender creativity, innovation, and problem-solving, that such spaces must be autonomous, allowing high degrees of freedom. Systemic action, therefore, requires a particular space to support it and a particular organizational form that is actively designed to be systemic in nature. This space is what I refer to as a **social laboratory**.

Starting a social lab

A social lab is a strategic approach to addressing complex social challenges. As a strategy, it is not too hard to grasp. It can be stated simply. Bring together a diverse, committed team and take an experimental, prototyping-based approach to addressing challenges *systemically,* that is, at a root-cause level. Keep going. That's it.

Addressing complex social challenges requires deep strategic commitment coupled with radical tactical flexibility. We are required by the nature of the challenge to take a long-term view, to make serious strategic commitments that survive short-term reversals of fortune. At the same time, we need to take an experimental approach, to try things out and hold them lightly. This combination of deep strategic commitment with tactical lightness is very hard to pull off because it simultaneously requires different temperaments.

In fact, dominant responses to complex social challenges often confuse what we need to hold fast to versus what we need to hold lightly. Our commitments should not be to tactics—to a particular plan or technique. Rather, we should reserve our deepest commitments for strategic goals.

Strategy is *not* sitting in a room coming up with a detailed plan and then instructing other people to implement that plan. That is planning. Tactics, on the other hand, are simply ways of achieving strategic goals.

Being unable to tell the difference between a strategy and a tactic means we risk treating social labs as short-term tactics, which is a recipe for frustration because when we fail to get short-term results, we will declare failure. A social lab is a strategy, requiring strategic commitment. Treating social labs as another tactic, methodology, or technique risks disappointment and eventually failure.

Having said that, it should be obvious by now that social labs are not silver-bullet solutions. No course of action or strategy will guarantee that we will be able to address a complex social challenge. All we can do is increase the probabilities of success and avoid courses of action that lead to the mathematical certainty of failure.

The newness of social labs means there is vast scope, not simply for improving things but for true breakthroughs. There is no venerated canon that we are obliged to follow. We don't have to spend years working up to a PhD. We can just get cracking. The vitality of prototyping-based approaches rests in their disregard as to how things should be done in favor of what actually works. But as the saying goes, if you are going to break the rules, then break them well and break them beautifully.

Here then are seven rules of thumb for starting social labs. Each can be done in a myriad of ways, and there is no one right way (even as there are plenty of wrong ways). Because these are rules of thumb—not laws— each needs to be shaped by the context of the particular challenge being considered. All successful social labs go through these steps, either consciously or unconsciously.

First: clarify intention

One of my early mentors, Toke Moeller, once remarked, "Clarity of purpose is a sweet weapon against confusion." So how do we clarify intention? Well, there is a range of options to suit the person trying to do so. Conventional approaches involve carving out time to think—ideally taking a sabbatical—and require coming up with ideas and then talking about them with a range of people.

Unconventional approaches (or less conventional in terms of the dominant culture) might involve a vision quest or a solo retreat of some sort, away from the hustle and bustle of life. But in either case, clarifying intention requires taking the time to be honest with yourself about what it is that you care about.

The person I learned the most from about clarity of intention was Joseph Jaworski, who has written extensively about his experiences. He once explained to me that intention is like a matchstick—when it flares into light, all the other matchsticks around it also flare, and this chain reaction of intention creates a force that has the capacity to change anything. Intention thus acts as a "strange attractor," and all sorts of help flow towards it. The education reformist Ken Robinson makes the point, "For most of us the problem isn't that we aim too high and fail—it's just the opposite—we aim too low and succeed" (Robinson and Aronica 2011).

Second: broadcast an invitation

The invitation is a way of communicating intention. An invitation, in contrast to propaganda, if genuine, is dramatically more effective. We, either as individuals, as leaders or as organizations, might feel alone in our intention to address a challenge. The question isn't simply how do we convince people to join us, but rather how do we find people who share our intention? The invitation is a way to find people. Invitations should make clear what the invitation is for. In other words, there is a spectrum between open and closed invitations.

An invitation is open if none of the variables have been nailed down and few, if any, decisions have been made. An invitation is closed if all key strategic decisions have been made. The most common mistake is to start completely open. The risk here is that people turn up in response to an invitation only to be asked, "And what would *you* like to do?" Then they look at each other and say, "Uh, we don't know—it's *your* thing." And so on till there is no energy left. In general, it is better to try for somewhere in between, make some key decisions but hold them lightly. "So here's my best guess on these decisions, but do you have a better idea? Is this how we should proceed? Does this make sense?"

Third: work your networks

Once a clear and compelling invitation has been formulated, get it out. Increasingly, the most effective way of getting your invitation out is through your networks, through people who know and trust you, and through your friends. This does not mean sending one mass email and then sitting back. Invite people you know and ask for a conversation, ideally in person. Once they are on board, ask them to invite ten others. Talk to people on the phone, on Skype and in person. Explain to them what you are doing, why you are doing it and what you are looking for (people, money, work space, companies etc.). If they can't help, ask them for names—who do they know who may be interested? If your invitation is good, you will start seeing results quickly. If your invitation is bad and people are not responding, ask for feedback. Iterate. Remember that getting a result requires a clear ask.

As our public spaces get more and more saturated with advertising, increasingly people will turn to people they know and trust, to their friends and family. Instead of trying to filter the deluge of information we are saturated in ourselves, we will rely on our networks to do it for us.

Fourth: recruit willing people

The convening strategy we usually adopt is first to try to find a small group of like-minded organizations or individuals with some convening power. We locate two or three key partners who are willing to lend their names and open their networks up to finding other aligned people. With these key partners, we try to locate at least 30 more individuals, representing different parts of the system we want to impact. From these stakeholders we form a lab team and a secretariat. The number of lab team members typically does not exceed 36 because it is hard to build trust in a starting group bigger than this.

One of the key challenges with starting to address any complex social challenge is that people will assess the seriousness of an effort. Why should they invest their time and energy in this as opposed to something else? This means that we can spend a lot of our time and energy trying to convince people who are skeptical.

Increasingly, as the nature of power shifts—and so the nature of influence shifts—I am convinced that we need to spend less time trying to convert people. Instead, we should move on. Obviously there may be actors who are key to the success of our effort, or we *believe* this is so. It is not necessarily true. Are we going home if a key politician does not support us? Really?

Operate on the assumption that the perfect team is out there. We have to go and find them—they will not come and find us. Instead of being blocked by a skeptic, listen carefully and then move on. Go to the next person. If one politician says no, well, there is always another politician to go to. Keep going until you find the right people, and then recruit them. Your problem will more likely be figuring out what to do with all the help you are offered.

Fifth: set direction

Instead of coming up with a grand strategic vision or plan, you can write a strategic direction—survival—and then go about doing what was needed for the group to survive. This is not a new idea in business. Gary Hamel and C.K Prahalad (1989) wrote about the importance of "strategic intent" almost two decades ago in the pages of *Harvard Business Review*.

Complex social challenges are too complicated for grand strategies. Instead, what are required from conveners of social labs are strategic direction and the creation of space. Within that space unfold multiple actions aligned in a strategic direction. That's strategy.

Sixth: design in stacks

All the social labs involve multiple activities. In the labs I have worked on, these activities were divided into different layers, or stacks.

1. **Innovation or problem-solving.** In the labs we have run, the basis for this layer has been the U process

2. **Information and learning.** This involves research, baseline surveys, documenting the process of the lab, and disseminating results

3. **Capacity-building.** This could involve building the capacity of the lab team or the secretariat

4. **Governance.** This may consist of a formal legal structure, or it may involve a steering committee or leadership group of some sort. Warning: overdo this one at your peril

Design your lab in stacks, and design a stack only when you need one. In other words, do not spend years planning your perfect lab on paper. Sketch out roughly what each stack might look like and its parameters. Then flesh them out and build them as and when needed.

There are endless options in terms of how, where, and when to design your stacks. For example, you may decide to run multiple innovation or problem-solving stacks, maybe in different neighborhoods, or with different demographics. Or you may decide to invite a partner to help design and run the information stack.

Seventh: find cadence

The issues are so heartbreaking and situations so urgent that the space of addressing complex social challenges is rife with burnout. One of the most difficult lessons I have learned in running social labs is about timing and, in particular, *cadence.*

"Cadence" is a term used in agile project management to refer to a pace that is sustainable. An agile coach, Mike Cottmeyer, coined the mantra, "Stable Velocity. Sustainable Pace." The origins of the term "cadence" come from the world of cycling. When professional cyclists are tackling particularly difficult stretches, they search for cadence, a rhythm of pedaling that is sustainable. Consider the case of the novice cyclist who changes gears while going uphill and gets pitched over the handlebars. That is anti-cadence, if you like.

When we first started using agile approaches, it seemed an impossible struggle. Initially, we just flailed about like a first-time cyclist hitting a steep, steep hill. People on the team questioned the process, asking if it made sense and why we were doing it. Persistence and learning are rewarded by the magic of cadence hitting a rhythm of activity that is stable, and hence sustainable. Finding cadence is not easy, but teams that find it can climb up any hill.

Recently, while convening a lab, one of our advisers said that the trick was to "make haste slowly."[3] And that's the key. Push but do not be aggressive. Keep going, find cadence, and you are on your way.

References

Adams, P. (2011) *Grouped: How Small Groups of Friends are the Key to Influence the Social Web* (Berkeley, CA: New Riders).

Hamel, G., and C.K. Prahalad (1989) "Strategic Intent," *Harvard Business Review* 67.3: 63-78.

Lefebvre, H. (1991) *The Production of Space* (London: Blackwell).

Naam, R. (2013) *The Infinite Resource: The Power of Ideas on a Finite Planet* (Lebanon, NH: University Press of New England).

Robinson, K., and L. Aronica (2011) *The Element: How Finding your Passion Changes Everything* (London: Penguin).

Watts, D.J., and S.H. Strogatz (1998) "Collective Dynamics of 'Small-World' Networks," *Nature* 393.6,684: 440-42.

3 Thanks to Hans Verolme for that phrase.

8

Inviting stakeholders to engage

Caroline Rennie

ren-new, Switzerland

The following chapter outlines the prime importance of the invitation in determining the success of a collaboratory. Caroline Rennie develops how the invitation embodies the purpose, sets the tone and makes a request, ultimately determining who steps forward. It sets out the sections, possible phrasings, and occasional examples.[1]

The Oxford English Dictionary beautifully defines "invite" as: "to ask a person graciously, kindly or courteously to come to a place or proceeding to which he is assumed to be pleased or willing to come." The word embodies pleasure, togetherness, the possibility of action and delight in the prospect—the very spirit of a collaboratory. Key in this is that the invitation, no matter how broadly distributed, involves those people who feel called to work together towards a common purpose, and only those who feel called.

The invitation—the gracious request—begins with the link to purpose, but only ends once the event begins. From the first contact until

---

1 The inspiration for this chapter is the section on Invitation in Peter Block's splendid book *Community: The Structure of Belonging* (2008).

the starting moment of the collaboratory, all contact needs to say "Welcome": the correspondence, the attentiveness to the invitee's needs and the directions. The invitation is not a summons, nor a letter alone, nor a call. It is the graciousness that reaches out to those who have a yearning to contribute and accompanies them into the event itself.

Who to invite?

Typically we see-saw between wanting to have specific people in the room and wanting to make collaboration available to everybody. The latter has even been codified in Open Space Technologies as the principle of "whoever comes is the right people."[2] The question is, is it *you* who should decide this, or is it the *purpose* of the collaboratory that should decide?

If it is you who should decide, there is already an important principle about what really matters—and the answer is evidently you. This will have an impact on discussions and outcomes because people will defer to you and your opinion, as you are likely to be seen as the top of the hierarchy.

If it is the call to purpose that decides who comes, the invitation's format, delivery vehicle, style, and so forth play a lesser role. When I was 19, in my second year of university, I was walking one evening through the campus in the dying light of a late autumn day, when my eye was caught by an A4 sheet of paper stapled to a tree: "Wanted: volunteers to work in a refugee camp in SE Asia. Support people whose lives have been exploded by the war so that they can regroup and find safety. Deadline: tomorrow." The sheet had details about what I needed to provide in the application and how and where to deliver it. I took the sheet and three months later was working in a refugee camp in the Philippines. It is not difficult to find flaws with the marketing and communications strategy behind the flyer except that it worked: a clear call to purpose can shine out of the darkness.

---

2 Open Space Technology is a framework for enabling rich discussion around a central, strategic question. Information and instructions can be found online at http://www.openspaceworld.org/.

To make the collaboratory vibrant and generative it should include people who do not generally talk to one another, whose fields and passions may be quite diverse, and who represent the various groups who are affected by the current situation. As a principle—you are seeking to get the system in the room.

When to invite

This is perhaps the most difficult thing to get right. Invite too far in advance and people park it with a view to making up their mind closer to the date. Do it too close to the event and people are already booked. This speaks to a campaign strategy—where you invite more than once. But it may speak to a more important strategy: people respond when they believe that they will be heard and seen, that their views and work will be valued and help shape the outcome and that the outcome will be satisfying to them. This is not something you can guarantee—but you can speak to how you are safeguarding this. And this may call for more than one meeting: early adopters come to the first meeting; if their experience is worthwhile they bring more people to the second meeting, who in turn bring more to the third … . Often people invited to a collaboratory have not had the experience of being able to participate freely and fruitfully with their whole selves. This trust needs to be built.

Elements of the invitation

To build this sense of safety and true invitation, the invitation should have the following elements:

1. Salutation

2. Statement of invitation

3. Possibility

4. Specificity of the request

5. The nature of the invitation

6. Who else has been and can be invited

7. Contacts for more information (and a warm invitation to do so)

8. What will be done with the outcome of the event

9. What they can expect before, during and after the event

10. Reiteration of welcome

Salutation

The more personal the invitation, the more likely people are to feel touched, safe, and engaged. We are hard-wired for reciprocity, and a personal letter invites a personal response (Cialdini 2007). In the act of responding we become more thoughtful and more likely to feel we need to explain why we can or cannot participate. This investment of time and thought dramatically increases the likelihood of people coming. "Dear Valued Customer" has become commonplace, but serves only to demonstrate that you are far from being a valued customer (they haven't even bothered to learn your name!). This is the moment to help someone feel valued by reaching out personally. If you want the message to be shared further, the recipient should equally forward the letter personally: "Dear (name), When I received this invitation it made me think of you because ..."

The initial statement of invitation

"Please join us in conversations and action to help build a sustainable world in our own lives." This was the template statement of invitation to people we were inviting to join us in Carbon Conversations, a series of conversations and group work to help us lower our carbon footprint and support each other in doing so. This was the hook, but to strengthen it, we would personalize it further by linking it to relationship, conversations, and anything we knew about that person that we felt linked well to the purpose.

The possibility

If the purpose of your collaboratory were fulfilled, what could that mean for your world? A peaceful community? Socially motivated business school students? High levels of youth employment? This is what you are seeking to bring forward in language that invites people to consider what life would be like in that world. This is the call that should feel irresistible and necessary. The invitation is to give time and energy and self to discussions around living into this possibility. There may well be project groups that come out of the collaboratory or even prototypes. This depends on the nature of the issue, the people who come and the nature of the discussion. There can therefore be no promises made here—this is not a quid pro quo: "you come and this is what you'll get." Instead it is a request for contribution and for engaging in tough problems. The possibility is what gives energy, and the invitation is for time and place and people with whom to make sense of it.

The specifics

What exactly are you inviting them to? Is this a series of discussions or a one-off? Is this a design jam or an in-depth probing? It is important to get clear here about what you do and do not know. For example, you may be inviting people to a three-day, facilitated on-site retreat whose purpose is to explore a subject, and you may not know if there will be a call for further meetings. You may be inviting them to a series of six one-day events with the intention of designing and testing prototype projects. What you do know and what you do not know need to be spelt out with great specificity. It may be that the purpose of the event is to have participants define how they might like to carry the conversation further. Here you are spelling out your understanding and intention around the event.

Then of course come the detailed specifics: where, when, what time, how long, map and picture of the location, how to participate online if that is a possibility, and so forth.

If you are asking them to sign up for multiple sessions, it is important that they realize they are requested to come to all the sessions because missing a session changes the dynamics of the group and considerably slows down progress.

The nature of the invitation

To be a true invitation, it is important that whoever receives it understands that they may say no to the invitation without suffering a consequence from you. If they are to suffer a consequence, this is not an invitation but a summons. Naturally if they are not there they will not have experienced what happened—but this is the place to explain what can and will be done to engage those who cannot be present. It can be useful here also to mention what you are not asking for. That is, you are not asking them to give up their other "belongings," to give up their interests. In fact you are asking them to bring themselves fully to this. And that also means bringing a spirit of inquiry and an acknowledgement that everybody present has an equal right to be there and be heard.

Who else has been and can be invited

It can be useful, and build a sense of trust, to note specifically or generally who else has been invited: specifically, by name or organization; generally, by organization/type of organization or by role in life, or by relationship to the possibility being discussed. If everybody in a community or at an event is being invited, that can be mentioned too. There is also a benefit to letting the recipient know how the invitation can be spread. It can be spread person to person, through larger networks, as an article in a paper, and so on. Are you seeking to limit this or spread the word?

A note of caution: some people may edit themselves out because they feel that invitees are too senior/junior to warrant their participation and this can diminish the diversity that builds richness in collaboration.

Contacts for more information

This is very often a pro forma "if you have any questions please contact xyz." In the spirit of invitation, this can be made more inviting: "We understand that you may have many questions about this. You are welcome to write to So&So (so-and-so@address), or to call So&So to discuss this more fully at xxx xxx. We welcome your call!" This is particularly important because the likelihood of someone coming who has not understood something is very low. Everything that you can do to smooth the path and make them feel welcome will increase the chance that they show up, and the spirit with which they participate.

What will be done with the outcome of the event

This can be addressed during the event, but the broad lines can usefully be spelt out beforehand to align expectations. Is this public/private? Are the results going to be captured in a formal document? Is the document going to be circulated and to whom? Are the outcomes going to feed into further events? And who decides all these elements?

Repeat and re-personalize the request: "Please join us! We are inviting you because we believe that you bring ..."; or if it is being spread more widely: "Please join us! We are inviting you to join us in making this possibility happen."

From the invitation to the beginning of the collaboratory event

That was part one of the invitation. Part two is each of the interactions you have with participants and possible participants between this first invitation and the event itself. A follow-up letter speaks volumes in terms of interest, as does even a simple answer: I recently received an answer to a follow-up in which the person wrote, "I'm not sure whether to come to your event or this other event." I wrote back, "I'm not sure what the difference would be, but I can tell you that if you join us you will be very welcome indeed!" And she did.

References

Block, P. (2008) *Community: The Structure of Belonging* (San Francisco: Berrett-Koehler).
Cialdini, R. (2007) *Influence: The Psychology of Persuasion* (New York: Collins Business Press).

9

Creating and holding a space

Learning circles

Janette Blainey[1]

The Earth Trust, Australia

This chapter offers an important insight into the age-old practice of how to create and hold the space in which important—transformative—work is to be done. Janette Blainey talks about the wisdom of the original Gumbaynggirr people who have lived on their land for 50,000 years. In Chapter 20 on Initiatives of Change at Caux, we see how such practices are transcultural.

The practice of creating and holding a space: learning circles

Through my learning from custodial peoples of the world, I now know that if we all could see, hear, feel, think of the Earth as our mother and

---

1 With thanks to some of those from whom I have learned: Gumbaynggirr Elders, Uncle Max Harrison, Uncle Bob Randall, Lex Grey, Arnold Mindell, Harrison Owen, my students over the last 50 years, family, friends, and colleagues.

all that lives on and in the Earth as our brothers and sisters, we would just naturally respect her and all our relations.

Learning is used here to include "knowing," as well as the acquisition of knowledge and skills. I use the word "knowing" to include that which is not always logical or able to be reasoned, but which can be known in other ways. I also consider that any gathering has a learning component, especially one that seeks to explore the "burning issues facing our world" today. *Circles* relate not just to shape and structure but to also what such a structure enables, in respectful sharing and caring, in a wisdom-enhancing mode. *Space* is, for me, the natural and built environment of place, as well as the "field" in which the circle and the learning take place.

Honoring place and acknowledging all present

The first thing I have learned to do when opening up the space to facilitate a gathering of people, be it for the purpose of sharing, learning or decision-making, is to acknowledge the place. Knowing about honoring the place became a conscious process for me through being with people who live with the responsibility of caring for the land and waters of their country.

Before setting up the circle I focus my attention out to the natural world. I see the land and the lie of the land and what surrounds it, be it waters or mountains or trees, whatever was there before the built environment was placed on it and which still is what holds the building etc. I notice the way the sky meets the land and the day or the night is included in my "view" of what surrounds where I am. I acknowledge the presence of all of this and offer my respect, for all that is there holding the space for what is about to happen. I also acknowledge the built environment, if we are meeting in a constructed place in a room or a shelter of some sort.

Indigenous people add a further element in their process of acknowledgement and I have come to a knowing of the value of this practice, such that I now follow their lead. They acknowledge the ancestors of the place and ask for their support in whatever it is they are undertaking in the space. This process of expanding the presence in a place through respectful acknowledgement enables a harmony to be present before any undertaking gets underway.

Now it is possible to step into the space in which I (as the facilitator) am to work with ease and grace; through respecting the place, it follows that we are then given the place to be there.

I find that setting up the space inside a building requires awareness of light and how it enters the room, of where there are clear walls, and of where there are images. If images of people or landscapes are there, I notice them and either acknowledge or "dismiss," according to what is the intention of the gathering and their appropriateness. If there is a need to create a feeling in the room, I have found music works well, even dancing works to move the air and create the ambience I am seeking. The use of aromatherapy can support the creation of clear and energized space (however, occasionally somebody may have a reaction or even an aversion to the scent). Placement of chairs or arranging the seating to suit the purpose of the gathering is something I do, while holding the intention of the circle deliberately and consciously in my mind.

There are native traditions, in particular Native American, where smudging is used to cleanse or clear the space. In other traditions, especially in the Pacific Islands, flowers are used to create the atmosphere for effective gatherings. In Australia, Aboriginal people use "smoking ceremonies" to clear and strengthen the field in which important events are to take place.

A critical part of acknowledging all present is to ensure everyone feels that they have a place in the circle.

Working with the circle

Circles have existed throughout Earth's history, across cultures, long before now. A circle has continuity and offers an image and an experience of "all in this together"; each person has a "place" in the circle, just like everyone else. In a sense the circle resonates with "we are all one." This, from an indigenous perspective, expresses in the gathering a fundamental universal law, which gives power to the work being done in the circle, especially if the facilitator works respectfully with this "knowing." In more simple terms the circle enables everyone to see and experience everyone else. It facilitates communication and supports connection.

There are traditions where the circle has been analyzed in geometric terms and in esoteric terms. To me what matters is that the people in the circle feel at ease, connected to each other, strengthened from within and supported to be present. Supported as they make their contribution either through listening or speaking, sharing a little of themselves, with as little sense of being separate as possible. Unless all participants feel that they have a place in the circle there is more chance that their thinking will include judgment, which will interrupt the collaborative process.

Whatever the tradition, I feel that where the circle is respected as a way to work together collaboratively, there is within it, an intention to engage the whole of the person in relation to the whole of every other person in the circle.

Opening the circle

Through sharing responsibility for holding the space with the members of the circle the facilitator sets the scene for the way the group will operate. By acknowledging the land and waters of the place where the gathering is happening, for all present to hear and join with, we enable a greater field to hold what we do together. In Australia we also acknowledge the ancestors of the place and respectfully ask for support from them in our endeavor.

This tradition of asking for support from the place and those who have cared for the place through generations is infused with respect for something greater than ourselves, greater than that which is happening in the gathering. It expands the field of the circle, provides an opportunity to lift the burden and share the responsibility for the success of the time spent together. This widening of the circle can be seen as a buffer to the central physical group, within the circle. It can be seen as a protection for what goes on in it.

The process used to introduce the intention of the circle gathering, the guidelines for working together, and the people to each other is important in setting the scene for the success of the learning or decision-making that is to follow.

Indigenous people like to acknowledge their parents or grandparents, even their ancestors, rather than just themselves, when introducing who they are. This helps to widen the circle and strengthens the "voice" of the speaker. I tend to look at a way to introduce ourselves, where we share a little of who we are, that is not just about labeling us or strengthening our sense of individual identity.

With the culture of "respect" firmly established, it is time to ensure that the purpose is clarified. Even if it has been articulated before the meeting takes place, it ultimately saves time to have a process of clarification that is collaborative.

Processes to enhance collaboration in circles

When it comes to creating and holding spaces there is a lot we can learn from ancient cultures. Here is a story that illustrates the power of circles and learning: the laughing way.

To give some background to the story I am about to relate: in the Aboriginal world as I have come to know it, a child comes into the world with her or his spirit as the guiding force. This positions the adults, parents, grandparents, aunts and uncles, of which there were many, as the ones to respect and support the life and spirit of the child. There is no taking over from the autonomy of the child's spirit. So when elders sit with a group for the purpose of learning there is respect for the spirit of everyone that those present need not be told what to do. The responsibility for the learning is firmly placed with the learner. This is best seen in the context of a collective world-view where "respect" is at the core, where everything about life is infused with respect for the spirit of everything and each has a place that cannot be fulfilled by another ... and together we are whole.

I will relate here a most significant learning that I have been privileged to experience. The story that follows informs the way I create and hold space.

More than 20 years ago I took a group of Aboriginal women from a number of different tribal groups to "sit with" (meaning to "be with" while allowing the time for what needs to emerge, to emerge) Elders of

Gumbaynggirr country. We were a group of about 20 women ranging in age from 19 to 50. The Elders were all senior women. We all crowded into a huge living room and sat on chairs or the floor (according to age). We were positioned around the perimeter of the room and pretty squashed, as the circle was required before anything happened. When we were all settled I offered to leave so that the business of the meeting could take place without an "extra" (me). My offer was conspicuously ignored and I was told to sit!

This is what happened that gave me the insight that I will share with you here. Those elderly women were shown respect by all of us as we sat waiting for the senior women to begin. We sat there while the "old ones" made jokes about each other, "jarring each other up" as they would say. Laughing began quietly in that part of the circle and occasionally one would explain something to us so we could laugh with them; before long we were all laughing, mostly about nothing in particular.

It was not until we were all laughing that anything that was important was shared. Never were the visiting women, who were there to listen, told what to do. Always they were given an idea to think about, or a way to connect and allow what they were seeking to come to them, while they went about their business with respect. They were not told anything as such but shown how to find what they were seeking. The women were given possible ways of how to proceed to access what they wanted to know. Everyone left feeling strong and clear, with a knowing that they could now go forward with the blessing of these Elder women.

The learning was profound. It was such that it could not be forgotten. What followed was further learning through dreams and experiences, which flowed from the gathering that day.

Just one small example of the way the learning occurred was about telling story through dance, as done in traditional times. The visiting women wished to learn about how to do this. They were not told what to do but instead were guided to listen to the natural world in such a way that they would know how to move to express the story. In the days that followed each seemed to contribute a part of the dance that became their inspired, collaborative creation. Not only did the women learn about dance, they gained real confidence in themselves, their identity, and their connection to country and to the ways of their people. All this happened at a pace that was right for each of them at this time in their own individual life journey.

My learning was more than I can write here. What was important and is relevant to learning circles is about the way laughing works to open the heart and the mind and allows us to take in more than information. It facilitates the integration of the learning in our minds and bodies, such that it cannot be forgotten, even if not easily articulated. Also of relevance is how the way space is held and can also hold the place for the responsibility of learning to sit with the learner. What is taken from the experience is what the learner is ready to integrate. The Elders open the doors of perception. The visiting women step through the doorway just as far as they are ready to go at that moment. Often this expands over time but at their own pace and without the need to be guided further.

As well as "laughing" and "sharing" rather than "telling," the art of listening is of vital importance. When I came to realize how people communicated within a predominantly listening-focused culture, it was like a light going on for me. The differences are marked. I will highlight two here, as they are particularly pertinent to creating and holding space in a circle.

Listening with all of who we are is quite different from just listening with our ears to words and meanings and tone and pitch. In a gathering where what is being shared is felt as much as heard, where the nuances of the words offered have a powerful bearing on the message being transmitted, the practice of listening with the whole body, mind and spirit is a critical factor, as we seek to collaborate effectively.

The other difference in listening-focused communication is that questions are less appropriate. Sharing is often with story rather than information alone. If a story is told, then the context is vital to the information being transmitted, as it holds feeling and background. Story is also given, with the intention that the receiver takes what it is for them to get at this time. There is respect for the person who is being given the story. They get what they are ready to take in, so that their world-view can expand or focus according to the way they are thinking and feeling.

People who share with story are often severely disturbed by interruptions and questions. Often the context for their holding of the story does not have any place for the questions to come in, or the time to address the question is not right for the person sharing. The disruption to the flow often means that these people who think, feel, listen, and share this way shut down and the circle is deprived of the contribution of a powerful listener or a pertinent story.

This is the reason why, when setting the scene for the process of the circle, I ask that those who are offering what they wish to say in the circle do so without interruptions and I suggest that questions be considered later. The "talking stick" is an effective technique that is used in some cultures to manage sharing without interruptions. However, with careful monitoring by the facilitator to see that respect for all is not transgressed in any way, everyone can share the holding of space together.

Closing the circle

I suggest that it is important to:

- Acknowledge with gratitude the land and waters of the place, the ancestors (if this is your practice) the building, if relevant, the support people, if relevant, and all present in the circle

- Offer participants the opportunity to share their thoughts and feelings of the experience

- Acknowledge the outcome such as can be articulated, while honoring the contribution of all

As the facilitator, the one who honored the place and set the space for the circle, it is important to clear the space after the circle is completed. This is with respect for all that happened in the circle and for the place and space that supported the circle. Finally, I like to offer my respect and give thanks to the place for holding our circle. I then ask that the ripples of learning continue to flow, in harmony and with respect, ever onwards.

In summary

- **Respect** for place, people and participation by all
- Honor the place
- Engage in a circle
- Honor everyone's place in the circle

- Create a clear opening of the circle, so all are aware of purpose and process

- Encourage openness in mind and body and remember to laugh

- Support an ethos of learners being responsible for their learning and of "listening"

- Close the circle with a moment of gratitude to all

- Do not ignore the setting in which the learning circle is to take place

- Do not assume that everyone present knows how to operate respect-fully in a circle

- Do not forget to share the holding of space with everyone in the circle

- Do not allow people to question others while they are sharing their perspective/story/idea

- Do not support people cutting others off as they offer their perspective

- Do not forget to close with respect and gratitude

The depth of knowledge that is held by elders still alive today is there, waiting to be shared. If we can learn to be respectful, "to stop, sit, be still and listen" as an old elder often says, then we too can share in the wisdom of the oldest living culture. The fundamental belief of "we are all one," the meaning of which I came to glimpse through the custodians of country, underpins the way I have learned to create and hold space.

10
Whole person learning

Claire Maxwell
Oasis School of Human Relations, UK

This chapter offers a perspective on how to go about engaging with
stakeholders in a collaboratory, engaging not only with the head, but
also with the heart, the soul and the body. "Whole person learning"
has emerged from the Globally Responsible Leadership Initiative
(GRLI) (see also Chapter 21).

It has become such a cliché to talk about living in turbulent, complex, and
chaotic times that there is almost a reluctance to start with those words,
yet we are experiencing an extraordinary pace of change and to not speak
of it is to deny the reality of our time, to somehow sanitize the experience
of day-to-day existence. As human beings, our lives have accelerated
beyond all known recognition and, unless we chose to remove ourselves
as completely as we can from the mainstream, we are in daily contact
with diverse and difficult challenges, experiences, and questions.

In addition, our relationship to the structures of hierarchical knowing is also changing. The safety we found in there being someone who
"knew," whether it be through religion or politics, has shifted. In the
developed world no one can really know the truth about living any
more. In that kind of reality, when structures are changing or even break-
ing down, we have to find more of what is inside ourselves to sustain the
self and the other. There is a need to retreat to a core of internal knowing
from which we can then reach out to the other.

The Globally Responsible Leadership Initiative, a partnership of businesses and business schools who want to be the best *for* the world rather than the best *in* the world, recognizes that people involved in globally responsible practice and leadership at whatever level need to prepare themselves differently if they are to make a difference in and to the world. Working beyond the cognitive and beyond ego requires an internal strength, a willingness to shift consciousness away from the "I" and towards the "we" and the "all of us."

In embracing the "all of us" we have to work with all of the self, with the practical, the physical, the imaginal, the affective and emotional as well as the conceptual. This is what whole person learning involves. It is a radical approach to how we learn and how we provide learning opportunities and experiences. It is much more than becoming informed and leaving the impact of the body of knowledge to influence the learner; it is about ensuring that when learners leave the learning environment they have been affected on all levels. The learners are more acutely aware of the impact of themselves on others and on their immediate environment.

It is not about telling people how to live, but in the context of the Globally Responsible Leadership Initiative there is a view about what it will take to work against the mainstream. To reframe management education as if people and planet really matter, to reconfigure business so that a triple bottom line has real meaning and impact, takes courage, strength, and persistence and, while the initiative may be led by one person, it requires more than simply the self to make things happen.

Being willing to really make a difference requires us to work differently. Working differently requires us to be willing to learn differently. This is what whole person learning is about, bringing more than the intellect to the table and being willing to deeply root the ability to learn in individual real-life experience and in real dialogue with others and their experiences. In so doing, there is recognition that collaboration, dialogue, communication, diversity, and active participation are all elements of learning for tomorrow.

The central tenets of whole person learning include an understanding of:

- How we relate to one another

- How we view the other

- How we teach and how we learn

- How we structure our decision-making forums

Working out of a whole person approach calls for us to be aware of, skilled in, and open to a depth of relationship that goes beyond the told and the teller. It is beyond student-centered learning as it places the student, the participant, at the very heart of the learning and calls for them be involved, influential, and able to shape their learning experience. At its most radical, the participants are also the main players in the assessment process, identifying, in the company of others and in recognition of their context, what it is they need to learn and develop and what criteria they will use to assess themselves and then be assessed against.

The rationale for encouraging such an approach is simple. Increasingly, in a global context, where systems and ways of operating are in question, a new paradox arises: individuals need to develop much higher levels of autonomy and a much stronger sense of self, while at the same time being able to shape the future in a way that involves and respects others. There is a need to be influential and influencing and to create an individual and societal context to meet the demands and requirements of this changing world. If our learning experience is only one of being told what we need to know and what to do and of regurgitating the same to meet externally validated criteria, then we have already internalized an unhelpful message: if we wait long enough, someone who knows will tell us what to do. We will be saved, not by our own actions but by the actions of others.

Already our life experience is telling us this is not going to happen. Of course, there are people with bodies of knowledge and expertise that are still relevant, vital, and necessary to the world. Whole person learning is not an anti-intellectual movement. In fact working with questions for which there are no easy answers and with deeply felt and complex dilemmas is an essential element of the approach. It is much more a call for those of us who have expressed a concern for and a willingness to engage with the complexity of globally responsible practice to be open to starting with the self; to working with our own deeply felt and complex dilemmas; to recognizing and embracing our core values; and to exploring how we manifest those in the world and how we work with those who hold different values and belief systems.

Collaboration, under these circumstances, goes much deeper than simply getting along without disagreement. There is a felt difference as we move from one level of operating to another deeper level and it is at this level that whole person learning flourishes. Full collaboration, among its many attributes, calls for a quality of listening with the whole self as much to what is not being talked about as to what is. This depth of listening is critical if real and difficult decisions are to be made and changes happen with people and to structures and systems to facilitate unique and long-lasting globally responsible practice.

At the heart of whole person learning is a relationship to and a love of power. Not power over but power with and power to. This position is not primarily for ideological reasons, although without doubt that plays a part, but more straightforwardly for the sake of high-quality, effective decision-making and effectiveness and efficiency in business and business education. Developing a relationship to whole person learning requires us to develop a relationship to and with power: our own, that of others and of the societal context in which we operate. In so doing we may discover some unpalatable truths about how much power and influence we really hold or how much more we will need to develop if we are to configure or reconfigure structures, systems, and relationships that enhance, encourage, and enable globally responsible practice.

At the heart of whole person learning is a commitment to working collaboratively, to encouraging the participation of others and of self, particularly in those decisions that most affect us, and a shift in forms of authority and power, particularly with regard to the usual relationship between learner and teacher. Whole person learning encourages:

- Individuals to relate to others in a more equal manner

- Honest, open dialogue and debate concerning the matter in hand, whether that be at board, team, or individual level

- A clarity of communication and understanding between all involved

- The recognition that differing perspectives all have a contribution to make

- Individuals to freely give voice to their authentic concerns

- Shared, "owned" decision-making

- A commitment to stand by what one agrees to and to work with the consequences and implications of the decision

- An aware understanding of the affective dimension when working with people

A whole person learning approach is transferable and translatable into any environment in which people meet together to make decisions, research topics, explore differences, and learn new processes or topics. All that is required is that those involved are open to bringing their authentic humanity into the room and allowing it to show rather than hiding behind role, title, or position. In so doing, working as a whole person does not deny hierarchy, indeed genuine hierarchy of knowledge, experience, and status is recognized and acknowledged in the development of relationship. What is discouraged is any retreat, during difficulty, to known positions of given authority, especially where challenging and demanding decisions need to be made.

In that sense, whole person learning calls for a meeting of minds, hearts, and humanity, in all aspects of what it means to be human: feelings, senses, intuition, connection to others and to the cosmos, as well as to the familiar ground of the mind and the intellect. This approach is often referred to pejoratively as "soft," as encouraging people to indulge themselves in navel-gazing rather than getting on with the job in hand.

From experience, working out of a whole person approach is anything but soft. As has already been suggested, revealing more of the self calls for a level of courage and openness that many of us find hard to deal with, preferring instead to retreat into or fall back on positional power and authority—a tactic that often allows us to act without being questioned or without having to show how we are affected by what we are seeing or doing. While sometimes this is a necessary stance, at its very worst it can encourage us to act in ways that are contrary to our deeply held beliefs or values or that allow our behavior to go unchallenged, often out of fear or an overly developed respect for position.

Summary

In whole person learning, adults stand in relation to one another as peers (or equals)—though they may have different roles and make different contributions. Aspects of good practice include:

- The encouragement, development, and practice of adult-to-adult relationships

- The willingness to work autonomously while also recognizing and accepting interdependence

- A willingness to work with the immediate and emergent

- Being authentic

- Holding the self accountable to and accountable with the other as a peer

- Remembering there are no "rights" or "wrongs," only consequences, both intended and unintended

- Tending to the development of the self in order to best serve the other (self as instrument)

We are entering an era where effective human relations and human relations skills are no longer a "nice add-on" to the "real job" of focusing on the task. The increased importance of ethical aspects of business, of stakeholder engagement, of concern for people and planet, and of being responsible for more than profit all call for a higher order of relational belonging and engaging.

If we accept that conflicts of interest are constant and there are no easy answers, then bringing a whole person learning approach to the business of business is a real-time response to current questions, dilemmas, and challenges. With an emphasis on deeper human engagement, authentic meeting, recognition of the need to work with issues of power and authority, practicing and bringing influence to bear on decisions that affect the future, being practiced in and unafraid of showing emotion, whole person learning is future-oriented: it is a way of preparing people for a world of complexity and, as Bryce Taylor (2010) put it, "deep and blessed unrest."

While the term "whole person learning" may be gaining greater currency in the world, the approach as understood by the Globally Responsible Leadership Initiative and developed and practiced by the Oasis School of Human Relations is new, challenging, demanding, and exciting. The Oasis School of Human Relations has been pioneering Whole Person workshops in business schools across the world as well as providing programs in the UK for the development of whole person facilitators and for people wanting to work with the deeper issues of people, purpose, and planet.

Adopting a whole person approach to life and learning ensures we are as best prepared as we can be to challenge, demand, and excite in order to ensure people and planet really matter. It is about change and evolution of the self, the other, the system, and the structure. Awareness, experience, and understanding are constantly changing and deepening. Whole person learning is very much a live and ongoing process that meets what the 21st century calls from us all.

References and further reading

Taylor, B. (2007) *Learning for Tomorrow: Whole Person Learning for the Planetary Citizen* (Boston Spa, UK: Oasis Press).

Taylor, B. (2010) *Whole Person Learning in Action Manual* (Brussels: GRLI Press/Oasis Press).

Taylor, B. (2012) *Ecology of the Soul* (Boston Spa, UK: Oasis Press, www.oasishuman relations.org.uk).

11

Building cooperative capacity for generative action

Appreciative Inquiry

Ronald Fry
Weatherhead School of Management, USA

This chapter provides insight into an often ignored yet important aspect, the *approach* taken to solving critical issues. A deliberately positive approach to how people, organizations, and issues can be addressed is suggested, which opens the space for entirely new dimensions and visions.

Appreciative Inquiry (AI) is a strength-driven process and approach to human system change and development. Through its deliberately positive assumptions about people, organizations, and relationships, AI is distinctive in that it eschews more modernist, deficit-oriented approaches to managing change in favor of leveraging individual and collective strengths to vitally transform ways in which we approach questions of organizational innovation, improvement, or effectiveness.

Practically, AI is a form of study that selectively seeks to locate, under-stand, and illuminate what are referred to as the life-giving forces of any human system's existence; its positive core. This realization of shared strengths then becomes a new platform for imagining possibilities for a preferred future. The new possibilities with the most attraction to the stakeholders engaged in the AI process then become opportunities for co-constructing future scenarios and launching self-managed change initiatives.

The Appreciative Inquiry method

AI assumes organizations are centers of vital connections and life-giving potentials: relationships, partnerships, alliances, and ever-expanding webs of ideas, knowledge, and action that are capable of harnessing the power of combinations of strengths. Founded on this life-centric view of organizations, AI involves the cooperative search for the best in people, their organizations, and the world around them. The key steps or phases include: (1) Discovery of the best of what is; (2) Dream to imagine what could be; (3) Design of what will be; and (4) Destiny: to enact change and improvisational learning to become what is most hoped for. These steps are all premised on the definition of an affirmative topic (or an issue in the language of the collaboratory)—the strategically relevant issue or opportunity that will be the focus of the inquiry. This issue or opportu-nity bounds the inquiry questions, determines who should be involved in the inquiry and signals the importance and aspirational intent behind the AI effort.

The purpose of the **Discovery phase** is to appreciate—uncover, artic-ulate, and illuminate—those factors that give life to when the human system has been at its best in relation to the chosen issue. Organization learning is fostered by sharing "best past" stories related to the topic and initial dreams about how the chosen issue could be better, enhanced, or improved in the future. This is the most fundamental departure from typical change methods and what most distinguishes AI in practice. Par-ticipants are not asked what they think about the issue or what change ideas they have, or what they would like to do next. The emphasis is on valuing stories first—before any of the typical diagnostic or expertise-based questions that provoke a predetermined list of opinions or facts. The outcome of the Discovery phase is an articulation of those strengths or success factors that connect across the most stakeholder stories; the system's positive core related to the chosen issue.

The **Dream phase** is about generating new possibilities for the future that capture the heightened aspirations and positive affect generated during the Discovery. Because these future images have been stimulated by asking positive questions (best past stories related to the affirmative topic) they paint a compelling picture of what the human system could or should become. By positioning this dreaming after the discovery of shared strengths, the participants have gained a greater sense of collective efficacy and so their future images of possibility expand beyond just incremental notions. They imagine bolder possibilities because of an enhanced sense of the capabilities of the total collective of participants based on the common strengths and success factors in the initial stories that were shared.

The **Design phase** translates future images into intentional action. By using such facilitation tools as mind mapping or Open Space, the ideas for change from the dreaming can be depicted or voted on to determine a subset that most energizes the participants and around which new change teams can form. The same group of stakeholders that did the Discovery now vote with their feet and go to the particular change idea they most want to make happen. Each new, multi-stakeholder change team now engages in design work including crafting an aspiration statement, brainstorming, prototyping, action planning, process mapping, role and decision charting, and other techniques to agree on a specific action path forward.

Destiny is a call to co-create the preferred future through action and innovation. The term "destiny" is meant to imply more of an open-ended quest or journey of continual learning. It is expected that the initial change team that formed in the Design phase will take on new members, drop others, alter its direction, and continue to improvise as it enacts its change journey. In some organization settings this will still look like a set of new projects that are monitored and tracked for progress and contribution, while in other contexts this phase will look like several autonomous and creative new ventures being nurtured and supported in less visible ways.

In sum, this "4-D" process juxtaposes grounded examples of the extraordinary (Discovery stories related to the chosen issue) with visionary images of positive possibilities (Dream and Design phases) to mobilize generative connections among stakeholders such that they want to work together to transform their shared future.

Distinguishing core principles behind the practice of AI

Suresh Srivastva, David Cooperrider, and their colleagues incorporated social constructionist perspectives in the initial framing of AI in their seminal article, "The Emergence of the Egalitarian Organization" (Srivastva and Cooperrider 1986). They argued that organizations were best viewed as socially constructed realities, and that forms of organization were constrained only by human imagination and the shared beliefs of organizational members. Following social constructionist thinking, organizing is the consequence of shared meaning about future possibilities in the minds of a critical mass of actors. This orientation and our analyses of large-scale social change (eradication of smallpox, end of apartheid, etc.) help frame the following core ideas or principles about human systems and organizing. These core ideas have since been validated in our lessons learned from numerous applications of the AI method and extended through the disciplines of positive psychology, positive organization scholarship, and neuroscience.

1. The constructionist principle: as we talk, so we make

The constructionist principle tells us that human systems move and grow in the direction of what they most talk about. In fact, we create the world that we call real through our forms of relational discourse—our conversations, symbols, metaphors, and stories. Our words create our world. This shifts the way we think about language, and places emphasis on conversation as an organizing force. The ways we talk and the language at our disposal are tools that help us construct and live in the world. Knowledge, then, is located not within the recesses of the individual mind, but within the nexus of human relationships—"between the noses" of those relating with each other.

It is no longer useful to think of words as pictures—as the "talk" being separate from the "walk." Instead, think of words as acts, potent tools that do something, and as navigation devices that allow members of a culture to move about and coordinate ongoing relations with one another. How we converse and what we converse about—the consequence of the questions we ask—is fateful.

2. The poetic principle: as we choose topics of inquiry, so we open new horizons of action

AI celebrates the notion that organizations are open-ended, evolving networks of possibilities open to an endless variety of interpretive perspectives. The poetic principle means that we can inquire into (study) anything in any organization, at any time: we can choose to notice the dynamics of stress, conflict, or competition, or we can choose to study the dynamics of hope, cooperation, competence, or joy. Virtually any topic is fair game. To study and learn more about low morale to lessen it is very different from studying to learn more about moments of high engagement in order to increase them. Both questions could be asked and pursued in any organization, anywhere. The choice is ours. It is not prescribed by an economic downturn, current morale, and the like. The poetic principle suggests that inquiry should be guided by an aesthetic imagination. In AI, the change agent is more like a poet crafting words than an archaeologist digging for hidden continents. Exercising the poetic imagination in choosing a positive, hopeful topic for further inquiry will dislodge patterns, interrupt taken-for-granted assumptions, provoke wonderment, and lead to transformation.

There is nothing about the organizational world itself that dictates what there is to be studied or talked about. The issue we study should be guided as much by the world we want to co-create as it is an effort to test or verify some underlying law or pattern in the world that already exists.

3. The principle of simultaneity: as we ask positive questions, so we transform

Change begins the moment we ask our very first question. Simply put, the simultaneity principle suggests that inquiry and change are not separate moments. Inquiry *is* intervention. The moment we begin to explore a topic, the moment we start to ask questions, even the moment we start to wonder about some social phenomena, we already change the "targeted" situation. The seeds of change are planted with the very first questions that we ask. If we ask organizational members about creative collaboration, we are laying the tracks for the "respondent" to recall such moments, to create or maintain a discourse that tracks the antecedents of creative collaborations and their consequences. Perhaps after leaving that conversation, one would begin to notice new spaces (possibilities) for better collaboration, tell others stories about recent collaborations, start to reframe "neutral" events as collaborative gestures, and so on. In short, our questions seed networks of conversations that create a backdrop that legitimizes certain categories of behaviors over others.

Every question into a social topic begins a conversation that creates, maintains or transforms a way of being and doing. There is no such thing as a "neutral" question.

4. The anticipatory principle: as we imagine, so we create

The anticipatory principle begins with what seems to be a counterintuitive hypothesis: if you want to change a human system, change the *future*. More specifically this principle suggests that perhaps the most potent vehicle for transforming human systems is our ongoing projection of a future image. The collective image of the future, as projected in questions we ask and resulting conversation, guides what there is to notice in the present and, in that way, guides action. The philosopher Martin Heidegger discussed how we are always creating anticipatory "forestructures," we are always projecting ahead of ourselves a horizon of expectations that brings possible future pathways into the present. People anticipate the future, project likely maps, and then proceed to live "as if" it were already happening.

One of the difficulties we face in this age of technological acuity is that we may blindly begin to assume that every human challenge can be solved with technology. We surrender our own dreaming to elite groups of experts who we assume will someday invent some technological innovation that will create a breakthrough. Studies of Olympic champions and the best professional athletes reveal that they learn and master the skill of imaging the perfect performance better than most. Recovering or developing such "image literacy" involves valuing multiple ways of knowing (not just mechanistic, deductive forms of knowledge) as well as multiple faculties—our intuition, our caring capacity, and our bonding instincts. Children do it all the time, but it is called daydreaming, and they are often punished for it.

Deep and lasting change comes from changing our anticipatory images of the future. In fact, positive images of the future may be so powerful that they guide us at the cellular level. Numerous medical studies have demonstrated that images of health and well-being might play an important part in actually releasing the mechanisms necessary for healing, recovery, and resilience.

5. The positive principle: as we express hope, joy, and caring, so we create new relations

The positive principle holds that organizations are affirmative and responsive to positive images and positive language. The more positive the questions we ask, the more opportunities to create and sustain a positive discourse. Experience of organizational change with AI suggests that people are deeply moved and committed when asked questions about those moments in their experience that were life-giving and hope-producing. Hopeful images of the future, when framed by past actual experiences, are compelling, attractive, and generative. Hopeful imagery attracts energy and mobilizes action and intention. Positive images in this sense *lead to* positive actions, not the converse.

It is important not to shy away from the "positive" in this formula. Humanistic psychology has outlined the power of positive regard and supportive affect in demonstrating that people and organizations are heliotropic; that is they tend to grow in the direction of the helio, or life source. To grow towards the light of a positive anticipatory image suggests that conversations of hope, joy, inspiration, and other positive affect are *key* (not by-products) to lasting change and enduring health. Committed and collaborative relations tend to flourish under interactive experiences of hope, excitement, and caring.

6. The narrative principle: stories weave a connectedness that bridges the past with the future

The narrative principle celebrates the power of stories as a catalyst for change. Relating through narratives preserves the concreteness of meaningful events and values; they have an illustrative appeal. Because they operate on emotional and metaphoric levels, stories move us before we "know" why we are being moved. They reach us before we have a chance to put up our defenses. By engaging in others' stories, we connect and learn through an analogic discourse; we listen, almost naturally, for connections, likenesses and similarities to our experience, instead of immediately searching for differences. Even more basic is everyone's individual conviction and experience that coherence, movement, and direction are central to "meaningful" life. Life is not series of random, discrete or unconnected happenings. The past, present, and future are not separate stages, but rather beginnings, middles, and endings of a story in progress. We constitute our lives as meaningful by seeing them and expressing them through stories.

Organizations and human systems are stories-in-progress. All the members are co-authoring a certain story every day. No human event in the system has meaning apart from a story. The system's culture is simply *a* story about itself that has been chosen to be *the* story for the time being.

Future trajectory for AI

The worldwide application and adaptation of AI, the growing body of empirical research and thoughtful critique of AI and the emergence of the fields of positive psychology, strength-based leadership, and positive organization studies all suggest AI is positioned well to become a widely applied method for change and innovation management. Those using AI are modeling a new form of leadership best articulated by the field of management's most prolific writer, Peter Drucker, who shared in an interview with this author that, "The task of leadership is to align a system's strengths such that its weaknesses become irrelevant."

References and suggested readings

The Appreciative Inquiry Commons: http://appreciativeinquiry.case.edu/.
Barrett, F.J., and R.E. Fry (2005) *Appreciative Inquiry: A Positive Approach to Building Cooperative Capacity* (Chagrin Falls, OH: Taos Institute).

Cooperrider, D.L. (1999) "Positive Image, Positive Action," in S. Srivastva and D.L. Cooperrider (eds.), *Appreciative Management and Leadership* (Westlake, OH: Lakeshore, rev. edn): 91-125.

Cooperrider, D.L., and S. Srivastva (1987) "Appreciative Inquiry in Organizational Life," in R.W. Woodman and W.A. Pasmore (eds.), *Research In Organizational Change And Development* (vol. 1; Stamford, CO: JAI Press): 129-69.

Cooperrider, D.L., D. Whitney, and J.M. Stavros (2008) *Appreciative Inquiry Handbook* (Brunswick, OH: Crown Custom Publishing, 2nd edn).

Srivastva, S., and D. Cooperrider (1986) "The Emergence of the Egalitarian Organization," *Human Relations* 39.8: 683-724.

12

Stepping into the emerging future

Principles of Theory U

Otto Scharmer

The Presencing Institute, MIT, USA

A core aspect that make the collaboratory different from any other co-creative approach is its deliberate and courageous concentration on the group consciousness and the visionary power that lies therein. As long as we take a problem-based approach, we limit our creative power to the same thinking we had when we created the problem. New solutions require new spaces for thought. Otto Scharmer's Theory U provides a concrete way to move a conversation to a space where the group connect into the future and drive home solutions that emerge from a different, future reality. Chapter 15 (at the University of St. Gallen) shows a beautiful application of how this can concretely work.

We live in a time of massive institutional failure, collectively creating results that nobody wants. Climate change. Hunger. Poverty. Destruction of the foundations of our social, economic, ecological, and spiritual well-being. This time calls for a new consciousness and a new *collective* leadership capacity to meet challenges in a more conscious, intentional, and strategic way. The development of such a capacity will allow us to create a future of greater possibility.

Illuminating the blind spot

Why do our attempts to deal with the challenges of our time so often fail? Why are we stuck in so many quagmires today? The cause of our collective failure is that we are blind to the deeper dimension of leadership and transformational change. We are blind to the *source dimension* from which effective leadership and social action come into being. We know a great deal about *what* leaders do and *how* they do it. But we know very little about the inner place, the source from which they operate.

Successful leadership depends on the quality of attention and intention that the leader brings to any situation. Two leaders in the same circumstances doing the same thing can bring about completely different outcomes, depending on the inner place from which each operates. The nature of this inner place in leaders is something of a mystery to us. We do know something about the inner dimensions of athletes because studies have been conducted on what goes on within an athlete's mind and imagination in preparation for a competitive event. This knowledge has led to practices designed to enhance athletic performance from the "inside out," so to speak. But in the arena of management and leading transformational change, we know very little of about these inner dimensions, and very seldom are specific techniques applied to enhance management performance from the inside out. In a way, this lack of knowledge constitutes a "blind spot" in our approach to leadership and management (see Fig. 12.1).

We know very little about the invisible dimension of leadership, even though it is our source dimension.

Slowing down to understand

At its core, leadership is about shaping and shifting how individuals and groups attend to and subsequently respond to a situation. The trouble is that most leaders are unable to recognize, let alone change, the structural habits of attention used in their organizations.

Learning to recognize the habits of attention in any particular business culture requires, among other things, a particular kind of listening. Over more than a decade of observing people's interactions in organizations, I have noted four different types of listening.

Listening 1: Downloading

"Yeah, I know that already."

I call this type of listening "downloading"—listening by reconfirming habitual judgments. When you are in a situation where everything that happens confirms what you already know, you are listening by downloading.

Figure 12.1 The blind spot of leadership

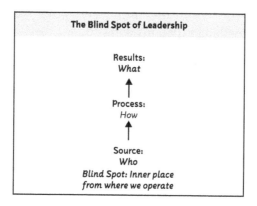

Listening 2: Factual

"Ooh, look at that!"

This type of listening is factual or object-focused: listening by paying attention to facts and to novel or disconfirming data. You switch off your inner voice of judgment and listen to the voices right in front of you. You focus on what differs from what you already know. Factual listening is the basic mode of good science. You let the data talk to you. You ask questions, and you pay careful attention to the responses you get.

Listening 3: Empathic

"Oh, yes, I know exactly how you feel."

This deeper level of listening is empathic listening. When we are engaged in real dialogue and paying careful attention, we can become aware of a profound shift in the place from which our listening origi-nates. We move from staring at the objective world of things, figures, and facts (the "it-world") to listening to the story of a living and evolving self (the "you-world"). Sometimes, when we say "I know how you feel," our emphasis is on a kind of mental or abstract knowing. But to really *feel* how another feels, we have to have an open heart. Only an open heart gives us the empathic capacity to connect *directly* with another person *from within*. When that happens, we feel a profound switch as we enter a new territory in the relationship; we forget about our own agenda and begin to see how the world appears through someone else's eyes.

Listening 4: Generative

"I can't express what I experience in words. My whole being has slowed down. I feel more quiet and present and more my real self. I am connected to something larger than myself."

This type of listening moves beyond the current field and connects us to an even deeper realm of emergence. I call this level of listening "generative listening," or listening from the emerging field of future possibility. This level of listening requires us to access not only our open heart, but also our open *will*—our capacity to connect to the highest future possibility that can emerge. We no longer look for something outside. We no longer empathize with someone in front of us. We are in an altered state. "Communion" or "grace" is maybe the words that come closest to the texture of this experience.

When you operate from Listening 1 (downloading), the conversation *reconfirms* what you already knew. You reconfirm your habits of thought: "There he goes again!" When you operate from Listening 2 (factual listening), you *disconfirm* what you already know and notice what is new out there: "Boy, this looks so different today!" When you choose to operate from Listening 3 (empathic listening), your perspective is *redirected* to seeing the situation through the eyes of another: "Boy, yes, now I really understand how you feel about it. I can sense it now too." And finally, when you choose to operate from Listening 4 (generative listening), you realize that by the end of the conversation you are no longer the same person you were when it began. You have gone through a subtle but profound change that has connected you to a deeper source of knowing, including the knowledge of your best future possibility and self.

Deep attention and awareness

While top athletes and championship teams around the world have begun to work with refined techniques of moving to peak performance business leaders operate largely without these techniques—or indeed, without any awareness that such techniques exist.

To be effective leaders, we must first understand the field, or inner space, from which we are operating. Theory U identifies four such "field structures of attention," which result in four different ways of operating. These differing structures affect not only the way we listen, but also how group members communicate with one another, and how institutions form their geometries of power (Fig. 12.2).

The four columns of Figure 12.2 depict four fundamental **meta-processes** of the social field that people usually take for granted:

- Thinking (individual)

- Conversing (group)

- Structuring (institutions)

- Ecosystem coordination (global systems)

Figure 12.2 How the structure of attention (Fields 1–4) determines the path of social emergence

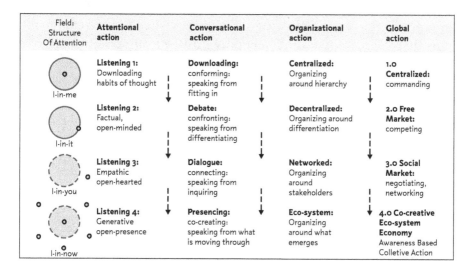

Albert Einstein famously noted that problems cannot be resolved by the same level of consciousness that created them. If we address our 21st-century challenges with reactive mind-sets that mostly reflect the realities of the 19th and 20th centuries (Fields 1 and 2), we will increase frustration, cynicism, and anger. Across all four meta-processes, we see the need to learn to respond from a deeply generative source (Field 4).

Summing up: the way we pay attention to a situation, individually and collectively, determines the path the system takes and how it emerges (Fig. 12.2). On all four levels—personal, group, institutional, and global—shifting from reactive responses and quick fixes on a symptoms level (Fields 1 and 2) to generative responses that address the systemic root issues (Fields 3 and 4) is the single most important leadership challenge of our time.

The U: one process, five movements

In order to move from a reactive Field 1 or 2 to a generative Field 3 or 4 response, we must embark on a journey. In an interview project on profound innovation and change that included 150 practitioners and thought leaders I heard many practitioners describe the various core elements of this journey. One person who did so in particularly accessible words is Brian Arthur, the founding head of the economics group at the Santa Fe Institute. When we visited him he explained to us that there are two fundamentally different sources of cognition. One is the application of existing frameworks (downloading) and the other accessing one's inner knowing. All true innovation in science, business, and society is based on the latter, not on the everyday downloading type of cognition. So we asked him, "How do you do that? If I want to learn that as an organization or as an individual, what do I have to do?" In his response he walked us through a sequence of three core movements.

The first movement he called "observe, observe, observe." It means to stop downloading and start listening. It means to stop our habitual ways of operating and immerse ourselves in the places of most potential, the places that matter most to the situation we are dealing with.

The second movement Brian Arthur referred to as "retreat and reflect: allow the inner knowing to emerge." Go to the inner place of stillness where knowing comes to the surface. We listen to everything we learned during the "observe, observe," and we attend to what wants to emerge. We pay particular attention to our own role and journey.

The third movement, according to Brian Arthur, is about "acting in an instant." This means to prototype the new in order to explore the future by doing. To create a little landing strip of the future that allows for hands-on testing and experimentation.

That whole process—observe, observe, access your sources of stillness and knowing, act in an instant—I have come to refer to as the U process because it can be depicted and understood as a U-shaped journey. In practical contexts the U-shaped journey usually requires two additional movements: an initial phase of building common ground (co-initiating) and a concluding phase that focuses on reviewing, sustaining, and advancing the practical results (co-evolving). The five movements of the U journey are depicted in Figure 12.3.

1. Co-initiating: build common intent. Stop and listen to others and to what life calls you to do

At the beginning of each project, a few key individuals gather together with the intention of making a difference in a situation that really matters to them and to their communities. As they coalesce into a core group, they maintain a common intention around their purpose, the people they want to involve, and the process they want to use. The context that allows such a core group to form is a process of deep listening—listening to what life calls you and others to do.

Figure 12.3 The U: one process, five movements

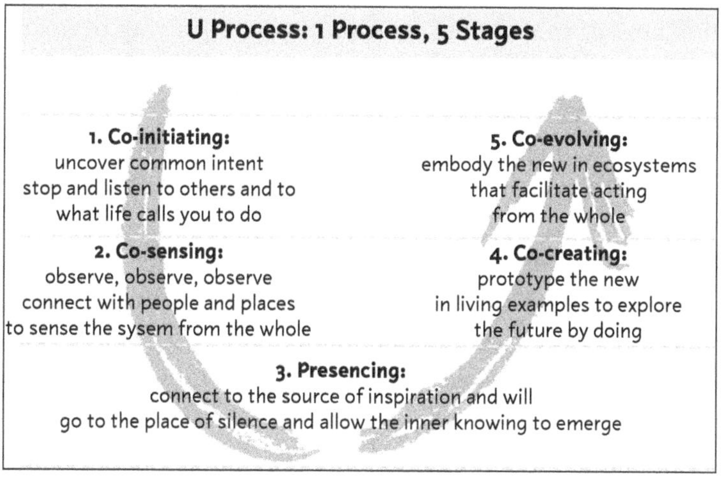

```
U Process: 1 Process, 5 Stages

    1. Co-initiating:                    5. Co-evolving:
   uncover common intent          embody the new in ecosystems
stop and listen to others and to        that facilitate acting
    what life calls you to do               from the whole

     2. Co-sensing:                      4. Co-creating:
   observe, observe, observe            prototype the new
  connect with people and places   in living examples to explore
 to sense the sysem from the whole      the future by doing

                      3. Presencing:
        connect to the source of inspiration and will
   go to the place of silence and allow the inner knowing to emerge
```

2. Co-sensing: observe, observe, observe. Go to the places of most potential and listen with your mind and heart wide open

The limiting factor of transformational change is not a lack of vision or ideas, but an inability to sense—that is, to see deeply, sharply, and collectively. When the members of a group see together with depth and clarity, they become aware of their own collective potential—almost as if a new, collective organ of sight was opening up. Goethe put it eloquently: "Every object, well contemplated, opens up a new organ of perception within us."

The late cognitive scientist Francisco Varela once told me about an experiment that had been conducted with newborn kittens, whose eyes were not yet open. They were put together in pairs, with one on the back of the other in such a way that only the lower kitten was able to move. Both kittens experienced the same spatial movements, but all of the legwork was done by the lower cat. The result of this experiment was that the lower cat learned to see quite normally, while the upper cat did not—its capacity to see developed inadequately and more slowly. The experiment illustrates that the ability to see is developed by the activity of the whole organism.

When it comes to organizing knowledge management, strategy, innovation, and learning, we are like the upper cat—we outsource the legwork to experts, consultants, and teachers to tell us how the world works. For simple problems, this may be an appropriate approach. But if you are in the business of innovation, then the upper cat's way of operating is utterly dysfunctional. The last thing that any real innovator would outsource is perception. When innovating, we must go to places ourselves, talk with people, and stay in touch with issues as they evolve. Without a direct link to the context of a situation, we cannot learn to see and act effectively.

What is missing most in our current organizations and societies is a set of practices that enable this deep kind of deep seeing—"sensing"—to happen collectively and across boundaries. When sensing happens, the group as a whole can see the emerging opportunities and the key systemic forces at issue.

3. Presencing: connect to the source of inspiration and common will. Go to the place of silence and allow the inner knowing to emerge

At the bottom of the U, individuals or groups on the U journey come to a threshold that requires a "letting go" of everything that is not essential. In many ways, this threshold is like the gate in ancient Jerusalem called "The Needle," which was so narrow that when a fully loaded camel reached it, the camel driver had to take off all the bundles so the camel could pass through—giving rise to the New Testament saying that "It is easier for a camel to go through the eye of a needle than for a rich man to enter the kingdom of God."

At the same time that we drop the non-essential aspects of the self ("letting go"), we also open ourselves to new aspects of our highest possible future self ("letting come"). The essence of presencing is the experience of the coming in of the new and the transformation of the old. Once a group crosses this threshold, nothing remains the same. Individual members and the group as a whole begin to operate with a heightened level of energy and sense of future possibility. Often they then begin to function as an intentional vehicle for the future that they feel wants to emerge.

4. Co-creating: prototype the new in living examples to explore the future by doing

I often work with people trained as engineers, scientists, managers, and economists (as I was). But when it comes to innovation, we all received the wrong education. In all our training and schooling one important skill was missing: the art and practice of prototyping. That's what you learn when you become a designer. What designers learn is the opposite of what the rest of us are socialized and habituated to do.

So the prototype is not the stage that comes after the analysis. The prototype is *part* of the sensing and discovery process in which we explore the future by *doing* rather than by *thinking and reflecting*. This is such a simple point—but I have found that the innovation processes of many organizations are stalled right there, in the old analytical method of "analysis paralysis."

The co-creation movement of the U journey results in a set of small living examples that explore the future by doing. It also results in a vibrant and rapidly widening network of change-makers who leverage their learning across prototypes and who help each other deal with whatever innovation challenges they face.

5. Co-evolving: embody the new in ecosystems that facilitate seeing and acting from the whole

Once we have developed a few prototypes and microcosms of the new, the next step is to review what has been learned—what is working and what is not—and then decide which prototypes might have the highest impact on the system or situation at hand. Coming up with a sound assessment at this stage often requires the involvement of stakeholders from other institutions and sectors. Very often, what you think you will create at the beginning of the U process is quite different from what eventually emerges.

The co-evolving movement results in an innovation ecosystem that connects high-leverage prototype initiatives with the institutions and players that can help take it to the next level of piloting and scaling.

The five movements of the U apply both to the macro level of innovation projects and change architectures and to the meso- and micro-levels of group conversation or one-on-one interactions. In martial arts you go through the U in a fraction of a second. When applied to larger innovation projects, the U process unfolds over longer periods of time and in different forms. Thus, the team composition in such projects usually changes and adapts to some degree after each movement.

Since introducing this framework of the U Theory in 2004 and 2007, many projects and initiatives have been using this method and process across organizations, systems, sectors, and cultures. What we learned throughout these applications is that there are three inner sources of resistance that leaders face when dealing with transformative change: the voice of Judgment, the voice of Cynicism, and the voice of Fear. We also learned that in order to deal with these sources of resistance, leaders need to engage in a new inner leadership work that focuses on cultivating three instruments of knowing: the Open Mind, that is the capacity to suspending habitual judgment, the Open Heart, that is, the capacity to empathize, to see a problem through the eyes of another, and the Open Will, that is, the capacity of letting go and letting come. For more detail in regard to the principles, practices, and learning experiences please visit www.presencing.com.

Transformative scenario planning

A new way to work with the future[1]

Adam Kahane
Reos Partners, USA

This chapter provides an important backdrop to understanding the complexities involved in solving "wicked problems" by involving societal stakeholders. It looks at conditions and potential solutions.

My first experience with transformative scenario planning, the Mont Fleur Scenario Exercise in South Africa in 1991 and 1992, left me feeling inspired and also uncertain. It was clear to me that the exercise had contributed to creating change in South Africa, but it was not clear to me whether or how this way of working could be used in other contexts. In which type of situation could transformative scenario planning be useful? To be useful, which outputs did it have to produce and which inputs did it require? And to produce these outputs, which steps were essential?

---

1 Reprint of Chapter 2 of *Transformative Scenario Planning: Working Together to Change the Future* by Adam Kahane with the kind permission of Berrett-Koehler.

These questions set me off on an exploration that I have now been on for more than 20 years. I sought out opportunities in South Africa and elsewhere to work with people who were trying to address tough challenges. I found colleagues, and together we worked on many different projects, on different challenges, of different scales, in different countries, with different actors, using different methodologies. These experiences gave me many opportunities for trial and many opportunities for error, and so many opportunities for learning. Gradually I found answers to my questions.

When to use transformative scenario planning

The South African context that gave birth to the Mont Fleur Scenario Exercise turns out to have been a particular example of a general type of situation. Transformative scenario planning can be useful to people who find themselves in a situation that has the following three characteristics.

First, these people see the situation they are in as unacceptable, unstable or unsustainable. Their situation may have been this way for some time, or it may be becoming this way now, or it may possibly become this way in the future. They may feel frightened or excited or confused. In any event, these people cannot or are not willing to carry on as before, or to adapt to or flee from what is happening. They think that they have no choice but to try to transform their situation. The participants in the Mont Fleur project, for example, viewed apartheid as unacceptable, unstable, and unsustainable, and saw the just-opened political negotiations as offering them an opportunity to contribute to changing it. Another, hypothetical, example might be people in a community who think that the conditions in their schools are unacceptable and want to change them.

Second, these people cannot transform their situation on their own or by working only with their friends and colleagues. Even if they want to, they are unable to impose or force through a transformation. The larger social–political–economic system (the sector or community or country) within which they and their situation are embedded is too complex—it has too many actors, too many interdependencies, too much unpredictability—to be grasped or shifted by any one person or organization or sector, even one with lots of ideas and resources and authority.[2] These people therefore need to find some way to work together with actors from across the whole system.

South Africans who wanted to transform the apartheid situation had been trying for decades to force this transformation, through mass protests, international sanctions, and armed resistance. But these efforts had not succeeded. Mont Fleur and the other multi-stakeholder processes of the early 1990s (which the previous forceful efforts had precipitated) provided South Africans with a new way to work with other actors from across the system. In the community example, changing the conditions in the schools might require the involvement not just of concerned citizens and school administrators but also of teachers, parents, students, and others.

Third, these people cannot transform their situation directly. The actors who need to work together to make the transformation are too polarized to be able to approach this work head-on. They agree neither on what the solution is nor even on what the problem is. At best, they agree that they face a situation they all find problematic, although in different respects and for different reasons.[3] Any attempt to implement a solution directly would therefore only increase resistance and rigidity. So the transformation must be approached indirectly, through first building shared understandings, relationships, and intentions.

The actors who came together in Mont Fleur all agreed that apartheid was irretrievably problematic and needed to be dismantled, but they came in with deep differences in their diagnoses of the ways in which it was problematic and their prescriptions for how it should be transformed. The scenario process enabled them to create common ground. In the community example, the administrators, teachers, parents and

2 I am referring here to the consequences of social, dynamic, and generative complexity respectively (see Kahane 2009: 5; Senge and Scharmer 2001: 23).

3 I learned this crucial distinction between problems and problematic situations from Kees van der Heijden.

students might have a long history of unproductive disagreements that means they cannot simply sit down and start to work together.

Transformative scenario planning is, then, a way for people to work with complex problematic situations that they want to transform but cannot transform unilaterally or directly. This way of working with the future can be used to deal with such situations at all scales: local, sectoral, regional, national or global (the stories in this chapter are all national because this is the scale at which I have done most of my work and that I know best). Transformative scenario planning is not a way for actors to adapt to a situation or to force its transformation or to implement an already-formulated proposal or to negotiate between several already-formulated proposals. It is a way for actors to work cooperatively and creatively to get unstuck and to move forward.

How transformative scenario planning works

In a transformative scenario planning process, actors transform their problematic situation through transforming themselves, in four ways.

First, they **transform their understandings**. Their scenario stories articulate their collective synthesis of what is happening and could happen in and around the system of which they are part. They see their situation—and, critically important, their own roles in their situation—with fresh eyes. In a polarized or confused or stuck situation, such new, clear, shared understandings enable forward movement.

Second, the actors **transform their relationships**. Through working together in the scenario team, they enlarge their empathy for and trust in other actors on the team and across the system, and their ability and willingness to work together. This strengthening of cross-system relationships is often the most important and enduring output of such projects.

Third, the actors **transform their intentions**. Their transformed understandings and relationships shift how they see what they can and must do to deal with what is happening in their system. They transform their fundamental will.

Fourth, the actors' transformations of their understandings, relationships, and intentions enable them to **transform their actions** and thereby to transform their situation.

The story of Mont Fleur exemplifies this four-part logic. The participants constructed a new way of understanding the political, economic, and social challenges that South Africans were facing and then created four scenarios as to how South Africans could try to deal with these challenges. The participants constructed new relationships and alliances, especially between leaders of hitherto-separated parties, sectors, and races. And they constructed new intentions as to what they needed to do in their own spheres of influence to try to prevent the "ostrich," "lame duck," and "Icarus" scenarios and to bring forth "flight of the flamingos." Over the years that followed, these new understandings, relationships, and intentions enabled the participants and others with whom they engaged to undertake a series of aligned actions that did in fact contribute to their achieving these intentions.

In the community example, a team of concerned citizens, administrators, teachers, parents and students might construct a set of scenarios (both desirable and undesirable) about what could happen in and around their schools and community. This work together might enable them to understand and trust one another more, and to clarify what they need to do to change the conditions in their schools. Then they might be able to take action, together and separately, to effect these changes.

Transformative scenario planning can generate transformations such as those in these two examples only if three components are in place. Transformative scenario planning is a composite social technology that brings together three already-existing technologies into a new way of working that can generate new results.[4] If any one of these components is missing, this new way of working will not work.

The first component is a **whole-system team** of insightful, influential, and interested actors. These actors constitute a strategic microcosm of the system as a whole: they are not from only one part or camp or faction

---

4   Brian Arthur (2009) says that new technologies arise from new and unexpected combinations of existing ones.

of the system, and they are not only observers of the system. They all want to address a particular problematic situation and know that they cannot do so alone. They choose to join this team because they think that if they can act together, then they can be more successful.

The second component is a **strong container** within which these actors can transform their understandings, relationships and intentions.[5] The boundaries of this container are set so that the team feels enough protection and safety, as well as enough pressure and friction, to be able to do their challenging work. Building such a container requires paying attention to multiple dimensions of the space within which the team does their work: the political positioning of the exercise, so that the actors feel able to meet their counterparts from other parts of the system without being seen as having betrayed their own part; the psychosocial conditions of the work, so that the actors feel able to become aware of and challenge (and have challenged) their own thoughts and actions; and the physical locations of the meetings, so that the actors can relax and pay attention to their work without interruption or distraction.

The third component is a **rigorous process**. In a transformative scenario planning process, the actors construct a set of relevant, challenging, plausible, and clear stories about what *could* happen—not about what *will* happen (a forecast) or about what *should* happen (a wish or proposal)—and then act on what they have learned from this construction. The uniqueness of the scenario process is that it is pragmatic and inspirational, rational and intuitive, connected to and challenging of dominant understanding, and immersed in and disconnected from the complexity and conflict of the situation. Furthermore, the future is a more neutral space about which all actors are more equally ignorant.

The transformative scenario planning process that was invented at Mont Fleur originated in the adaptive scenario planning process that had been invented at Shell two decades earlier (see Shell 2008)—but it turns this adaptive process on its head. In an adaptive scenario planning process, the leaders of an organization construct and employ stories about what could happen in the world outside their organization

---

5 This container principle is explained in Stookey 2012.

in order to formulate strategies and plans to enable their organization to fit into and survive and thrive in a range of possible futures. They use adaptive scenario planning to anticipate and adapt to futures that they think they cannot predict and cannot or should not or need not influence.

But adaptive scenario planning is useful only up to a point. Sometimes people find themselves in situations that are too unacceptable or unstable or unsustainable for them to be willing or able to go along with and adapt to. In such situations, they need an approach not simply for anticipating and adapting to the future but also for influencing or transforming it. For example, an adaptive approach to living in a crime-ridden community could involve employing locks or alarms or guards, whereas a transformative approach could involve working with others to reduce the levels of criminality. An adaptive response to climate change could involve building dikes to protect against higher sea levels, whereas a transformative approach could involve working with others to reduce emissions of greenhouse gases. Both approaches are rational, feasible, and legitimate, but they are different and require different kinds of action and alliance.

The key difference between adaptive and transformative scenario planning is, then, one of purpose. Adaptive scenario planning uses stories about possible futures to study what could happen, whereas transformative scenario planning assumes that studying the future is insufficient, and so it also uses stories about possible futures to influence what could happen. To achieve these two different purposes, adaptive scenario planning focuses on producing new systemic understandings, whereas transformative scenario planning assumes that new understandings alone are insufficient and so also focuses on producing new cross-system relationships and new system-transforming intentions. And to produce these two different sets of outputs, adaptive scenario planning requires a rigorous process, whereas transformative scenario planning assumes that process alone is insufficient, and so it also requires a whole-system team and a strong container.

Transformative scenario planning enables people to transform their problematic situation through building a strong alliance of actors who deeply understand the situation, one another, and what they need to do.

The five steps of transformative scenario planning

I have learned how to do transformative scenario planning through 20 years of trial and error. I have observed when these projects fail to get off the ground and when they succeed in launching, when they get stuck and when they flow, and when they collapse and when they keep on going. In this way, I have been able to discern what works and what does not and why, and to piece together a simple five-step process. The five steps are as follows: convening a team from across the whole system; observing what is happening; constructing stories about what could happen; discovering what can and must be done; and acting to transform the system. This process is like an old cow path: although it is not the only way forward, it is a way that has, after many alternatives were tried out over many years, proven to provide a reliable route. Those undertaking transformative scenario planning projects have available to them many options for processes to use in each of the five steps (for and overview of resources see Box 13.1 at the end of this chapter).

These five steps can be framed as an application of the U process to the transformation of complex problematic situations.[6] The U process is a model of transformation that includes five movements: co-initiating (in transformative scenario planning, this is the convening step), co-sensing (the observing and constructing steps), co-presencing (the discovering step), and co-creating and co-evolving (the acting step) (see Figure 13.1). The U process is an indirect process—a detour—in that it is a way to get unstuck and move forward to transform a problematic situation through pausing and stepping back from the situation. It is a creative process in that what can and must be done on the right-hand side is not visible from the left-hand side but can be discovered only along the way. And it is a fractal process in that each step along the U contains within it a smaller U, so that the actors repeat the five movements from co-initiating to co-evolving over and over.

6 The U process is outlined in Senge *et al.* 2005 and Scharmer 2009. I have also learned about the U-Process from Jeff Barnum. See also Chapter 12 in this book.

Figure 13.1 The five steps of transformative scenario planning

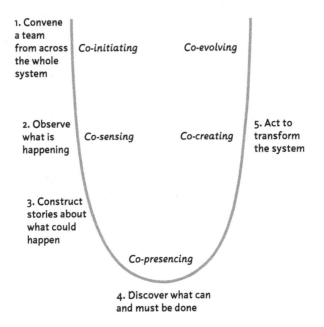

Transformative scenario planning addresses problematic situations slowly and from the inside out. Over the course of the five steps, the actors gradually transform their understandings, relationships, and intentions, and thereby their actions. Through this process, the transformation ripples out from the individual leaders to the scenario team, the organizations and sectors they lead, and the larger social system.

A transformative scenario planning project can be broad or narrow, large or small, long or short. My experience suggests, however, that for a complex problematic situation to be transformed, certain ideal parameters exist. You can succeed outside of these parameters, but you will find it harder, or you will have to use methods different from the ones outlined in this book.

In the first step, a convening team of five to ten people builds a whole-system scenario team of 25 to 35 leading actors (including the conveners themselves). Convening or scenario teams that are smaller than these will be unlikely to have the diversity required for whole-system insight and influence. Convening or scenario teams that are larger than these will find it difficult to develop the intimacy and engagement that the process requires. There are other methods for working with much larger teams, but these are not compatible with the structured combination of rational and intuitive processes of scenario work.

The scenario team undertakes the second, third, and fourth steps in three or four workshops of three to four days each (with supporting work being done in between the workshops), spread over four to eight months. A process with fewer workshops or workshops that are shorter or closer together will be unlikely to provide enough time for the team to go deep enough (and get lost enough) to transform their understandings, relationships and intentions. (My partner Bill O'Brien said about the time needed for transformational work: "It takes nine months to make a baby, no matter how many people you put on the job.")[7] A process with more workshops or workshops that are longer or more spread out will find it difficult to maintain the requisite energy and momentum.

Finally, the scenario team, with others, undertakes the fifth step over another four to eight months or longer. A shorter process will be unlikely to provide enough time for the team's actions to transform their situation. But their actions could well ripple out for years, either within the scenario project or beyond its end. A transformative scenario planning project can get a process of systemic transformation started, but the process may take generations to be completed.

Transformative scenario planning is simple, but it is not easy or straightforward or guaranteed. The process is emergent; it almost never unfolds according to plan; and context-specific design and redesign are always required. So the only way to learn this process is to practice it in a range of contexts.

7 Personal communication with Bill O'Brien, 2000. Also see O'Brien 2008.

Box 13.1 Overview of resources for transformative scenario planning processes

Step 1: Convene a team from across the system

- Seek out potential allies
- Identify and enroll a convening team and then a scenario team
- Conduct dialogue interviews of scenario team members and other actors
- Make a project plan and mobilize necessary resources
- Build the project container

Step 2: Observe what is happening

- Share and reflect in the scenario team
- Go on learning journeys
- Commission research papers
- Interact with resource people
- Search for structural driving forces
- List certainties and uncertainties

Step 3: Construct stories about what could happen

- Choose key certainties and uncertainties
- Construct scenarios deductively
- Construct scenarios inductively
- Write logical narratives of hypothetical future events
- Find metaphors, images and names for each scenario
- Compare and contrast the scenarios
- Prepare reports in different media

Step 4: Discover what can and must be done

- Take an adaptive stance
- Consider your strengths and weaknesses in, and the opportunities and threats of, each scenario
- Take a transformative stance
- Develop options for joint and separate actions
- Draw conclusions about what you will do

Step 5: Act to transform the system

- Hold individual, organizational and public meetings
- Disseminate the scenario using print, broadcast, and social media
- Launch spin-off initiatives of all kinds
- Cultivate and coordinate an ongoing network of inspired and aligned actors

Process instructions, project case studies, web links, and other resources are available at http://www.reospartners.com/scenarios.

References

Arthur, W.B. (2009) *The Nature of Technology: What it is and How it Evolves* (New York: Free Press).

Kahane, A. (2009) *Power and Love: A Theory and Practice of Social Change* (San Francisco: Berrett-Koehler Publishers).

O'Brien, W. (2008) *Character at Work: Building Prosperity Through the Practice of Virtue* (Boston: Paulist Press).

Scharmer, C.O. (2009) *Theory U: Leading from the Future as It Emerges* (San Francisco: Berrett-Koehler Publishers).

Senge, P.M., and Scharmer, C.O. (2001) "Community Action Research: Learning as a Community of Practitioners, Consultants and Researchers," in P. Reason and H. Bradbury (eds.), *Handbook of Action Research: Participative Inquiry and Practice* (Thousand Oaks, CA: Sage Publications).

Senge, P.M., C.O. Scharmer, J. Jaworski, and B.S. Flowers (2005) *Presence: An Exploration of Profound Change in People, Organizations, and Society* (New York: Crown Books).

Shell (2008) *Scenarios: An Explorer's Guide* (The Hague: Shell International).

Stookey, C.W. (2012) *Keep Your People in the Boat: Workforce Engagement Lessons from the Sea* (Halifax, Nova Scotia: ALIA Press).

Part 3

Examples of the collaboratory

In Part 3 we are looking at concrete examples of the collaboratory across the world in a diversity of settings and involving different degrees of complexity:

- The collaboratory in the classroom—Bentley University

- Students leading collaboratories—University of St. Gallen

- Creating connection, conversation and courage—the Exeter collaboratory

- Transforming an organization—participatory leadership and art of hosting

- Regional organizational change—community-building in action

- Transforming collaborative institutions—Australian business schools

- Long-term stakeholder engagement—Initiatives of Change

- A meta-collaboratory—the Globally Responsible Leadership Initiative

We start with the most simple example of using the collaboratory in an undergraduate classroom at Bentley University (Chapter 14) and follow how the collaboratory was used to encourage student-led stakeholder engagement at the University of St. Gallen, which includes a step-by-step process guide that can be applied to many other situations (Chapter 15). From there, we are inspired to learn about how the collaboratory is used in yet another university setting at the University of Exeter to gather and unite a dispersed faculty (Chapter 16).

The collaboratory idea has also been used in more traditional organizational settings to transform a pharmaceutical company in Switzerland (Chapter 17) offering a fascinating view and powerful facilitation narrative of designing and co-creating systemic change. A deep insight into community-building as a transformational change practice at Unilever in Asia is presented in Chapter 18. Both examples show how a collaboratory can work in a process over a certain period of change and what key enablers for success are. Chapter 19 looks at a collaboratory initiated by the Australian Business Deans Council to run a practice innovation trial based on the 50+20 vision. Initiatives of Change, which started seven decades ago in Caux, Switzerland, offers profound and extensive insights into how a collaborative idea can be held alive both across space and time (Chapter 20). In a global perspective we look at two specific examples from the Globally Responsible Leadership Initiative, a meta-collaboratory founded in 2004 assembling corporations and learning institutions to advance responsible leadership worldwide (Chapter 21).

While these examples are only a few hand-picked best practices from around the world, there are many others that have taken place, are in the middle of their co-creative process or are in the process of being launched. This sample is thus meant to serve as a source of inspiration for those interested in bringing about change in their own environment through a collaborative stakeholder approach.

If you have additional thoughts, examples or questions, please contact katrin.muff@gmail.com.

14

The collaboratory in the classroom

Bentley University

Anthony Buono
Bentley University, USA

This chapter looks at a specific application of the collaboratory method in an undergraduate setting and considers its effect on the learning and development of concerned students.

Reflections on pedagogy and undergraduate student development

The application of the collaboratory methodology as a way to engage stakeholders, promote in-depth dialogue and interaction, and open avenues for further learning, development, and exploration reflects a promising way to tackle both local and global challenges. I was initially struck by the potential of this practice through ongoing exchanges with Thomas Dyllick (University of St. Gallen) and the 50+20 group at two Principles for Responsible Management Education (PRME) forums and the first meeting of the Aspen Consortium on "Rethinking Undergraduate

Business Education." Based on that experience, I decided to experiment with the approach in one of my undergraduate electives—the Sociology of Work and Organizations.

A central component of the course focuses on the transition from an industrial to a post-industrial society and the underlying ramifications for the various ways in which we think about management and organization. As part of the course, new perspectives on business and its social role are also explored, including such topics as the UN Global Compact and the PRME initiative, the 50+20 vision of management and management education, and conscious capitalism, a new approach to business that is based on commitment to a higher purpose (beyond profitability per se) and a stakeholder-centric perspective for conducting business (see Buono and Sisodia 2011; Mackey and Sisodia 2013; Sisodia 2011). My initial thought was to create a single collaboratory experience for the students within this module of the course, with the dual focus of facilitating their exploration of different views about conscious capitalism and illustrating how this pedagogical approach might be used.

The collaboratory in the classroom

Framing an intervention

During an earlier class session, we had discussed the 50+20 framework, focusing on the need for globally responsible leaders to have broad reflective awareness with the ability to act as enlightened statesmen. Within this context, we examined the concept of the collaboratory as a way to educate and enable such leaders, drawing out its transformative potential for engaging stakeholders.

Because the ideal of conscious capitalism runs counter to traditional corporate models—as well as many of the perspectives they are exposed to in other business courses—I felt that it was important to provide the students with an open space to explore and share their ideas. Thus, as a way of bringing the concept of conscious capitalism as well as the collaboratory to life, we created a collaboratory class session in which students were asked to share their views on this approach to business, drawing out its pros and cons, possibilities and limitations, and how it might evolve.

Staging the collaboratory

Creating a circle with five chairs in the front of the classroom, the discussion started with volunteers to "kick off" the conversation. While I wanted to create another two or three rings of chairs around the inner circle to create a "fishbowl" experience, the physical nature of the room—a tiered classroom with movable chairs—limited what we were able to construct. Students were instructed to "filter into" the dialogue when they felt they had something to contribute—from supporting, questioning, and critiquing viewpoints to adding new perspectives—by approaching the individuals in the circle and tapping them on the shoulder. The only other ground rules were that all students had an equal opportunity to contribute, they had to leave the circle when tapped but could rejoin the conversation after at least one other person entered, not interrupt others as they were speaking, and were expected to *listen* to others and be respectful in their comments and exchanges. Any criticism was also to be constructive in nature, allowing for the further development of the initial ideas. Following roughly 30 minutes of exchange among the students, we debriefed the collaboratory approach and the extent to which it influenced their views and perspectives on conscious capitalism, and explored its potential to influence how we think about pedagogical approaches to management education.

Although I was generally pleased with the way in which the experience unfolded, a lingering concern was that the conversation was still dominated by the more vocal students in the class, in essence, the same people who always speak up with something to contribute. It was also more of a challenge than I had initially envisioned (given the tiered classroom seating) getting students to move around the room to enter and leave the circle. Still the collaboratory did facilitate a thoughtful exchange among the students and many of them reported that the openness of the discussion raised points about the topic they had not considered. Thus, despite the physical constraints of the tiered classroom and a smaller number of participants than I had hoped for, after debriefing the experience with the students I decided to revisit the approach later in the semester.

Instead of using the method to explore a particular topic as I had done with conscious capitalism, I decided to use collaboratories as a way of reviewing and reflecting on material covered throughout the course.

Since the first collaboratory took place relatively early in the semester, we were able to utilize the approach three more times, at intervals two to three weeks apart. Over the course of the semester, collaboratory conversations gradually became more animated, the students seemed to be increasingly engaged in the exchanges, and students who did not engage in the first one or two exercises began to get involved. As the process evolved, one of the outcomes that I was especially struck with was the extent to which the students in the circle drew on earlier course materials to frame their comments, integrating different segments and topics and creating what might be thought of as a new level of learning. I also found that the in-class dialogue that took place in more traditional class discussions improved as well—becoming more thoughtful and more extensive.

Although I debriefed the class after each exercise, drawing out their thoughts about the experience and raising questions for them to consider about the exchange (e.g. "How could you be more constructive when critiquing someone's idea?"; "How might concept x have contributed to the discussion?"), my role throughout the process was largely as a facilitator rather than the classroom expert. One of the things that I wrestled with was my comfort level with silence during parts of the exchanges. Knowing my own tendency to "fill in the blanks" to keep the conversation going, I purposely held back—which was not all that easy—and found that the less I talked, the more they did.

The collaboratory circle as an intimidating place?

Reflecting back on the experience, another thing that caught my attention came from the comments of one of my students, a bright but shy young woman who said she had a difficult time speaking up in class. One of the realities we often downplay as professors is that speaking up in class can be difficult for many of our students and, within this context, the collaboratory's inner circle can be a very intimidating place—especially at first. Looking back to highly interactive collaboratory sessions during the Rio+20 Earth Summit and the 2013 PRME Summit, for example, I saw similar hesitation among some of the professionals in attendance—individuals one would expect to be quite comfortable in that environment. It is important to realize that it can be much more intimidating for students, especially undergraduates and those who might be more introverted.

Over time, however, the collaboratory approach engaged this student and, as she expressed, she felt compelled to join the conversation (it was not mandatory). Although she did not participate in the first exercise, she did get involved towards the end of the second session. In each of the subsequent collaboratory exchanges her participation and engagement increased—and at the end of the semester she approached me. As mentioned above, she noted that she was very shy and had a difficult time contributing to class discussions—but observing other students in the collaboratory, and her reflections on those observations ("I can do that")—gave her the confidence to join in the conversation. The content of the discussion and the constructive way that students raised their points and questioned others gave her the confidence that she had good ideas to share. The experience also gave her the self-assurance to engage in more traditional classroom discussions—something she noted she had avoided as much as possible.

Reflections

Writing this brief chapter provided the opportunity to reflect on my experience with the collaboratory, attempting to make sense of that experience and think about its possibilities in the classroom. Looking back, I was drawn to a number of conceptual linkages, from Stein's (1994) insightful work on "listening deeply," my own work on "guided changing" (Kerber and Buono, 2005) to more recent developments focused on "presencing" (Senge, Scharmer, Jaworski, and Flowers 2005) and "Theory U" (Scharmer and Kaufer 2103).

Stein (1994) underscored the need to engage all parties involved in a given situation, getting those participants to listen to each other with greater attentiveness, compassion, and understanding—especially on issues where there are strong differences of opinion. I have used this approach in the past within my own merger and acquisition consulting (Buono 2009) as well as my work on guided changing (Kerber and Buono 2005), a highly interactive approach to conceptualizing and approaching the change process, as a type of collaboratory without the circle. Guided changing is an iterative process of initial interpretation and design, implementation, and improvisation, learning from the change effort, and then sharing that learning system-wide, leading to ongoing re-interpretation and redesign of the change. The resulting spiral of learning, innovation, and development contributes to both continuous improvement of existing change efforts and the ability to generate novel changes and solutions. An underlying goal is to bring people into the present, encouraging them to openly probe and explore the challenges they are facing.

The idea of presencing—in essence creating a physical and mental environment that increases awareness of the present moment, encouraging reflection, insight and creativity (Senge *et al.* 2005)—raises some interesting challenges in our attempts to transform our classrooms into true learning laboratories. The traditional classroom approach—not matter how interactive—reinforces old patterns of seeing and acting, what has been referred to as "downloading," supporting habitual ways of knowing and doing. The collaboratory methodology brings such presencing to life, as Scharmer and Kaufer (2013) have called for, "holding the space of listening" on several levels, from listening to others, to oneself and, ultimately, to the larger group or collective. Moving from observing and sensing to truly participating, however, takes confidence and self-assurance, especially in multi-stakeholder gatherings where they are trying to shift from debate and argument to "co-creating the new." This requisite level of knowledge, insight, and confidence, however, may not necessarily reside in many of our undergraduates, at least initially.

Using collaboratories as a way of "flipping" the classroom (Bergmann and Sams 2012) inverts our traditional approach to education. In a typical classroom, students listen to lectures in class and perform other learning activities—for example, dealing with practice problems—as "homework." In a typical flipped classroom, in contrast, students go through content-based assignments—readings and video lectures for example—before class and perform other learning activities in class, attaining deeper knowledge via class activities. The resulting interaction leads to deeper learning, as the class as collective grasps more meaningful and pertinent direction for their understanding of the subject matter.

One of the ongoing challenges we face is balancing the time it take to create the reflective awareness that is at the heart of the collaboratory paradigm with coverage of content-specific material in our courses. By flipping the classroom we can accomplish both goals. My experience underscores that it take multiple collaboratory exercises to truly engage students, helping them to build the confidence and self-assurance they need to engage in such interaction and exchanges on a meaningful level. Despite what may initially seem like an intimidating experience, putting oneself in the circle can be a powerful way of building that self-assurance.

References

Bergmann, J., and A. Sams (2012) *Flip Your Classroom: Reach Every Student in Every Class Every Day* (Washington, DC: International Society for Technology in Education).

Buono, A.F. (2009) "Consulting to Integrate Mergers and Acquisitions," in L. Greiner and F. Poulfelt (eds.), *Management Consulting Today and Tomorrow: Perspectives and Advice from 27 World Experts* (New York: Routledge): 303-29.

Buono, A.F., and R.S. Sisodia (2011) "A Conscious Purpose," *Global Focus* 5.2: 56-59.

Kerber, K.W., and A.F. Buono (2005) "Rethinking Organizational Change: Reframing the Challenge of Change Management," *Organization Development Journal* 23.3: 23-38.

Mackey, J., and R. Sisodia (2013) *Conscious Capitalism: Liberating the Heroic Spirit of Business* (Cambridge, MA: Harvard Business School Press).

Senge, P.M., C.O. Scharmer, J. Jaworski, and B.S. Flowers (2005) *Presence: An Exploration of Profound Change in People, Organizations, and Society* (New York: Crown Books).

Sisodia, R.S. (2011) "Conscious Capitalism: A Better Way to Win," *California Management Review* 53.3: 98-108.

Scharmer, C.O., and K. Kaufer (2013) Leading from the Emerging Future: From Ego-System to Eco-System Economies (San Francisco: Berrett-Koehler).

Stein, H.F. (1994) *Listening Deeply* (Boulder, CO: Westview Press).

15
Students leading collaboratories

University of St. Gallen

Thomas Dyllick
Institute for Economy and the Environment, University of St. Gallen, Switzerland

Katrin Muff
Business School Lausanne, Switzerland

This chapter looks at a full-fledged application of the 50+20 collaboratory as invented for Rio+20 and including a step-by-step approach through the entire process in all detail in order to be applied to other applications within a university, business or community situation.

Besides this useful step-by-step approach, another interesting element of this example is that it shows how to involve a large number of stakeholders in the facilitation of collaboratory events (in this case students). This may be of interest for collaboratories where it is important to assure a deep involvement of stakeholders.

The collaboratory described below took place in the semester-long master's specialization course "Strategies for Sustainable Development" at the University of St. Gallen and was co-created by the two authors.[1]

---

1 The course syllabus can be downloaded from: http://www.iwoe.unisg.ch/~/link.aspx?_id=ED3FE263734D445C9AA23754FD114755&_z=z, accessed 6 April 2014.

Context and overall objectives

At the University of St. Gallen we used the Collaboratory as the guiding principle and method for a 12-week master's course "Strategies for Sustainable Development" for the first time in Spring 2013. It sought to address and resolve three critical sustainability issues on a local level (creating a breakthrough for climate-friendly food, promoting the bicycle as a viable mobility alternative in the city of St. Gallen and at the university, making tap water the favorite drink in Switzerland). Each issue was introduced in one session followed by two collaboratory sessions that took place every three weeks. The Collaboratory 1 uses all three phases of Scharmer's Theory U (downloading, visioning, and prototyping) (Scharmer 2009). A crucial element of Theory U is the visioning process, as it directs the attention and intention from a past space of experience to a future space of possibility. The Collaboratory 2 shows an important continuation and deepening of the Collaboratory 1.

This chapter presents a detailed description of our Collaboratory approach and process for 50 students split into three groups of equal size. The Collaboratory can be run with much smaller groups making the organization easier. To illustrate the process we will provide detailed descriptions of the Collaboratories 1 and 2 and hint at some of the outcomes. We hope that our process, experience and learning serve as inspiration for others who wish to use the Collaboratory approach in an educational setting.

Collaboratories are live processes, which cannot be predicted or planned in all detail in advance. It is important to remain open and flexible. Being prepared extremely well is a pre-condition for being flexible. A collaboratory is a careful collective improvisation rather than a strict procedure. Being spontaneous and having fun is very important for a creative atmosphere. Everything will happen as it should—and you cannot do more than be well prepared. The organizing team will help each other spontaneously and support those in need of help or getting stuck.

Introductory session

The professor invites three subject-matter experts to introduce the topics and related challenges (climate-friendly food, bicycles and tap water) in an introductory session.

The invited experts included the CEO and founder of a start-up offering climate-friendly food services, the head of communications of the Swiss Association of Water Works, the Head of Slow Mobility of the City of St. Gallen and the Head of Infrastructure at University of St. Gallen. The tap water issue is used in the remainder of this chapter for illustration purposes.

The Q&A part of the introductory session is particularly important to reveal crucial issues related to the topic and stakeholders to be invited for the Collaboratory sessions. Each of the (three-hour) sessions is prepared, facilitated, and evaluated by the student team in charge of the topic.

In the follow-up to the Introductory Session a crucial task for the student group is to structure the issues and to invite stakeholders to the two Collaboratory sessions representing the real issues at stake. The depth and relevance of the debate, but also the degree of engagement of all participants are directly correlated with the presence of the relevant stakeholders.

In the tap water collaboratory, for example, the stakeholders present were the Head of Communication of the Swiss Association of Water Works, the General Secretary of the Swiss Association of the Mineral Water Industry, the Head of Quality Assurance of the St. Gallen Water Works, and the manager and cook of a popular St. Gallen restaurant.

Collaboratory 1

The objectives of the Collaboratory 1 are:

- Understanding the issue/challenge/problem and its context
- Developing a comprehensive overview of all perspectives concerning this issue

- Creating a group engagement process through the collective vision-ing process which sets the stage for overcoming polarities and opposing views through the emergence of a group consciousness and the embodied experience of all participants

- Further developing a vision of what the world would look like if the issue was resolved

- A first round of ideas of how we could make concrete steps in resolving the issue at hand (using the method of back-casting, e.g. starting with the future and working back to now)

- Providing a set of concrete "prototype" ideas that can be developed further in a next session

The net process time is designed to be completed within three hours (180 minutes). Additional time is required for set-up and clean-up (before and after). It is sensible to reserve a room for at least four hours. The Collaboratory 1 process is structured in six steps:

1. Set-up of room (for approximately 50 participants, student team)

The team in charge (a group of 15 students—there should be no less than five) prepares the room and ensures that all the required tools (talk-ing stick: can be a microphone, a stone or something else) and support materials (phase 1–3 visuals, previously prepared) are brought to the location. Two students act as coordinators of the team throughout the different phases of the collaboratory.

Five or six chairs are placed in the middle of the room in a circle (one chair per expert, one student member from the group plus one empty chair). Around this inner circle two bigger circles of chairs are formed (in two rows); a gap is left at every four or five so that people can get to the inner circle without obstacles. Those gaps should be small enough, however, to create the overall picture of well-rounded outer circles.

Four flipcharts (with a lot of paper and colored pens) are placed behind the circles with four students placed next to them for taking notes.

In the middle of the inner circle a talking stick (or stone) is placed on the floor.

At the walls of the room, on flipchart paper (but not on the flipcharts themselves) the central question or issues discussed, the objectives of the collaboratory and the Theory U process should be represented in a clearly visible form. They are prepared beforehand.

The professor is informed in advance who are the two coordinators, the note-takers, the team leaders and supporters (see step 5). It is crucial that the group organizes itself internally from the start and is fully aware of this challenge. They should come well prepared with clear responsibilities, with moderation guidelines and tools ready.

The student team had autonomously organized a blind tasting of tap water and a popular still mineral water, the results of which were presented during the introduction. Tap water turned out to be the preferred water.

2. Introduction (professor and coordinators: 15–25 min)

The session begins with a 5 min introduction into the collaboratory process by the professor. This is followed by a short introduction to each expert in the inner circle.

The group coordinators then present a succinct summary of the topic and the challenges to be addressed. This can be a short film, a summary, collection of points of view, or anything else that sets the stage for the following discussion (10–20 min maximum).

3. Downloading (professor and student team: 60–75 min)

The downloading step consists of two parts:

1. An exchange of the experts in the inner circle, whereby their different perspectives are presented and taken note of ("downloaded"). These perspectives are compared and discussed among the experts (some 40–50 min)

2. This is followed by a deliberate and active involvement of the participants in the outer circles, to gain further insights, questions and ideas, but also to draw as many participants as possible into the discussion (20–25 min)

The downloading is guided by the professor and documented by the student team. The coordinators guide the four writers at their flipcharts and are responsible for summarizing the key insights at the end of this step. From this results a rich picture and deep understanding of the issues at stake and the positions of the different stakeholders. For the summary a separate flipchart paper should be used. The designated team leaders of step 5 (see below) take notes to make sure the results are well captured.

4. Visioning (professor: 30–40 min)

In the first part of step 4 (approx. 10 min) the professor guides the visioning process in which the participants get out of their heads and dive into a deeper level of the "group consciousness." The objective is to change the inner space from the past to the future and to allow images of a future world to emerge in very concrete and specific ways, in which the issue at stake has been solved. It is important not to include leading assumptions in this process but to enable each and every participant to pursue his/her own personal visioning journey through the development of inner images, sounds, etc., which are anchored through physical experience (see Otto Scharmer's Theory U).

The guided journey ran like this: "Imagine a world where tap water has become the new normal in St. Gallen and in Switzerland. Picture such a world. Let real situations of your world appear, with specific pictures, colorful images, moving pictures. Imagine what this world looks like when you are at home and drink something. What does it look like at breakfast, at lunch, at dinner? Maybe you have friends over at your place and go out for drinks later? What does your life at home look like? What strikes you as different? What does everybody drink? How do they drink it? How is it being served? Where is stored? Where does it come from? What does it look like? How does it feel? What do you see, hear or smell?

Now you go to school, on your regular route. Maybe you stop by at the café bar and get something to drink? What does it look like? In which way is it different? What do you drink? What do the others drink? Do they serve tap water? How is it being served? What does it cost? How popular is it? For lunch, maybe you go to the cafeteria. What does it look like there? What do you drink? What do the others drink? What role does tap water play?

On your way home you may stop at the supermarket or where you usually shop. You go the beverages section. What strikes you as different in this new world? What do the beverages look like? How are they being presented and marketed? Where do they come from? What do you buy? What do the others buy?

In the evening, imagine you go to a restaurant with friends. Imagine your favorite restaurant and look at the beverages listed in the menu. What is different in this new world? What do they offer? At what price? You order tap water. How does your server react? How do your friends react? How do they serve the drink? What does it taste like? How do you feel?

Back home you read the newspaper or watch the news. What do you note concerning beverages, water and tap water? What topics and issues are dominant? How do you react to them? Are you surprised about what you read? Why? What thoughts pass through your head?

Now we leave this future world where tap water has become the new normal and return to Switzerland, to St. Gallen and into our today's world."

The visioning phase is critical to the whole process as the majority of the participants will not be familiar with and used to this kind of experience. Therefore, it should be facilitated by the person most comfortable with this, most likely the professor. It is important that there is total silence and that nobody moves around or leaves the room. All cellphones have to be turned off (it is probably better to mention this already at the beginning of the session). The members of the student team in charge take a seat and participate, too. The team discreetly helps to ensure the silence and concentration needed.

In the second part of step 4 (approx. 30 min) the visions and images of all participants are shared. This is done by handing over the talking stick from one participant to the next, so that everybody can share his or her vision. This is done by the person who conducted the visioning. Four team members document the contributions on flipcharts, supported by the two coordinators. The challenge is to ensure fast documentation (for example, by picking up one input after the other clockwise from one flipchart writer to the next). This process should be defined in advance, so that the documentation process does not need to be commented on publicly.

The coordinators' task is to create a coherent vision of the colorful images, stories and impressions shared (not a very easy task). Therefore it may be useful to prepare a flipchart sheet that can be glued or written on. The designated group leaders of step 5 are taking notes to ensure continuity.

5. Harvesting (coordinators and group leaders: 30–40 min)

In step 5, the results of the visioning process are connected to the over-all objectives of the collaboratory to define specific starting points for action ("harvesting"). All participants now split into groups of at most eight members, with each group being led by one team member with one additional team member taking notes. The coordinators ensure that all groups have about the same number of participants and that the stake-holders and experts are equally spread over the groups (the art lies in explaining this as simply as possible). Each new group forms a circle and sits around one of the flipcharts, situated in the corners of the room. The purpose of this phase is to collect first rough ideas for prototypes that will be worked out in Collaboratory 2.

Each group leader starts out by summarizing the vision as an experi-enced but relatively abstract image. It is recommended that the group leaders go to their flipcharts at the end of step 4 and write down the key issues that are summarized by the coordinators. After this, the key insights from the Introductory Session are brought up again. The group leaders may have prepared this on a flipchart or on a separate piece of paper. The crucial question in this phase is: What can the different stakehold-ers, including the students, do concretely in the next three months to work decisively and effectively towards the ideal vision?

Initially, it is recommended that everyone gets five minutes to reflect silently on this question. Then the brainstorming rules are applied: all ideas brought up are written down without comment (no criticism, no questioning). The group leader starts the brainstorming, moderates it lightly, ensures the overall timing, and ends with a short summary.

After some 20–30 minutes all participants take their chairs and return to the plenary: the chairs are returned to their original position in the big circle. The coordinators now moderate the discussion of the group leaders, who present the results of their respective brainstorm-ing. The goal is to generate and record 10–20 key aspects or ideas as input for the Collaboratory 2. This also includes ideas regarding which stakeholders should be invited. These stakeholders will be selected and invited with a view to developing and implementing the emerging practice projects.

Main insights of the harvesting step included:
- Mineral water is perceived as a useful alternative to tap water, in particular in situations where tap water is not available/not suitable
- Tap water is already being offered in some restaurants, but the customers are typically not ready to pay for the service
- Availability of tap water is crucial for tap water consumption
- Communication has a central role to play in creating a positive image of tap water, similar to what is being done (on a massive scale) for mineral water

6. Wrap up (professor: 5–10 min)

The coordinators acknowledge the experts and hand over a small present. At the end, the professor collects short comments from all participants of the collaboratory, its procedure and its results. For this, the team members working on the specific topic are invited to open up the round with short statements. Finally, the professor thanks the student team and their coordinators.

Collaboratory 2

The objectives of Collaboratory 2 are:

- Using the "harvested" ideas of Collaboratory 1 as a starting point
- Developing specific action plans for the most relevant ideas
- Involving experts that could implement the action plans

The net collaboratory process time is designed to be completed within three hours (180 minutes). Additional time is required for set-up and clean-up. The Collaboratory 2 process is structured in seven steps.

1. Preparation (student team and professor)

The team in charge determines together with the professor the prototype ideas from Collaboratory 1 to be further elaborated and the experts and potential implementers to invite to the Collaboratory. Convincing stakeholders to join includes explaining the larger objectives of the exercise.

Two team members act as coordinators during Collaboratory 2 (they may be the same as in Collaboratory 1). Two more team members are defined as group leaders for each project selected. The professor knows in advance who plays what role.

2. Set-up of room (student team)

Same as in Collaboratory 1: large circle with experts being placed in the inner circle, at the beginning.

3. Introduction (coordinators: 20 min)

The group coordinators welcome all guests and participants and provide an overview of what has happened so far in the Introductory Session and Collaboratory 1 and what the larger context of the session is. They clarify the objectives for Collaboratory 2 and outline the planned process. Each prototype idea that has been selected for further elaboration is briefly presented. The estimated impact and the probability of an implementation are explained.

In the case of the tap water project, three priority areas were defined for further elaboration: University of St. Gallen, City of St. Gallen and restaurants.

The experts who take part in the collaboratory and are new to the process receive particular attention. The coordinators introduce the experts by providing a short biographic overview and explaining why they have been invited. This clarifies their areas of expertise and perspectives of contribution.

The invited experts were: Head of Infrastructure, University of St. Gallen; Head of Marketing and Director of the Public Services, City of St. Gallen; General Manager Switzerland of an international water dispenser company; President of the Association of Restaurants, Canton of St. Gallen.

4. Group work to define core ideas (group leaders: 45 min)

All participants are split up into groups each consisting of a maximum of eight 8 people (bigger teams would lower productivity) to work on the defined prototype ideas. The groups are formed based on a prior Doodle online scheduling request. One expert and a potential implementer of the prototype idea are present in each group.

Each group works separately with a flipchart on one topic. All group members take their chairs and gather around their flipchart. Each group is facilitated by two group leaders, with one of them moderating and the other writing.

A professional facilitation includes: welcoming and opening of the discussion; clarification of the goals and rules; facilitation of the discussion; focusing; summary; and ending of the discussion. If different groups work in the same room the discussions need to be held in a quiet voice.

It needs to be clear what output is expected from the groups; therefore a form with goals, results, members of the group, etc. should be prepared by the team beforehand. These forms need to be completed by the group leaders and handed over to the professor at the end of the collaboratory.

The two coordinators circulate between the different teams and make sure that everything runs smoothly. Timing is kept to (an alarm app might be helpful), and substantial results are produced.

The following procedure is recommended:

- Short introduction by the two group leaders to the topic, background, goals and own expectations, procedure (5 min)

- Silence for five minutes, so that each participant can concentrate and note down his or her ideas concerning the prototype idea

- Brainstorming (the rules should have been explained) (15 min)

- Reduction of all ideas to the ten ideas with the strongest implementation potential (5 min)

- Input of the expert and short discussion on which of those ten ideas are most relevant, realizable, and promising. Selection of five implementation ideas and summary by the two group leaders for subsequent presentation in front of the whole class (10 min)

The participants may want to take a short break (15 min).

5. Presentation and selection of the best ideas for implementation (coordinators and group leaders: 30 min)

All participants turn their chairs round and return to the big circle (setup at the start). The two coordinators moderate the session.

The group leaders present their five implementation ideas (5 min/group; 15 min in total).

After each group presentation the whole class selects the top three ideas based on a plenary vote (5 min for each group, 15 min in total).

Five ideas for University of St. Gallen and three selected (in bold):
1. Introduction of water dispensers
2. Improve infrastructure and directions for water faucets/fountains
3. Attractive bottle of water for each student
4. Information campaign to increase knowledge and awareness about water issues
5. Water week, organized by student organization oikos

Five ideas for City of St. Gallen and three selected (in bold):
1. Information campaign to increase knowledge and awareness about water issues (water day)
2. Awareness raising and education in pre-schools and schools
3. Improve infrastructure and directions for water fountains and create attractive bottle
4. Collaboration with local companies
5. Co-sponsoring with local companies

Five ideas for restaurants and three selected (in bold):
1. Tap water refinements (e.g. different tastes)
2. Adaptation of water dispensers to different locations (restaurant versus nightclub)
3. Information campaigns for different cities (St. Gallen water, Zurich water, etc.)
4. National branding for Swiss tap water
5. Harmonization of pricing structures for tap water

6. Developing definitive action plans (group leaders: 40 min)

The groups return to their flipcharts in order to develop action plans for the three selected ideas. They split up into sub-groups to work separately on the selected ideas. The issues discussed are: (a) the crucial actions and the time needed, (b) critical resources/support/stakeholders, and (c) expected impact of the project (25 min). The sub-groups present their results to the whole group. The group leaders sum up the results and record them on the pre-established form (15 min).

7. Presentation of the results (coordinators and group leaders: 30 min)

The participants return to the big circle set-up and the group leaders present their results to the whole class. The results consist of clear action plans with suggestions on how to proceed, including points a, b and c mentioned above (5 min/group, 15 min in total).

The two coordinators sum up the most important results, highlight next steps to implement the projects and end the session (10 min). The professor acknowledges the experts and offers a small present. He thanks the student team and their coordinators (5 min).

Learning outcomes of the three sessions

The learning outcomes can be related to the following four aspects: the collaboratory method, the student experience, the observed learning, and the impact noted by the participants. They have been extracted from comprehensive reflection papers submitted by the students on their key experiences and learning at the end of the course. The selected quotes include learning outcomes that were mentioned most frequently by the students (see Box 15.1).

Box 15.1 Students' learning outcomes

Related to the collaboratory method:

- The method allowed for a much more profound insight, understanding and engagement with the topic than traditional methods; the extent of commitment, engagement, drive and determination of my fellow students to work on these subjects was very high, which is very rare
- The lively and interactive atmosphere inspired a highly active thinking and reflection process; what we did didn't feel like work
- It turned traditional learning methods upside down with a focus on developing visions and practical solutions

- Biggest learning effect was due to the amazing preparation of the collaboratories
- Initially, the speaking stick reminded me of an educational measure for children, in hindsight, I must admit that it enabled a respectful exchange of positions and made great sense
- I was surprised how constructive the experts were. Their ideas were innovative, even visionary, despite the fact that they held contradicting views
- The open circle created a space where everybody was invited to partici- pate. The professor held back on purpose, thus opening the door for all of us to participate and engage; but not everybody was willing or able to embark on a journey into a visionary future
- I was fascinated by the diversity of proposals emanating from the process. It demonstrated to me the need to have many different stakeholders and perspectives around when we want to come up with innovative ideas

Related to the student experience:

- I was most skeptical as I have never seen anything similar in my university. Yet I was most amazed about the degree of my own learning and the learn- ing about myself
- I started to feel more comfortable in the second Collaboratory of the first group.
- I was astonished at the wealth of creative and innovative ideas of my fellow students
- I never thought so much learning was possible
- After Collaboratory 2 I told my team that I would go to war with them and how deep a level of trust I had developed
- I spent many hours in my free time to understand these topics better. I experimented with new recipes, new shopping, all of which are really important for my learning success

Related to the observed learning by the participants:

- I was required to step outside my comfort zone and realized that I have never so far critically reflected my own behavior and actions
- The course enabled me to drop my mostly legally formed, fact-based think- ing and to embrace a more joyful and maybe naïve approach. I realized that my talent for imagination was very weak

- I realized that my past experience of mostly having to memorize for exams is not the only form of learning. I have learned by communicating with experts and my fellow students—a totally new and enriching experience
- I have never worked in such a large group (15) and this has been the best team experience ever
- My brain was massaged to develop a consciousness for sustainability. This consciousness now flows into many daily considerations in the three topical areas: climate-friendly food, mobility, and water

Related to the impacts noted by the participants:

- I realized I had no clue which vegetables were in season. As soon as I arrived home, I printed a seasonal table of veggies and put it on my fridge. But I also realized that there were a number of things I did not want to live without. I chose to eat less meat and to avoid veggies and fruits from overseas
- The continuous exchange of ideas with my fellow students resulted in so many ideas that we have now decided to launch a start-up
- It took much courage to contact new people and encourage them to spend their valuable time in our collaboratory—but my related learning curve was steep
- My way of managing the group was much appreciated despite much hesitation on my side
- We produced nine concrete ideas of how to solve our issues; two of the experts embraced these and agreed to implement them
- The concept "my town–my water" will be implemented by the city of St. Gallen—totally amazing
- Besides the various changes in my own life, I was also able to influence my family and friends: my aunt now receives a weekly local veggies basket and my friends order tap water in restaurants

In conclusion, we were very positively surprised by these early conclusions, which suggested that the collaboratory offers more profound insights and deeper learning through more engagement and an active process of both group and individual reflection. We believe that these were enabled and triggered by the collaboratory setting, which enabled an equal learning environment of students, experts, and professors. We had entirely underestimated the impact of the large group team work among students in terms of enhancing the learning breadth and depth, which included an unusual dimension (for university courses) of innovative and entrepreneurial ideas. An important implicit aspect was the deeper dimensions of interpersonal relationships and friendships that had developed.

We are continuing with another 40 students engaged in three new burning societal issues this year and look forward to evaluating the learning of this new co-creative process. We wholeheartedly invite others to embrace such experimentation and remain available if we can help in this process.

Reference

Scharmer, C.O. (2009) *Theory U: Leading from the Future as it Emerges* (San Francisco: Berrett-Koehler).

16

Creating connection, conversations, and courage

The Exeter collaboratory

Jackie Bagnall
Centre for Peace and Global Studies, UK

Stephen Hickman
University of Exeter Business School, UK

This chapter offers insights into the strategic appliance of the collaboratory in an environment where the sense of belonging and collegiality is being eroded by the drive for resource efficiency, highly productive delivery systems and service quality.

The chapter presents a particular perspective of the collaboratory as a proven instrument to both build and unify a community as well as facing and resolving issues that had otherwise no forum to be addressed, appropriately discussed or satisfactorily resolved. An institution that has explored the collaboratory as such an enabling method is the University of Exeter Business School in the UK.

In what is essentially a reflexive piece of writing the authors will oscillate between recollections of an unfolding story of connection, conversation, and courage, and their own experience of playing storyline characters.

The chapter is sited in a higher education (HE) environment facing change on a grand and rapid scale where those working in this milieu ask the question, **Where do the people tasked with making this change happen go to make sense of this increasingly challenging experience?**

Figure 16.1 Collaboratory: a sense-making forestructure

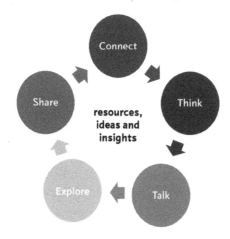

It is about an idea that sought to bring together a few individuals to talk about teaching. An idea hatched in the vestibules of the University of Exeter Business School, galvanized over coffee, and advanced as a campaign for a social space where educators could meet, think reflectively about their actions and experiences (Schon 1983), and inform each other about their teaching practice.

A sense-making narrative

As a reflexive piece the narrative is first person, as we look critically at our story so the reader is invited to listen in on the evocative "leadership in learning" voice. The voice is that of a group of educators, dealing with persistent problems in the throng of the academic year and facing up to the undesirable effects of change (Goldratt 1986). This is the story of our attempt to establish the foundations of community encouragement, as a forestructure of understanding (Gergen and Gergen 1991) out of which we can make sense of our predicament.

The need for a place to connect

In a world in which teachers do not have sufficient time to form their ideas, research and update their knowledge, reflect upon their teaching, manage their emotions or sharpen their practice opportunities for progression of thinking or attaining and maintaining quality of teaching are limited. Yet if pedagogic practice is anything but progressive, HE is unlikely to continue to effectively serve and support the intellectual development of undergraduates (O'Donovan 2010). Such progress can only be manifested when, on an individual level, educators are collaboratively supported, afforded appropriate time to self-question and self-evaluate, and offered space to critically reflect, not alone but in conversation and counsel with their peers as critical friends. This logic was to be our start point for enlisting a handful of colleagues that we knew would be willing to discuss teaching matters openly and reflectively. Using our immediate network we carried forward our new ethos of collaborative learning, believing that more connections needed to be made and that the wider community's views on teaching should be sought. This, we calculated, would create conversations that were notably informed and relevant, and would produce practicable ideas that might, in turn, gain momentum through others as collaborators (McNiff, Lomax, and Whitehead 1999).

The Exeter Collaboratory

The aim was to create a space for connection, a place in which those who teach could gather together to share best practice, deliberate, ask developmental questions and generally connect to others who faced the same isolation and challenge. "Communities of practice are formed by people who engage in a process of collective learning in a shared domain of human endeavour" (Wenger 1998).

We couched our intention in the science of education and pronounced that there was a need to "pump up the pedagogy," beginning with a spirit of equality and a genuine desire to create a community of practice (Wenger 1998).

We proposed the term Collaboratory as a sort of virtual community kiosk: "a metastructure, an evolving platform that can be established anywhere, virtual or real, within companies, communities or within a management school."[1]

Creating a presence

In need of a permanent physical space we negotiated with senior school management for the special room in which we wanted to hold the sessions to be named the Collaboratory. Neither securing a room for non-teaching activity in a space-pressured university, nor naming room 0.28 was straightforward. Eventually, however, with some support from our dean we readied ourselves to hold a modest naming ceremony and launched our community space. The Collaboratory room breaks away from the norm of tiered lecture theatres in which students face the front and receive the broadcast from the professor. This room is flat and flexible, with movable chairs and tables to facilitate learning through conversation; a social space that has evolved into the ideal space in which to invite the teaching community to meet; a rendezvous with a collegial atmosphere.

In a world increasingly filled with mandates and instructions our invitation to all colleagues centered on what the Collaboratory was *not*: "Not a staff coffee time. Not a whinge fest. Not an imposed initiative. This is not an event run as a committee or a club. Not something we will not make time for." And was most certainly "not possible without our peers." We had something much more audacious in mind.

The Collaboratory would become a space for individuals from completely different departments (fiefdoms) to open up their respective teaching worlds to their peers. A safe place and a confident space designed to encourage boundary-less storytelling so as to convey the idea of a community of practitioners, working together and learning from one another towards collaborative, progressive pedagogic development.

---

1   http://www.50plus20.org

Foundational work

The first session was well attended albeit, we reflected, a rather over-controlled affair because of some bossy facilitation. The teacher tendency to need to control proceedings and the need to mitigate this was an early "key learning" for us as the organizers. We used the launch to explain the Collaboratory aims and shared our aspirations to spark a dialogue, but this was the one and only occasion that anything during Collaboratory time would be broadcast from the lectern!

The inaugural dual-chaired discussion invited suggestions for future Collaboratory topics. Successively we recruited some of the more experienced teachers, familiar with interactive methods to facilitate a roundtable discussion, which offline from the sessions we labeled "collabora-stories." The format of **collabora-stories**, as a sort of dialogue button, remains at the heart of the sessions, albeit these are regularly reinvented, refreshed and communicated under different guises, such as "show and tell," "beleaguered and inspired," as a means of collecting and sharing "ground truths" about teaching in our school on an ongoing basis. This "connection and conversation" process has developed into an unwritten routine now: practitioner meets practitioner, and colleagues plough into a succession of conversations. And while the mood is relaxed, the yield of ground truths is generally plentiful. Feedback from Collaborators is that they find a level of stimulus and support that is not readily or typically afforded them on a regular basis elsewhere in the institution. In all, during the 2012/2013 academic year there were six Collaboratory sessions, generally bi-monthly and as far as practicable on different days of the week to recognize the constraint of regularized teaching timetables.

Community-building

Posing the question "What is bothering you about HE teaching at the moment?" was perfect fuel for the succeeding sessional conversation and gave us proof of concept; teachers as active participants with collective purpose offer HE huge potential for doing the right things right.

Something else soon emerged from these bi-monthly get-togethers, something that we had not consciously considered when establishing its purpose. This gathering in this room became a place of sanctuary, a quiet space in which the hurly burly of institutional life had no place. The room was calm and there were no interruptions. In our university college there is no staff common room, no mustering point where the hundred or so people teaching across the college can meet to share their happiness or frustration. There is no sheltered enclave where people tell the stories of life at the chalk face, stories which help others to make sense of their own experience.

We have learned that facilitation of these events requires energy and commitment, and our experience is that a sort of facilitator-carousel, whereby the same three or four people, appropriately skilled in facilitation, work as a watchful team and interpose only when they sense it is necessary to do so. This light-touch approach is serving us well and achieves just the right balance between having a completely open conversation and having a little bit of focus to get people started. What is more, this approach seems to ensure the sessions are not over-facilitated or impeded in pursuit of conversations that are legitimate, emotionally honest, and produce learning. This learning is often particular to an individual and has at times evolved into action research with people "working intentionally towards the implementation of their ideas" (McNiff, Lomax, and Whitehead 1999: 9) on an inter-departmental basis in response to common predicaments. The Collaboratory is all about connection and voice, and because each "connection" is bundled up with ownership and integrity, with colleagues simply wanting to "talk teaching" and share their wealth of good ideas and experiences, excesses of posturing and PowerPoint are shunned. Connection at all times is at a human level.

In the absence of bureaucracy, status differentials and hierarchies that often play out in public-sector settings, unusually the Collaboratory, with no set agenda has, extraordinarily, no dominant voice. With facilitation being proportionally distributed among contributors these gatherings are well-mannered affairs, with each participant cognizant of the need to balance their individual learning needs with the collective learning of *their* "community." Typically, however, conversations will be heartfelt, and occasionally exchanges become feisty, such as the sessions on budgetary constraints that we discuss later.

The Collaboratory sits outside the normal organizational structure and is not owned by a particular department. It belongs to the community and as such there is neither need nor desire to managerially curb and control as a means to silencing human emotion. This is a place in which we learn about each other and about our frustrations and where we can build a shared academic identity, a collective social identity (Haslam, Reicher, and Platow 2011) centered on teaching. From this shared identity we hope to develop empathy and through empathy a way to offer each other better support. As some of the same people began to return each time we saw that people began to turn to each other and sought solace in this regular meeting, as in the story that follows. This in turn enabled them to locate others in teaching-focused roles facing the same reality.

This was at its most poignant when a colleague committed suicide. This is not the place to explore why that suicide happened, but what shook the community was the fact that in our busyness and in our disconnected practice we had let a colleague in trouble go unnoticed. The sign on her office door saying "absent due to ill health" was noticed but not really comprehended. Her death sent shock waves around the college; how had we become so disconnected from each other? There was an uncomfortable understanding that in our fight for our own survival and in our attempt to manage the increasing workloads we had lost our connection to others and with that our compassion. The Collaboratory suddenly had a very important role to play, one that we had never envisaged.

Commemorative conversations

A miserable shudder seemed to traumatize everyone. The school was unusually solemn. Coincidentally, two days after this tragedy, on the spur-of-the-moment we replaced a timetabled Collaboratory session with a commemoration of our departed colleague. Noticeably on this occasion, Room 0.28 uncharacteristically filled up around the fringes first, as though the front tables and chairs were being left for absent family members. The immediacy of this event and the obvious fragility of that day produced a touch of awkwardness for everyone. The awkwardness was channeled into steering, not too quickly, the Collaboratory participants towards a sense of readiness for receiving our visitor: the university's multi-faith chaplain. Although the community had morphed into a congregation, and had been consoled by our visitor's words, the impossibility of predicting how to follow our Chaplin's address left a gap in proceedings. What to do next? This unexpected hiatus demanded content. The impromptu act of reading aloud a tenuously relevant poem "The Lecture" (McNaughton 1988), a children's nonsense poem, although tensely recited, seemed to reward the deep thoughtfulness of the congregation. The poem, which was delivered by a teacher friend, provided some camouflage and halted a clumsy hesitation in dialogue. The unintended outcome was a precious moment for individual reflection. A colleague later remarked that they had learned that even when there is nothing that can be said, it is important to be ready to say something.

The poem signaled the end of the commemoration. People, customarily and respectfully silent in these circumstances, took to reconnecting in whispers and subtle collegiate gestures, and softly voiced conversations began to fill the Collaboratory once more. This social interaction was a critically important part of the grieving process as it allowed individuals to make sense of their thoughts by connecting to others. The conversations this particular day, in our special space and what we now regard as a collective courage all helped to lift the numbness that had befallen our community. At this difficult time, we were, as a community ensemble endeavoring to say in one voice "we care." Our mourning was indeed a rare expression of common life amid intensification of work and financial constraints.

What emerged in other conversations?

There are a variety of other exchanges and engagements from this early phase of establishing our Collaboratory that exemplify our new-found level of connection and sense-making—best practices modestly tucked away in tutorials, seminars and lectures.

How do I know what I'm feeling if I never get the chance to air my thoughts, to make sense of my thoughts by connecting to others? Our Collaboratory, we believe, offers this space; a chance for people to say out loud to an audience that will listen, just what they have experienced. Some of those conversations serve as a validation of the work that people undertake.

It provides an opportunity to share what works well: one colleague shared with her peers the process that she uses with students at the start and end of each class. After a "check-in and check-out" process she found that her students really began to feel a sense of place within her weekly session. This sense of place in turn had a very positive effect on attendance rates. This simple story, sharing with colleagues a practice that she was most committed to, opened up in others the understanding that as teachers we are the architects of the learning space. That our choice in how we choose to engage with those that attend our classes has a very real impact on them as people, and in turn we can solve the issues that plague us, such as poor attendance.

Other "shared" pieces include conversations about:

- Staggering assessment due dates to ease timetabled workloads and lessen student anxiety

- Lobbying for the scaling up of our e-learning usage

- Making tutorial and seminars more participatory

- A peer-led "internationalization" initiative to improve colleagues' confidence in student name pronunciation

All this sharing means that mandates imposed from the centre of the university have a place to be reviewed. Colleagues no longer need to sit at the end of an email alone and frustrated at the lack of respect or understanding behind such commands; they have a chance to air their point of view. Through discussion and debate colleagues have the opportunity to find consensus and importantly their voice.

An example of this came at the end of a busy academic year when after delivering successful degree programs to an ever-increasing number of students there was a central announcement about budgetary constraints. Collaboratory session topics are not as such chosen; they tend to emerge through conversations. So much so, that the last two Collaboratory events of 2012 focused on the educational consequences of the Business School's budget challenges. Conversations both in corridors and at the Collaboratory at this time were generally about little else. Academic colleagues from all departments and job families from across the College were represented at these two events, expressing quite an extraordinary strength of opinion on management's imposed cuts. People understandably wanted a say in matters and anticipated an opportunity to exercise influence.

Even with some skilled and often quite stringent facilitation it was tricky to overcome the initial anxiety about how on earth the "teaching community" could respond to this complex challenge. The need to wrestle the first few conversations away from a negative route, gradually eliciting more constructive suggestions demonstrated just how problematic this would be. The complexity of this issue, and taking on what is essentially a management task, produced more disagreements than any other topic discussed in the Collaboratory. It also produced a considerable amount of offline work for the facilitators.

Nonetheless, this budget challenge, as unwelcome as it was, signified the importance for everyone to work together to find solutions that minimized the effects both on student experience and on staff workload and well-being. This extramural activity in the form of a community's creative exploration for solutions pushed the Collaboratory forward as a "space" that facilitates collective conversations about these things, and to find creative solutions that might mitigate the impact of this financial imposition. The output from the Collaboratory sessions was tangible and certainly constructive: a "risk register" comprising (1) the risks, (2) the implications of the risks, and (3) possible actions we could take, with a focus on our "top ten" concerns. The key points from this ground-up appraisal were shared with senior management. In some departments (although we accept not all) staff were subsequently commissioned by their respective director of education to undertake their own detailed risk assessments, investigating peak work loading and critical points in the academic year. This is fine example of teachers and management working collaboratively rather than competitively to offer each other new insights.

In pursuit of permanence

The very nature of the contemporary university means that teaching is scheduled over two intense semesters. This means that for many a year's workload is delivered in about 28 weeks of the year. This is taking its toll on teachers and professional staff. The existing structures and the systems are not sufficiently supporting the delivery of the modern "pile 'em high" financially driven education goals. In reviewing the intention of our meeting place we can see how the Collaboratory will play an increasingly important role in how educators and education managers deal with these new HE realities.

We seek to keep humanity and compassion at the heart of the teaching community; we seek for this place of collaboration to be valued and cherished as a place of sanctuary where through shared identity colleagues find solace and connection. We draw on Wenger's (1998) idea that a community of practice is where those facing the same reality come to learn from each other. We have much to learn about the human condition, to understand the impact that the changing HE landscape is having on the people tasked with bringing change to life.

In the main, our institution's administration is pretty robust, and on the whole management are trusted to make decisions about resources and resource efficiency. However, sometimes the human factor in all this needs to be drawn together without any instrumental reasoning by HE managers. The Collaboratory is an example of human factor agency that can positively impact the rather disparate jumble of individuals that academics sometimes become as they come to terms with their collective working lives, constrained by powerlessness, disheartened and disconnected.

Through connection and conversation pedagogic practice is now less of a nonentity and what was a cacophony of isolated teachers is becoming a more valued community: a community with a voice, an academic identity, and, as we showed with our risk register initiative, a community with confidence and courage.

We are proud of what we have achieved at Exeter, but it has been hard work, and we recognize there is much still to do to. The Exeter Collaboratory is a useful example of what can be achieved when teachers are treasured and pedagogy underpinned as much by a community of practice as it is by policy, procedures and workload models. The permanency of the Collaboratory as a place of fellowship is assured all the while it is served by the community and remains self-sufficient. Our immediate internal priority is to maintain the momentum kindled thus far. We have observed what can be achieved when reflective teaching becomes a more lived experience through connection, conversation and collaboration, and we like what we see.

We would now like to stir up and encourage other HE practitioners to nurture their own community in a similar direction. If, subsequently, the approach used at and by Exeter can facilitate a larger movement around stakeholder engagement and ground-up transformational change in higher education, then this will have exceeded the humble beginnings of an idea propagated during a casual coffee conversation. In that conversation we put forward a courageous notion to push education and scholarship from the periphery to centre stage, and in so doing created an off-stage refuge for business and management educators.

References

Gergen, K.J., and M.M. Gergen (1991) "Toward Reflexive Methodologies," in F. Steier (ed.), *Research and Reflexivity* (Trowbridge, UK: Redwood Books): 76-95.

Goldratt, E.M., and E.F. Fox (1997) *The Race* (New York: North River Press).

Haslam, S.A., S.D. Reicher and M.J. Platow (2011) *The New Psychology of Leadership* (New York: Psychology Press).

McNaughton, C. (1988) *There's an Awful Lot of Weirdos in Our Neighbourhood* (London: Walker Books).

McNiff, J., P. Lomax, and J. Whitehead (1999) *You and Your Action Research Project* (New York: Routledge).

Muff, K. (2012) "The 50+20 Collaboratory: Methodology and Approach for Short One-time Sessions," http://50plus20.org/wp-content/uploads/2013/02/50+20-Collabo ratory-Approach.pdf, accessed 6 April 2014.

O'Donovan, B. (2010) "The Motivations to Study of Undergraduate Students in Management: The Impact of Degree Programme and Level of Study," *International Journal of Management Education* 9.1: 11-20.

Schon, D. (1983) *The Reflective Practitioner: How Professionals Think in Action* (London: Temple Smith).

Wenger, E. (1998) *Communities of Practice: Learning, Meaning, and Identity* (Cambridge, UK: Cambridge University Press).

Transforming an organization

Participatory leadership and the Art of Hosting

Caroline Rennie

ren-new, Switzerland

This chapter offers insights into how a collaboratory can work in a situation that requires fast and unconventional organizational change to respond to a complex challenge. It is a first of a series of examples of collaboratories that have been applied to a corporate environment. Caroline Rennie introduces the important notions of participatory leadership and the Art of Hosting to create a co-creative environment for stakeholders that are not necessarily used to working together.

The Art of Hosting and participatory leadership embrace a number of practices that are best explained through illustration. Better even would be to experience such a session. This example takes place within a large multinational organization with tens of thousands of employees in dozens of countries—a highly complex system. We thus believe that learnings from this story may be applicable to other complex systems with people who have different interests, cultural backgrounds, or attachment to the issue in question.

The design department of a pharmaceutical company in Basel, Switzerland, was concerned that they could not make legally required changes to a drug's information materials fast enough to meet regulatory deadlines. There were many complications: as regulation in one country changed, they needed to determine if there were contradictions between requirements in different countries and how to manage those, impacts on printing length, mechanical folding and costs, and so forth. Historically such questions fell to logistics and project management teams who would analyze the situation, develop methods for solving them, and then send out instructions to everybody concerned. In practice this had slowed things down rather than sped them up, and the result was rampant blame-storming. What follows is the story of how the organization managed to dramatically reduce the time and people involved in the process, and a discussion of how this demonstrates some of the principles of participatory leadership and the Art of Hosting.

A better way?

Seeing that interventions designed to improve efficiency were actually doing the reverse, the company decided it should address things differently. Perhaps, it reasoned, if it could bring together the loudest complainers from the different departments and countries, it could have them design a better system. In light of the high emotions surrounding the task it was determined that the meeting(s) should be facilitated, and techniques brought in that could help keep the discussion focused on the purpose and solutions. It was clear that this was not just about the redesign—it was about finding ways to ensure that the new processes would be implemented effectively and efficiently—without generating the conventional hostility and resistance. This called for designing not just the meeting but also how participants to the process would be selected and invited, how the results of the meeting(s) would be disseminated and implemented, and how the effectiveness would be assessed.

Key principle:
Design of any intervention (a workshop, a process, a system...) needs to include design for acceptance and implementation.

They used as a framework the Art of Hosting's "eight breaths of design":

1. **Call.** Naming the issue

2. **Clarify.** Moving from need to purpose

3. **Invite.** Determine how to ensure the parts of the system you are seeking to change should be represented, and by whom. Structure the invitation

4. **Meet.** Design the meeting to ensure you can build trust, deepen understanding, and design prototypes for action

5. **Harvest.** Make sense of what emerged in and from the meeting(s) and how that informs future action

6. **Act.** Determine how to implement the agreed actions and implement

7. **Reflect and learn.** Explore both the results and the "how did this process work for us? How did we work together? What does this tell us about how we could do this again?"

8. **The breath that holds the whole**

As imposing a participatory system rather undermined the message, the head of the design department invited everybody affected by a design change to volunteer if they wanted to be a part of this, asked them to name the people they absolutely felt should participate, and explained that for logistical and financial reasons they wanted to limit the number of attendees to 30. The process was transparent on the intranet, and soon they had their participants.

The program itself needed to determine what was working well (to help protect it), where the system was getting bogged down, how it might be redesigned to be more effective, and how the changes could be implemented without resistance. Historically there was a good deal of bad blood between many of the actors who would be present. Their careers had been shaped by protecting their interests (and those of their part of the company) against the depredations of the others. Consequently, the first activities in the meeting needed to establish an understanding of one another as people, as well as people in a role. The 35 people met in a large room, cleared of all furniture except chairs that had been assembled in a large circle. In the centre was a small hippopotamus carving to be used as a talking piece. (The facilitator noted that in Africa the ears of the hippopotamus are often all you can see—but underneath lies a hugely powerful and potentially very dangerous beast. In using this as a talking piece we are reminded how powerful what we *don't see* can be—and how we can help each other understand more and better about what lies under the surface.) The question they were asked to use to introduce themselves was: What in your life and work inspired you to step up for this project? Using the circle practice they started the process of introducing each other with respect to the project.

The circle practice
First described by Christina Baldwin and Ann Linnea (2010), the circle practice sets out the standard elements in creating the conditions for deep listening, intentional speech, and attentiveness to the well-being of the group.

Key principles:

- Design participatory processes to be participatory from the earliest stage (that is, invitation rather than demand; transparent principles rather than hierarchical decision)

- Provide sufficient structure that people feel safe because they know how a session will work, how long it lasts, etc.

- Provide conditions that help participants speak to their dreams and hopes

Building rapport and trust

This was followed by Appreciative Inquiry (AI) interviews (see Chapter 11 on AI) in groups of three. The questions flowed as follows:

1. Tell me about a peak experience or high point in your professional life ... a time when you felt most alive, most engaged, and really proud of yourself and your work

2. Without being humble, what do you most value about yourself? Your work? Your team? Our company?

3. Thinking back to a time when you experienced a powerfully collaborative process in your life, how did it feel? What factors made it so effective?

4. What are the core factors that give life to our organization when it is at its best?

5. If you had a magic wand and could have any three wishes granted to create a lightning-fast design process, what would they be?

This built rapport, connection, and admiration between the participants and a surge of buzzy energy. One participant even said "for the first time my job makes sense to me now!" Each team was asked to capture the feel of the interview, the common themes, and all the wishes. These were put up on the wall and participants were invited to fan out and interview others about what they had learned about their colleagues and organization. Then the "three wishes" from each participant were clustered by theme.

Key principle:

Rapport and trust are the ground on which effective change work can be built.

Clarifying the situation and developing solutions

Following the Appreciate Inquiry interviews was a full group session to describe visually the entire process from request for change to the final design. Using sticky notes they described all the loops that slowed things down, and how often they might occur at any given stage. The group agreed that it took up to 134 days to get from design-change request to finished product.

In small teams participants addressed what needed to change in the process to bring down the time radically. Keeping in mind the purpose, ideas for solution, who should be involved, and implementation, they started to design new systems. Leaving one person with the design, they then fanned out to see other designs and ask questions about the thinking, how it would work, etc. In a third round they regrouped and revisited their design to see what they wanted to change and how they wanted to change it. Each group pitched their prototype to the others, and then they gradually merged all the designs (pairs of groups merged their design, then pairs of the remaining groups merged, and so on, until there was one representative design.

To test the final design, people were asked either singly or in small groups to determine "what's missing" and "what needs strengthening" in the final design. Before going through a final "final" design, we opened up the possibility to discuss "what questions do you still hold that you would like to explore around this project?" This fleshed out areas that did not seem to fit well in other discussions and enabled them to be explored in light of the proposed system. Ultimately, it brought out unexpected areas of interaction with people and processes that had not been considered in the early stages but that needed to be involved in a successful implementation. We used Open Space Technology for this, in which people held parallel discussions on the areas they felt most compelled to discuss.

Open Space Technology (OST)

OST is a simple framework for enabling rich discussion around a central, strategic question. Information and instructions can be found online at http://www.opens paceworld.org/.

Key principle:

The invisible needs to be made visible in such a way that people are ready and open to see it. This can be done visually, but also as theatre, dance, physical models, etc. Groups can be asked to describe the same situation or issue from different perspectives (e.g. the point of view of the paper that needed to be approved; or from each of the repetitive points; or as experienced by the patient) to enrich understanding of the whole.

Implementation, buy-in and assessment

There was now a rich understanding of the issues involved, possible solutions and areas for concern. To establish what the group found most important and most doable, participants were invited to develop a collective mind map that made the themes and elements visible to everybody and were given seven votes that they could distribute freely. The key areas were then explored more deeply in small groups, which considered implementation and how to get buy-in (and from whom).

Collective mind map

In a collective mind map the question that called people together is at the centre. People then put their ideas up as a theme, or as a sub-theme to somebody else's ideas. This can be done electronically or with sticky notes but can quite quickly generate an overall picture of what people find matters with respect to the issue at hand. Discussion will often arise about links between themes and new constellations can appear as a result, with links between areas drawn up.

Finally, they designed how to assess results (including how to assess the redesign process) and developed questions such as: "What has shifted/changed in the organization since we started to redesign the process?" This enabled them to capture the more subtle and intangible changes such as better working relations and a more harmonious and healthier work environment, as well as the more direct resource efficiencies.

Key principle:

The value of participatory processes comes from the ability of participants to help practices spread in the organization, community or system. Therefore, have them design these elements too. Furthermore, as a low-resistance change often goes unremarked, it can be useful to consider how things were before the change and what has shifted since—this tends to surprise people and help them see what has been achieved.

At the end of the process I asked one of the participants what these changes meant to her. "Oh, I won't have a job!" she said cheerfully, "but this totally makes sense."

The final outcome: the process was redesigned to decrease time from 134 days to 15, and the people who would suffer as a result were proud of their work and optimistic about going forward—which meant that the change was unlikely to be resisted by the parties most likely to seek to block it.

Key principles and findings

- A common purpose creates the call to interact

- Effective change processes need to create the conditions in which people master themselves, are open to hearing what others are saying to increase their own understanding, participate in a productive fashion, and help take care of the group. This is what participatory methods do—often by creating formal roles (e.g. guardian, scribe, timekeeper)

- The knowledge you need to change a system is already alive in the system. The people who hold it just need to be invited to discuss it together and, with common purpose, together develop the path forward

- To work together fruitfully and efficiently people need trust and relationship

- The setting and conditions for the interactions therefore need to be designed to provide safety and minimize fear

- Respectful listening not only diminishes fear, it releases the speaker from his or her point of view and enables willingness to work together

- Plan not only for the event but also for the outcome(s) of the event and how they will be distributed, implemented, and assessed—including the more intangible assessments

- When you are unsure what to do, turn to the affected people and have them work together to design the change

- To get meaningful change you need to feel that things are a bit out of control because the most vital and generative area lies on the edge of what feels chaotic—where order and chaos meet

- Many techniques will bring you good results. A mix of techniques can help the discussion stay fresh and broaden perspectives. The Art of Hosting thus uses established techniques and practices such as World Café, Open Space Technology, the Circle Way, Appreciative Inquiry, and Pro Action Café

- Each session needs to be linked in a way that delivers

The thinking that went into this intervention drew heavily on the Art of Hosting trainings and workbook. More information at www.artofhost ing.org/.

References

Baldwin, C., and A. Linnea (2010) *The Circle Way: A Leader in Every Chair* (San Francisco: Berrett-Koehler).

18

Regional organizational change

Community-building in action

Philip Mirvis
USA

In this chapter we look at how deep transformative change can be brought to a global organization through community-building as a central aspect of collaborative co-creation. The deep space created through processes embracing and working with the phenomenon of group consciousness enables a deep transformation of a highly diverse and culturally challenging group.

Go faster, think smarter, and focus on the subject at hand! The prevailing wisdom is that groups engaged in problem-solving, innovation, business planning and the like can benefit from preparatory activities and facilitation that helps them to form more quickly and function more efficiently (Daly and Nicoll 1997; Katzenbach and Smith 2001). Often this involves a regimen of team-building to accelerate group development. There are also a variety of tools (some covered in this volume) that can *speed up* team talking, thinking, and learning.

Yet, in *How We Think*, philosopher and educator John Dewey (1910) opines, "Time is required in order to digest impressions, and translate them into substantial ideas." This raises questions as to when it is appropriate for a group to *slow down* and reflect more deeply about fundamental questions of "who we are," "what we are doing," and "where we are headed." One such case is when attention turns to sustainability. Here the issues are complex: different people may have different views on their relevance and action implications; competing visions, interests, and values are sometimes at stake; emotions can run high; and often there are few apparent "win–win" options, at least at initial stages of consideration. So time is needed to develop open and fruitful dialogue among participants. And care must be taken to contain the heat and even the hurt that may arise as a multi-sided group confronts its differences and attempts to arrive at a common conclusion.

There are many frameworks on airing differences and resolving conflicts (Fisher, Ury, and Patton 1991; Levine 2000) and practical tools for capitalizing on diversity in groups (Gordon 2007; Ferdman 2013). Of interest here is the theorizing of M. Scott Peck (1987) as outlined in *The Different Drum: Community Making and Peace* and the methods developed by Peck and his colleagues (myself included) through the Foundation for Community Encouragement (FCE) that aid groups to confront differences gradually and with care and thence to develop a "group mind." This chapter describes some of the methods used in community-building and illustrates them in development of a community of leaders in Unilever Asia as they devised a new business model based on sustainability in the Asia–Pacific region.

Community-building

Drawing on elements from human relations training, spiritual traditions, 12-step programs, and large group intervention, community-building efforts aim to increase a group's capacity to function as a *single intelligence*. The process of building a community involves deep dialogue among people typically arrayed in a circle. Programs can run from intensive two-to-three-day workshops to periodic dialogues extending over weeks and months. The building blocks are for individuals to understand and express "who I am" and make a conscious choice to join with others. Conversation that deepens person-to-person relationships, in turn, creates a sense of trust and unity that is needed to bring a collection of individuals into community. Thoughtful, if sometimes heated, reflection on "who we are" yields a collective identity and oneness that, at the same time, preserves individuality and diversity in the community.

The next layers of community-building engage collective consciousness and apply it to complex problems in such a way that every individual thinks and acts mindful of the "whole"– in an organizational context this means the individual, fellow employees, and the enterprise, as well as customers, shareholders, other stakeholders, and of course society and the planet. Much of the writing and practice on community-building in business concerns its applications to problem-solving, organization learning and culture change (see, for example, Peck 1993; Kofman and Senge 1993; Gozdz 1996; Mirvis 2002). The case here is unique in that it shows its use by business leaders in not only developing their internal processes but also inquiring into "what we do" and reframing the very purpose of their business.

Background on Unilever Asia

To build a sustainable, profitable foods-and-beverage business in Asia, Unilever Food's Asia Chairman Tex Gunning worked with the author to build a leadership community among 250 managers spread across 17 countries in Asia–Pacific (Mirvis and Gunning 2006). We two first met based on our interest in the work of M. Scott Peck who pioneered an approach to community-building that emphasizes group consciousness to open up a sense of wonder about human purpose and the presence of a higher power. The practical intent is for the assembled group to develop deeper connections and ultimately find common ground. Tex had used these methods, along with other group development and learning tools, to join together 180 business team leaders and turn around Unilever's foods business in Holland—going from years of losses to double-digit growth (Mirvis, Ayas, and Roth 2003). He brought this philosophy with him to Asia when he took charge of the foods-and-beverage business.

But it is one thing to unite people from a single country with a relatively egalitarian culture; quite another to bond leaders of so many different nationalities, and in many cases from ethnic cultures that favor hierarchy and social distance. Furthermore, the Unilever Asia leaders were based in historically independent country business units and, to this point, had progressed through single-country career paths. Tex's operating model called for the creation of pan-Asian business models and management practices. Behind this was his desire to build the capacity of this entire leadership body to think, feel and work together, that is, to operate as a community of leaders. Could the Asian leaders find common cause and learn to work together?

Community-building concepts

The generic model of group development, based on studies of small 8–12-person groups, involves stages of forming, storming, norming and performing (Tuckman 1965). There are obvious parallels between the development of small groups and large ones (or communities) but key differences as well. To begin, the theories behind community-building, which has people in a large forum open up about their lives and speak from their heart about coming together with others present, certainly incorporate group dynamics but also reference trans-personal psychology and spirituality (Mirvis 1997). Dialogue, a community-building practice, has individuals speak to the "group as a whole" about matters of interest and simultaneously scan their feelings, assumptions, and reactions to the experience. As such, it also reflects ideas about the interconnection of human thought and energy (Isaacs 1999; Scharmer 2009). A look at the conceptual stages of development in small groups, dialogue groups, and community-building forums highlights some similarities and differences between them (see Figure 18.1).

Figure 18.1 Stages of development in groups, dialogue, and communities

Group development Tuckman	Forming	Storming	Norming	Performing
Group dialogue Isaacs; Scharmer	Talking nice	Talking tough	Reflective dialogue	Generative dialogue
Community-building Peck	Pseudo-community	Chaos	Emptiness	Community

Practices of community-building also differ in key respects from the standard regimen in team-building or guided small group facilitation (Schwarz 2002). In team-building programs, for instance, the facilitator often adopts an active leadership role, at least at the start, and steers the group into structured conversation about roles, goals, and working processes. At the start of a community-building workshop, by contrast, everyone sits in a circle to signal norms of shared leadership and responsibility. In FCE programs, facilitators begin by speaking to key principles of community-building: to welcome and affirm diversity, deal with difficult issues, bridge differences with integrity, and relate with love and respect. In this sense, community-building advances by the "positive values=positive action" equation that guides groups involved in appreciative inquiries. They also highlight the importance of speakers personally "owning" comments ("I" statements) and of attending, as in Quaker meetings, to when they are "moved to speak" (see Box 18.1).

Box 18.1 Key FCE principles of community-building

- **"I" statements.** Use the first-person singular pronoun to claim knowledge, feelings and observations rather than ascribe them to "we" or to "everyone"
- **Moved to speak.** Follow the Quaker injunction to wait until you are personally moved to say something and, when so moved, to speak
- **Emptiness.** Share personal thoughts and feelings, especially those that prevent you from being fully present in the dialogue
- **Witnessing.** Welcome and affirm others' stories and points of view and, in the spirit of community, bridge differences with love and respect
- **Difficult issues.** Face difficult issues that arise rather than deny, disregard or downplay them

At the same time, facilitators are admonished that they cannot "lead" a group to community. They and anyone else present can, however, share their own thoughts, call the group into silence, or slow the discussion down. Let us see these practices in action across the stages of community-building among the Asian business leaders.

1. Pseudo-community

In the formative phase, individuals in a group have to deal with their purpose in coming together and form relationships with one another and with formal leaders. This raises issues of "inclusion" and begets questions about how much a person wants to be included and is inclined to include others. Peck labels this phase "pseudo-community." Here, a new group often adopts a culturally comfortable form and rhythm that allows each individual to bring forth his or her needs, style, and ideas. In dialogue, this has people "talking nice." The drive is to incorporate everyone, blur individual differences, and establish a common, familiar baseline of relating.

Coming together for the first time as a leadership circle from 15 different countries in Asia– Pacific, the leaders of the foods business struggled with the process of opening up, talking together deeply and making space for and including divergent points of view. A facilitator intones: "This is an effort to build a leadership community where everyone thinks and acts mindful of the whole. It is one based on shared understanding among people and deep communication, a community that values personal reflection, deep listening, and authentic conversation." Sitting in a circle, the 250 leaders present are asked to take a moment of silence, attend to their feelings and any discomfort, and heed when they are "moved to speak"; they are encouraged to speak up when they are so moved.

There is a long, awkward silence. The leaders sit on little benches, thinking and squirming, as a huge fire throws sparks into the blackness. The chairman finally begins to talk, by way of example. A few more speak up, with long stretches of nothing in between. There are genuine attempts at sharing, but the bulk of the talk takes the form of stand-up speeches, filled with logical reasons to come together and occasional references to ancient wisdom or poetry on such matters, followed by polite applause. Most of the speakers are from central Asia—India and Pakistan—or with origins in Europe, all fluent in English. One Chinese leader finally speaks directly to the chairman, "It's hard to have a conversation with two hundred people at a time."

The talk winds down and the gathering ends in silence. Some leaders talk quietly in clusters of two or three. Most walk wordlessly away. One participant reflects:

> The evening dialogue was very frustrating, despite my own pitiful efforts at involvement. The exercise left a sour taste in my mouth, and some anger as well, for forcing such an uncomfortable and culturally insensitive situation on us all. I felt so much empathy for my South Asian colleagues. I also come from a more publicly conservative culture, unlike our [European and Central Asian leaders]. I went to bed feeling very pissed off.

Not everyone shares the same anguish and anger: "There are moments that things happen and moments when they don't," says a Pakistani leader. "I did feel a little let down when we failed to dialogue with each other but then I quickly used that opportunity to question my beliefs, the status quo, the easy and comfortable solutions," says another. Others continue to reflect and question more deeply why it was such a struggle:

> Why was I not open and honest during that night when we tried to start-up up a dialogue? I believe there was a barrier of judgment … of my mind not letting me reach my heart. I was hiding myself in that darkness behind self-centered and mind-driven judgment, resulting in neither giving or receiving, though my heart was forcing me to share.

2. Chaos

In the next phase of group development, individual differences come to the fore and a group faces conflict and constraints—and begins to "storm." Group members have to deal with issues of control—how much to exert and how much to accept from others. This conflictual phase is called "chaos" in community-building language and in dialogue terminology has people "talking tough." Throughout this phase, boundaries are being set and a collective culture begins to take shape. One common collective issue concerns a leadership crisis: who is in charge? Can a community lead itself?

The next day's dialogue begins in chaos among the Asians. One leader challenges the chairman for seeming to question him about speaking up. At issue is the strength of his leadership. Several speak of their disgust with having "rules" for talking together and with the inefficiency of a whole group conversation. In some respects, this is akin to the "revolt" found in encounter groups where members turn against their leaders and the group begins to establish its own independent identity. A revolution is forestalled here when a young female leader from Thailand speaks up and tells a personal story of experiencing fear. More stories then follow in sequence about personal adversities, trials, and even triumphs. In the community-building vernacular, people begin to "empty."

> I sat there wondering why it was so easy for us to put our messages across but so difficult to listen to others' points and build on them. I was not sure if this was arranged intentionally, but it really pushed my colleagues and me to the border of discomfort, so much that we exploded implicitly afterwards and explicitly the next day.

3. Emptying

In group dynamics, confrontation segues a group into "norming" and has it finding its own direction, setting rules, and getting "organized." This is sometimes sped up through techniques such as role negotiation, structured problem-solving, or conflict-resolution interventions—common tools in a group facilitator's regimen. On a larger scale, it involves setting direction and defining rules for collective behavior.

Methods for setting norms and addressing conflict take a different form in large groups involved in building community. In groups intending to form a learning community, for instance, conversation is directed not towards negotiation or problem-solving but to what learning theorists characterize as collective "inquiry" (Argyris 1982; Schein 2003). In FCE programs, people are encouraged to talk personally about what is keeping them from connecting to the group. By "emptying" themselves, as in meditation or prayer or as one would in self-help groups or Quaker meeting, people open up to others present and comprehend their own lives and circumstances afresh. This entails personal vulnerability and the surrender of formal roles, agendas, and even goals. As this phase unfolds, self-awareness increases and feelings of empathy with others often emerge. A sense of community is born as people start then to see themselves in another and another in themselves (Fromm 1956; Dutton and Heaphy 2003).

Among the Asians, a Filipino says, "I know now that the experience drove me and a colleague with whom I had never had a discussion before to open up. We shared deeply our thoughts and difficulties and experience." "While there were differences in our appearance, speech and food yet we were bonded by feeling of friendship and caring," says an Indian manager, "sharing innermost feelings and fears so openly bonded us emotionally." Says another, "We all have different backgrounds, so I have to look into that deeply and I have to open my mind up and be big enough to accept each one of you in my heart. Then we can have some sort of understanding and then become more united together."

What makes the second day's dialogue fascinating is that nearly all the speakers are South Asian leaders (from Indonesia, Thailand, Malaysia, Vietnam and China) who to this point have not spoken to the group as a whole. The more expressive English speakers from India and Pakistanis have seemingly emptied themselves of their need to speak. They are giving space to and welcoming the diversity of other voices. There is no applause. No speeches. People are standing up one at a time, as they are moved to speak, not competing for airtime but attentively listening and building on what is said. This is a glimmer of what true dialogue can be. Now that it has begun, what will the leaders talk about?

4. Community

In solo, in small groups and as a community, the Asians probe deeply into existential questions of Who am I? Who are we? and, finally, What are we here for? The result of their collective inquiry is a shared aspiration to make their work more relevant to the communities they serve in Asia. Says one,

> I started getting the feeling that my work need not be confined to producing and selling as efficiently as possible but has a higher purpose of community service to the people of Asia. Maybe I can call it [a shift] from a mercenary to a missionary view [of our business].

Ongoing dialogue brings them closer to the conclusion that organizations have to be driven by their missions rather than by numbers and processes. "We should be able to serve the larger community by being relevant for them—not by just being providers of products," said one. An imperative emerged: the leaders needed to puts flesh into these caring aspirations and translate them into a mission and a way of life that would emphasize the healthy, nourishing aspects of food. Hear one of the statements:

We want to be responsible partners with the people of Asia, to provide health, vitality, and the development of the children and families through better food and beverage. We can do this by earning the trust of people everywhere, having authentic standards for what is right food. We can do this by being at the leading edge of nutrition science and technology. We need to be actively involved in communities, to understand all their needs, especially the needs of the economically underprivileged and children. We need to do so with humility, truth, and authenticity. That means we have to do what we say.

Build community, then organize

In its mature or performing phase, a group of whatever size dedicates more of its time and resources to its tasks—whatever they may be.[1] The interpersonal agenda has people asking how much to give of themselves to the task and how open and intimate to be to one another. A dialogue group asks "generative" questions about its tasks and about itself. And, in the FCE community-building vernacular, a maturing group looks for spiritual guidance on its purposes asking what actions are called for or emerging from conversations. Peter Senge and colleagues (Senge 1990; Senge, Scharmer, Jaworski, and Flowers 2005) term this "presencing."

Testimonials abound about the creative breakthroughs that groups can experience in consciousness-raising programs, when engaged in theatrics or the arts, or in meditation or other mediums where the experience of wholeness translates into creative insight or action or both (Mirvis 2008). Several variants of the spiritual sciences also reference this

---

1   Some key points about the development of groups. First, progress through stages is by no means smooth or inevitable. On the contrary, groups often seemingly get 'stuck' at one or another phase and either do not face or fail to master more complex developmental challenges. Second, rather than a sequence, developmental stages might be better depicted as a spiral. Changes in setting and circumstances mean that groups must continuously cycle through activities involving forming, storming, norming and performing. In the ideal, new challenges can be managed more quickly and effectively by 'mature' groups. In practice, however, many other factors can either increase progress or lead to regression.

dynamic. The order to be found in chaos, for instance, revolves around an aptly named "strange attractor"; Margaret Wheatley (1993), among others, suggests that its human equivalent is meaning. William James (1902), speaking of the common core of spiritual revelation, says we find *more* of that quality "which is operative in the universe outside of [ourselves]."

Peck (1993) likens the oceanic feeling to a "state of grace" and describes the experience of making community as transcendent—a term that means literally to "climb over" or, more colloquially, to achieve a "peak experience" or find one's "higher self." On these matters, two Asian leaders reflected:

> I realized that words like emotions, feeling, moods may not sound businesslike; however, once used in their best and sincere form have real consequences for getting work done. I began to understand that building a resonant culture, one where all of us can bring out the best in us, would bring us to greatness.
>
> I feel very close to the Asia group. There was some weird sense of bonding that developed even though I didn't know more than half of the people. I really can't explain it well but it was a sense of oneness or being together. It is strange because I felt this when weren't even talking. It was a nice feeling. For the first time I experienced it outside my family. Maybe this is what we call community feeling.

A sense of community grew easily as the Asian leaders strove to speak authentically, build on comments, challenge gracefully, and help new thoughts and intentions to emerge. The process was maturing to the point of collective thinking. Said one,

> Initially it was hard, it was painful to talk so openly as we are so new to each other. Now it was great to see that words just poured out from everyone. We are starting to see the connections with each other.

Another said,

> I was struggling with the concept of community in a business corporation such as ours but the layers unpeeled over the days slowly. It is a very powerful thought and I am still trying to soak it in. I saw a deeper meaning of life in all this ... understanding, belonging, affiliation, caring, working

together in a responsible and dedicated fashion like a family, a sense of fulfillment and so on. While family is so central to me in personal life, I feel that similar core thoughts need to be internalized and become a way of life in work life.

Facilitating community-building

There is a growing literature on methods for building community and a "group mind" and training programs, in universities and elsewhere, where facilitators can develop their skills in these regards. Those seasoned at team-building and group facilitation, or in leading T-groups or other small group experiences should note, however, that some of the practices in community-building call for a distinctive facilitative style (see Box 18.2).

Box 18.2 Facilitating community-building: key practices

Self-reflection

Many group development workshops encourage participants to give one another feedback. In community-building, the notion of offering Rogerian-type counseling in a group—to help people see themselves more clearly through questioning or clarifying—is discouraged as it equates to "fixing" someone. Instead, participants are urged to self-reflect and be aware of their filtering and judgments. The idea, as expressed by William Isaacs (1999) is that by "observing the observer" and "listening to your listening," self-awareness of thoughts, feelings, and experiences, past and present, seep gently into consciousness.

"Letting go"

Groups typically mature by "working through" issues (e.g. membership, authority, control, trust) that are posed at each stage of development. In the community circle, people are encouraged instead to talk personally and to witness one another do so. The rationale is that people progress towards community not by "working" issues but rather by "letting go" of thoughts, feelings, wishes, and everything else that gets in the way of being "fully present." In so doing, individuals begin to open up to the "others" in their circle and comprehend their own lives and circumstances afresh.

A container

The intent in community-building is not to confront conflicts directly. Instead, the group serves as a "container"—to hold issues and conflicts up for ongoing reflection. This keeps potentially hot conversation cooled sufficiently that people can see the "whole" of the group mind. Physicist David Bohm (1989) likens the resulting state to "superconductivity" in a group—the elements of the conversation move as a "whole" rather than as separate parts.

How about the emphasis in community-building given to spirituality and an "unseen order of things?" Peck and the FCE are adamant that community-building is *not* religion and that its principles are by no means sacred. Religion is about answers, so they say, and spirituality is more about questions. But however we characterize the experience of community and its spiritual dimensions, it is plain enough that vast numbers of people, from all walks of life, are searching for new relationships, attachments, and "something more" in their individual and collective lives. In my view, the case of Unilever Asia provides a strong example of how sustainability, in its ethical, social, and environmental dimensions, can provide people and organizations a sense of "higher purpose" and meaning (Mirvis 2008).

Fine words and uplifting sentiments, but the challenge facing Unilever Asia going forward was how to transform their aspirations into a socially responsive business model and new way of life. Peck was fond of saying, "first build community, and then organize." Here, community-building was threaded through a set of learning journeys that took 250 or more of the Asian leaders to Sarawak, China, India, and Sri Lanka to see first-hand the social, environmental and economic issues connected to their business. This effort at "educating for sustainability" had the Asian leaders survey economic, social and environmental conditions on the ground, engage myriad customers, community leaders, political figures, and their critics in dialogue, and then fashion a new business model based on sustainability. Later they introduced social and environmental content in Unilever's brands. Their innovation platform ultimately worked its way to the corporate offices and ultimately shaped development of Unilever's Sustainable Living Plan (Mirvis 2011).

References

Argyris, C. (1982) *Reasoning, Learning, and Action* (San Francisco: Jossey-Bass).

Bohm, D. (1989) *On Dialogue* (Ojai, CA: David Bohm Seminars).

Daly, R.E., and D. Nicoll (1997) "Accelerating a Team's Developmental Process," *OD Practitioner* 29.4.

Dewey, J. (1910) "Natural Resources in the Training of Thought," in *How We Think* (Lexington, MA: D.C. Heath): 29-44.

Dutton, J.E., and E.D. Heaphy (2003) "The Power of High-quality Connections," in K.S. Cameron, J.E. Dutton, and R.E. Quinn (eds.), *Positive Organizational Scholarship* (San Francisco: Jossey-Bass).

Ferdman, B. (2013) *Diversity at Work: The Practice of Inclusion* (San Francisco: Pfeiffer).

Fisher, R., W. Ury, and B. Patton (2011) *Getting to Yes: Negotiating Agreement without Giving In* (New York: Penguin Books, rev. edn.).

Fromm, E. (1956) *The Art of Loving* (New York: Harper & Row).

Gordon, J. (2007) *The Pfeiffer Book of Successful Conflict Management Tools* (San Francisco: Pfeiffer).

Gozdz, K. (ed.) (1996) *Community Building in Business* (San Francisco: New Leaders Press).

Isaacs, W. (1999) *Dialogue and the Art of Thinking Together: A Pioneering Approach to Communicating in Business and Life* (New York: Doubleday).

James, W. (1902) *The Varieties of Religious Experience: A Study in Human Nature* (New York: Longmans, Green & Co.).

Katzenbach, J.R., and D.K. Smith (2001) *The Discipline of Teams* (London: John Wiley).

Kofman, F., and P. Senge (1993) "Communities of Commitment: The Heart of the Learning Organization," *Organization Dynamics* 22.2: 5-22.

Levine, S. (2000) *Getting to Resolution: Turning Conflict into Collaboration* (San Francisco: Berrett-Koehler).

Mirvis, P.H. (1997) "'Soul Work' in Organizations," *Organization Science* 8.2: 193-206.

Mirvis, P.H. (2002) "Community Building in Business," *Reflections* 3: 45–51.

Mirvis, P.H. (2008) "Executive Development Through Consciousness Raising Experiences," *Academy of Management Learning and Education* 7.2: 173-88.

Mirvis, P.H. (2011) "Unilever's Drive for Sustainability and CSR: Changing the Game," in S. Mohrman, A.B. Shani, and C. Worley (eds.) *Organizing for Sustainable Effectiveness* (vol. 1; London: Emerald).

Mirvis, P.H., and W.L. Gunning (2006) "Creating a Community of Leaders," *Organizational Dynamics* 35.1: 69-82.

Mirvis, P.H., K. Ayas, and G. Roth (2003) *To the Desert and Back: The Story of One of the Most Dramatic Business Transformations on Record* (San Francisco: Jossey-Bass).

Peck, M.S. (1987) *The Different Drum: Community Making and Peace* (New York: Simon & Schuster).

Peck, M.S. (1993) *A World Waiting to be Born: Civility Rediscovered* (New York: Doubleday).

Scharmer, C.O. (2009) *Theory U: Leading from the Future as it Emerges* (San Francisco: Berrett-Koehler).

Schein, E.H. (2003) "On Dialogue, Culture, and Organization Learning," *Reflections* 4.4: 27-38.

Schwarz, R. (2002) *The Skilled Facilitator: A Comprehensive Resource for Consultants, Facilitators, Managers, Trainers, and Coaches* (San Francisco: Jossey-Bass, 2nd edn).

Senge, P. (1990) *The Fifth Discipline: The Art and Practice of the Learning Organization* (New York: Doubleday).

Senge, P.M., C.O. Scharmer, J. Jaworski, and B.S. Flowers (2005) *Presence: An Exploration of Profound Change in People, Organizations, and Society* (New York: Crown Books).

Tuckman, B.W. (1965) "Development Sequences in Small Groups," *Psychological Bulletin* 63: 419-27.

Wheatley, M.J. (1993) *Leadership and the New Science: Discovering Order in a Chaotic World* (San Francisco, CA: Berrett-Koehler).

19

Transforming collaborative institutions

Australian business schools

Eddie Blass

Learning Innovations Hub, University of New England, USA

Peter Hayward

Swinburne University, Australia

This chapter outlines the use of a collaboratory approach to facilitate transformative group work among a disparate group who did not necessarily know or work with each other prior to the group forming. The process design and implementation is outlined here rather than the results in terms of content, as it demonstrates an alternative use of collaboratory engagement as a stimulus rather than as the generator of the outcome itself.

Swinburne University of Technology received funding from the Australian Business Deans Council to run a "practice innovation trial" in the form of the creation of a collaboratory, bringing together a range of academics across disciplines, representative parties from industry, peak bodies and government agencies, with the purpose of exploring, in particular, objective one of the 50+20 Agenda: to refocus education to ensure we educate and develop globally responsible leaders. The short film of the launch of the 50+20 Agenda at Rio[1] was used to open the retreat and individuals were invited to share their reaction to the film.

The 50+20 project outlines their philosophy of the collaboratory involving a circular space that is open to concerned stakeholders for any given issue (Muff 2012). It represents an open-source metaspace: a facilitated platform based on open space and consciousness-building technologies, as described in Muff 2012 and in Chapter 2 in this book.

Drawing on Open Space Technology, the process requires little formal preparation. Harrison Owen (2008) suggests that a detailed agenda, plan, reading materials and so forth in advance can detract from the process, and it is better simply to have a compelling theme and committed group with a leader to facilitate the process.

> Open Space Technology is effective when real learning, innovation, and departure from the norm are required. When you aren't quite sure where you are, and less than clear about where you are headed, and require the best thinking and support from all those who wish to be involved, Open Space Technology will provide the means (Owen 1997).

The stated objectives of the innovative practice trial were:

1. To establish a "collaboratory" of academics from across the university, industry representatives, and government and peak body leaders to explore the notion of a management education for the world

2. To develop a curriculum for the development of responsible leaders for a sustainable future drawing on the outcomes of the collaboratory

3. To test the curriculum ideas with current and future students and future employers

4. To prototype elements of the curriculum for testing in the current "classroom"

5. To disseminate an "alternative model" to the current management education offering to encourage debate and be a trigger for change

---

1 Viewable at http://www.youtube.com/watch?v=pRCVrZSUyzM&list=PLL7UFp_pBVO_byryqxHtSGSSXYwb-BNGp, accessed 6 April 2014.

6. To contribute to the further dissemination and development of the 50+20 Agenda to develop management education for the world in partnership with the Global Responsible Leadership Initiative and Principles for Responsible Management Education

Design and collaboratory methodology

The design of the workshop was informed by two main bodies of theory.

The first was Adam Kahane's work on *Transformative Scenario Planning* (Kahane 2012, and see Chapter 13 in this book), which recounts a series of change initiatives that started out looking at problems that appeared on first sight too big to solve. Kahane has brought together groups opposing ends of the spectrum to resolve issues that appeared unresolvable by creating scenarios for the future in which every stakeholder had a stake and appreciated how their stake impact both positively and negatively on each other. Through this process, stakeholders started to take responsibility for not causing harm to each other and mutually beneficial futures were created. This process of sharing responsibility for different stakeholders was one we sought to emulate in the collaborator as industry and academia recognized the planet as a stakeholder that also needed a voice.

The second body of theory we drew on for methodology, which focused more on the process of taking the individuals into a transformative space, was Otto Scharmer's Theory U (Scharmer 2009 and see Chapter 12 in this book). This work outlines "the social technology of presencing" which is a necessary state for individuals to reach in order to achieve transformative change. This is achieved through diving down a U, requiring the individual to open their mind first, then open their heart, before finally opening their will. At the point of open will the individual can be present and a group engaging in presencing can bring about powerful, transformative change together.

The third element contributing to the design of the process was the information for moderators of collaboratories issues by the 50+20 project itself (Muff 2012: 17; see also Chapter 2 in this book).

The 50+20 Collaboratory Moderation states that the basic set-up of a collaboratory is always circular, with an inner circle embedded within an outer circle. The inner circle was seated on "benches," which we formed by putting two chairs together, and the outer circle stood and walked around. Each bench had a single person sitting on it. Anyone from the outer circle wishing to join the inner circle in order to contribute to the conversation, moved and sat down next to someone on a bench. The person already sitting on the bench then stood and moved back to the outer circle. In this manner, in order to join a conversation, a contributor had to displace someone already in the conversation.

A talking-stone approach was used to slow down and deepen the conversation. A stone was placed in the center of the circle and, in order to speak, an individual had to get up and pick up the stone, then sit down again on the bench before starting to talk. On finishing speaking the individual replaced the stone in the center. The next person who wanted to talk then had to move to pick up the stone and sit down again before starting to talk. While this slows the conversation down, participants fed back to us that they could not believe how quickly the time passed. It also makes people very aware of how much they are talking within the circle as some people tend to take many more turns at speaking in a conversation (Bales, Strodtbeck, Mills, and Roseborough 1951), and rules regarding turn taking in conversation are an intrinsic feature of the conversation (Wilson, Wimann, and Zimmerman 1984). By shifting the conversational rules, participation activity moves away from roles reasonably attributed to the participants' normal operation and changes the nature of the interaction away from role to one more of who they are (Gibson 2003).

We did not get members of the group to introduce themselves to each other. We did not want their position, status, role, employment sector, or other differentiating factor to impact on how they were included in the conversation (Goffman 1983) so we simply introduced names and our reaction to the film.

We held three collaboratory cycles on the first day of the retreat. We gathered at lunch and then went into the workshop space, watched the video and then introduced ourselves giving our names and our reaction to the video. As a means of parking preconceived ideas and freeing the mind in order to be able to transform understanding, our first activity was to brainstorm in small groups what we thought the current leadership problems were and what the current leadership solutions tended to be. We captured this on a flipchart and tacked it to the walls. We did not discuss it. The point of the exercise was for people to park what they had come in to the experience thinking about as their agenda. We had captured it and written it down so they no longer needed to think about it. They had permission to let it go to allow space for new thoughts. We then moved into the collaboratory circle process. Each circle ran for just under one hour with a short break in between each. The three topics of discussion were:

1. Who will the leader of the future be?

2. What will globally responsible leadership look like?

3. Can globally responsible leadership be learned?

The essence of the conversation was captured on flipchart paper and is discussed below. The process had moved the participants from their start point, through "open mind" towards "open heart." To open the heart more fully, we sent the participants off on a walk in the park to find something to bring back that was their "teacher," so the artifact they returned with had to represent something that they were taught or felt needed to be taught in order to be a globally responsible leader. We finished the evening by sharing our artifacts and positioning them on the table to represent our sculpture. We did not use the visioning process straight away as the energy in the room had reached an exploratory point that needed reflection.

Building on the collaboratory stimulus and concluding the process

The next morning we started by hearing reflections on where people were at, given the day before. We then moved on to a quick brainstorming task to start to generate ideas to move forward. On the premise that every good idea about the future sounded ridiculous when it was first mooted, we asked people to put down any and all of the ridiculous ideas that were coming into their heads around the agenda.

In order to start to find actors to take action, we moved into a task that identified who the stakeholders and actors were in globally responsible leadership. Once this long list was compiled, small groups mapped some of the stakeholders on a grid in terms of current position and preferred future position. The grid axes were impact and influence on globally responsible leadership on the Y axis and strength of interest in globally responsible leadership on the X axis.

The groups then worked on ideas that would help move the stakeholders from their starting point in the direction of the preferred end point. These ideas were then put through a rapid democratic prototyping process[2] before being adopted as a feasible intervention to pursue or not. A total of eight interventions made it through the prototyping process. Finally the group reconvened after lunch to explore what the role of the business school was in developing globally responsible leaders.

The outcomes from the whole process were slightly disappointing as the stakeholders visioned actions that they did not own themselves; hence they attributed the responsibility for action to others. This might, on reflection, have been avoided had we carried out the visioning process immediately after the collaboratory circles. In a follow-up day, to recover the process, we ran a single collaboratory circle followed by an activity based on future scenarios. This led to a much more focused outcome.

References

Bales, R.F., F.L. Strodtbeck, T.M. Mills, and M.E. Roseborough (1951) "Channels of Communication in Small Groups," *American Sociological Review* 16: 461-68.

Gibson, D.R. (2003) "Participation Shifts: Order and Differentiation in Group Conversation," *Social Forces* 81.4: 1335-81.

Goffman, E. (1983) "The Interaction Order: 1982 Presidential Address," *American Sociological Review* 48, February: 1-17.

Kahane, A. (2012) *Transformative Scenario Planning: Working Together to Change the Future* (San Francisco: Berrett-Koehler).

Muff, K. (2012) "The 50+20 Collaboratory Methodology and Approach for Short One-time Sessions," http://50plus20.org/wp-content/uploads/2013/02/50+20-Collaboratory-Approach.pdf, accessed 6 April 2014.

Owen, H.H. (1997) "A Brief User's Guide to Open Space Technology," http://www.openspaceworld.com/users_guide.htm, accessed 6 April 2014.

2   See www.holacracy.com for a rapid prototyping, democratic process.

Owen, H. H. (2008) *Open Space Technology: A Users Guide* (San Francisco: Berrett-Koehler, 3rd edn).

Scharmer, C.O. (2009) *Theory U: Leading from the Future as it Emerges* (San Francisco: Berrett-Koehler).

Wilson, T.P., J.M. Wimann, and D.H. Zimmerman (1984) "Models of Turn Taking in Conversational Interaction," *Journal of Language and Social Psychology* 3: 159-83.

20

Long-term stakeholder engagement

Initiatives of Change in Caux

Louie Gardiner

Potent 6, UK

This chapter looks at a very particular form of a collaboratory process. It explores the systemic conditions that have supported the emergent evolution of Initiatives of Change (IofC), a global community and movement that has endured over more than seven decades. Each year members converge in Caux, high above Montreux in Switzerland to catalyze dialogue and inspire action to address issues affecting people in communities across the world.

The chapter offers interesting insights in how to create and hold a community space, how to integrate "quiet time" into a community-building process enabling transformation at personal, group and systemic levels. We would love the use of the collaboratory to endure over time. It may be too ambitious to imagine it to be used across decades and continents, but IofC gives us hope of what can unfold when groups of passionate stakeholders meet around an important cause.

Being touched

In August 2010, after a sodden journey across rain-filled skies and mist-covered, mountainous terrain, I found myself entering the Mountain House to contribute to a conference called "Leading Change for a Sustainable World." This majestic building—once a salubrious hotel for the wealthy—is set high above Montreux, Switzerland, in a tiny hamlet called Caux. As I walked into the large, rather dark entrance hall I felt something … I sensed that in this place, I had a place. By the end of those first ten days, I had heard many people talk of the "spirit of Caux"—something that was felt, yet was hard to define. I knew that, like me, they too had been touched. Certainly there was a quality of being and engaging in this place that we sensed and appreciated and to which we were drawn but could not explain.

Initiatives of Change (IofC)

My first encounter with IofC happened to be in my professional capacity as a leadership consultant, facilitator, and coach. Arriving in time for afternoon tea, I was greeted by Cain[1] at the door and was escorted to the terrace. Three things took my breath away: the rear spectacle of Mountain House; the view overlooking Lac Leman with its dual Swiss and French panorama; and the visible diversity of people—clearly coming from multiple continents. Cain gave me my first introduction to IofC and Caux, talking about Frank Buchman (the founding catalyst); the practice of "quiet time" to access inner guidance; using the "Four Standards" of honesty, purity, unselfishness, and love to guide personal decisions and action; and finally, that this was not just a conference, it was a way of living, sharing, and being in community—and as such, everyone who attends is invited to join a "community group." He told me that each group undertakes several work shifts during the conference—taking it in turns to cook, serve, or clean up after meals. My theme for the week

---

1   Cain Ormondroyd works as a barrister and is a practicing Christian. He has been involved with IofC for seven years as a conference participant and volunteer organizer.

ahead was to be about leadership and "response-ability" and I noted the connection between what I was to explore and the pattern of "responsibility and service" that seemed to be embedded in the design and practice of what happened here in Mountain House.

Seeds are sown

In those first moments Cain introduced me verbally and practically to what is at the heart of IofC. I heard his words but did not consciously take in that he was modeling a spirit of service. I had been side-tracked, noticing my own internal resistance to taking part in the work shifts—I heard my inner, unpalatable voice of arrogance claiming to myself that "*my* service will be what I contribute in my conference sessions." It did not take long to come face to face with my false pride and to realize that, in this context, I was more student than teacher.

In trying to understand what was happening around me, I found myself drawing on an area of study in complexity sciences called "simple rules" (Reynolds 1987), introduced to me by Dr Glenda Eoyang who suggested calling them "seed" behaviors within the IofC context. These refer to behaviors or exchanges that emerge among individuals in a human system, which then produce "patterns" or "culture," for example, "the spirit of Caux." In 2012, I started engaging others in naming obvious "seed" behaviors that were happening around us, which seemed to express the spirit of Caux.

The first was strikingly apparent from Cain's exchange with me:

- **Serve and receive service, joyfully.** Service is central to all IofC gatherings. Everyone shares in running the house. Lifetime volunteers such as Jean Brown[2] continue to source action on the ground that transforms countless lives. She recognized that conflicts in

2 Jean Brown, an Australian, has worked for over 45 years as a full-time volunteer with IofC, much of that time in India and more recently in Africa. She has been involved in reconciliation initiatives, in training—for ten years with her husband on the faculty of the Action For Life leadership program—and, as an International Coordinator of Creators of Peace, is the author of the Creators of Peace Circle, a methodology now used in 40 countries to engage women in peace creating.

communities were often perpetuated through the stories told by women—by mothers and grandmothers. She realized that they had a key part to play in healing and reconciliation. Today, Creators of Peace[3] is perhaps the most well-established program of IofC supporting women across the world to heal wounds within families and divided communities. Iman, a teacher, in her passionate determination to sow the seeds of peace is, against all odds, finding a way to run Peace Circles in Damascus, Syria[4]

The power of valuing difference

Every year in Caux, an extraordinarily diverse mix of human beings converge—every continent is represented; multiple nationalities, religions, ethnicities; people with little or great material wealth; those with and without formal status; intergenerational; multilingual—and the list goes on. As human beings, we are hard-wired[5] to categorize, judge, and seek alliances with those who are similar, with a tendency to separate from those who are not like us. Daniel Kahneman (2011) illuminates the process in our brains—that thinking "fast" is our default reaction to what happens around us. "Slow" thinking faculties require conscious, effortful attention. So to get beyond our hard-wired categorizing minds and unconscious bias we need to slow down enough to challenge ourselves to open up to each other. People in IofC are no less mortal than the rest of us, yet countless individuals have embraced courage and forgiveness over fear and shame, let go of hatred in favor of healing, relinquished blame in favor of compassion and righteousness in favor of love, and chosen connection over conflict. How?

3 Creators of Peace: http://www.iofc.org/creators-of-peace.
4 Jean Brown supporting Iman to run Peace Circles in Syria: http://www.iofc.org/cir cles-syria-%E2%80%93-creators-peace-circles-heart-damascus?bc=node/21827, accessed 6 April 2014; to find out more about Iman's story, see: Gardiner 2014.
5 Professor John Powell, Director of the Haas Diversity Research Center, University of California, diversity researcher, speaker at the Healing History conference in Caux, Summer 2013, speaking about unconscious bias.

- **Turn judgment into curiosity.** IofC gatherings are designed to encourage deep listening and inquiry between people who might ordinarily be adversaries. Space is given for individuals to share without interruption. Those listening are encouraged to open their hearts and minds to each other's humanity—to act with love, honesty, unselfishness, and purity of intention—to forgive and make restitution for one's own wrongdoings. Caux made it possible for Irène Laure, a lifelong socialist, labor leader, and French Resistance fighter in the Second World War to admit her consuming hatred of the German people and to seek forgiveness from them. In the post-apartheid years in South Africa, this context made it possible for Ginn Fourie to forgive and befriend Letlapa Mphahlele, the man whose orders had her daughter killed[6]

Revisiting the roots

IofC, originally called Moral Re-Armament (MRA), took shape in the first half of the 20th century in an era that included the rise of communism and two world wars. MRA's embryonic beginnings were evangelist, centered on Frank Buchman, a Lutheran Minister, born in the United States with Dutch heritage.

He wanted to change the world. As he travelled the globe he moved away from large-scale methods because he found that intimate, informal exchanges with individuals and smaller groups, were more effective in bringing about lasting personal change. From these explorations, the central notion of "changing the world starting with oneself" took root. In 1921 he visited Oxford University in the UK. Students were inspired, and out of the "house parties" that took place, the Oxford Group was formed. In these intimate community gatherings, people engaged in quiet time, learning to listen deeply to "God" or to the "still voice within," sharing what arose for them.

---

6 Ginn and Letlapa bear testament to what becomes possible in a film, *Beyond Forgiving*, Producer and Director: Imad N. Karam, http://www.iofc.org/beyond-forgiving-documentary-wins-golden-award-inspiration, accessed 2 April 2014.

Quiet time: group consciousness in practice

It took several years of attending Caux for me to realize that three systemic factors were embodied in quiet time. First, it is simple—which makes it potentially easily replicable. Second, it connects across scales—from individual to group to global.[7] Sharing quiet time enables individuals to extend their reflection beyond themselves. Listening to the similar and different struggles of others connects people to each other and links their personal change to global concerns. Third, it is iterative—enabling rapid-cycle, regular reflection supporting one's (and the system's) capacity to adapt to complex, shifting conditions. Quiet time invites "connection" to what is; making sense of what needs "correction"; and discerning what "direction" or actions to take. By another name, it is the systemic, action-oriented reflective practice of "adaptive action" (Borton 1970; Driscoll 1994; Eoyang and Holladay 2013) (see Table 20.1).

Engage in quiet time. Every morning in Caux a space is opened up for shared quiet time. Sometimes an individual shares a personal story or reflection; this may be followed by a period of quiet self-reflection, after which, in small groups, individuals may be invited to contribute their insights. The invitation is to seek "connection, correction, and direction" within. It is not simply an event with a fixed time and place. It is a "way of being" that facilitates a deeper connection with oneself, others, the "here and now" and future intent. There is no prescription, only an invitation for individuals to do it in whatever way is best fit for them. Moments of quiet reflection are often used to open meetings, community groups, creators of peace circles, conference plenaries

---

7   In HSD (Human Systems Dynamics) the field founded by Glenda Eoyang, we talk about the "whole," "part," and "greater whole" and recognize that in wanting to influence systemic change, we need to act on at least three connected levels of a wider system.

Table 20.1 Quiet time and adaptive action

QUIET TIME: Listening for guidance	Generic activity	Adaptive action
CONNECTION: Reflecting on one's life, actions, impact in the world	Noticing what is present internally, externally; whole, part, greater whole	WHAT? Looking for "patterns" and what holds them in place
CORRECTION: Exploring what repair/ restitution one could make	Making sense of what is present; exploring options for action	SO, WHAT? Explore meaning within and across system scales
DIRECTION: Taking action and following through on commitments	Deciding what to do + doing it—observe impact; Connection/ "What?"	NOW WHAT? Taking action—whole, part, greater whole—going for simple, scalable, replicable

However, setting aside quiet time and space does not, by itself, necessarily bring about useful action and change. When we understand the complexity of reality we know that the best we can do is influence. In IofC, best-intention influence comes through applying the Four Standards (purity of intention, honesty, unselfishness, and love) as reference points to guide one's internal reflections and decision-making. These are crucial in setting conditions for what arises out of "quiet time" and the invitation to:

Share and learn through honest conversation. IofC's philosophy suggests that looking at our own lives honestly equips us for personal change. Using the Four Standards brings an internal check to our thoughts, feelings, and actions. In a conference plenary, Mike revealed how he had been judging a colleague for his actions; instead of speaking to him, he had distanced himself. In sharing his story, he moved himself forward, choosing to reconnect, apologize, and open an honest conversation with his colleague. Having others bear witness to our truth-telling requires us to be vulnerable. This opens us up to potential personal transformation. It is no easy process, but when held in the context of a bigger community committed to the shared "practice," each is supported to step beyond the fear that obstructs honest conversation and reach across the divide of judgment that keeps people apart

Irène Laure, Ginn Fourie, Letlapa Mphahlele, Mike, and many more bear testament to the transformation that is possible when we dare to speak honestly and to listen with open hearts as others do the same.

Changing the world in community

The above insight was profound because, while Buchman was committed to changing the world he believed that this could only happen if it started with the individual and in the relational space between people who were connected in some way or for some reason. The patterns of being supported and challenged in "community" were established in Buchman's time and continue today: Creators of Peace women meet in small circles to share and transcend personal stories of conflict, tragedy and loss. Participants at Caux conferences join a community group and meet to reflect, connect and share. In all settings, individuals are encouraged to practice deep listening without interruption; hearing all voices and turning judgment into curiosity.

Buchman acted systemically whether or not he knew it. He recognized the importance of thinking globally, acting locally and making it personal. In the aftermath of the Second World War, he played a central role in convening crucial dialogues in Caux, between people who had previously been enemies. He championed the notion that a Europe united against war would not become reality if Germany were not included in the post-war conversations. To this day extraordinary healing between peoples in conflict continues to take place in the cultural "container" of Caux:

Care for others, the planet, and ourselves. IofC is about making the world a fairer, safer, sustainable place for all. In 2013 a large team of IofC volunteers headed to South Sudan to train local peacemakers across regions within this newest of nations. After attending the "Leading Change for a Sustainable World" Conference in 2009, Yahaya left a lucrative job in Belgium to return to Nigeria. He was inspired to take action on desertification and the increasing conflicts over land, fuel, and water—all exacerbated by deforestation. Community Groups at Caux conferences bring individuals together during which their time is divided between reflecting, connecting, and serving others in the house. Here individuals get to share the power of meaningful collaborative endeavor—actively experiencing trust-building between strangers and across differences while also benefiting from the care of others

In IofC, inspired action is birthed and unlikely coalitions are forged in service to something greater than any individual in the mix.

Patterns across space and time

Over the decades, the work of Buchman, the Oxford Group, MRA, and IofC has changed shape and form, responding to the needs and challenges of the times. Paradoxically, what has enabled this network to endure across place and time is, in large part due to what has stayed the same. Stuff happens. Lots of stuff happens. Every summer some six to eight conferences take place at Caux Palace (Mountain House). Such activity has endured, not through central control but through an enduring commitment to:

Engage with purpose. IofC nurtures the ability in people to respond to their unique "call," even if others do not see the point, for example, Foundations for Freedom, a change-makers program connecting young eastern Europeans, began from one man's determination. Caux conferences are sourced and served almost entirely by volunteers—beyond the more obvious organizing teams there are numerous contributions: Jan comes each year, baking the most amazing cakes for afternoon tea; Elisabeth, in her 70s, attends the entire summer, each day creating the most exquisite flower arrangements throughout the house; she now passes on her gift to young trainees to continue the service. Volunteers travel from the furthest reaches of the world at the beginning and end of the summer to "open" and "close" Mountain House. All are humbling examples of the myriad personal contributions that enable IofC to continue to play its part in changing lives and changing the world

How come all this continues? There is a helpful HSD model called STAR, created by Brenda Zimmerman, that points to four conditions that help a group to be generative (able to do useful work, repeatedly): each individual's purpose and passion aligned to a shared bigger purpose (R: Reason for being); a focus on doing something specific, for example, running a conference (A: Authentic work); having a relevant mix of people with similar and different contributions (S: Similarities and differences);

and with a quality of exchanges (T: Talking and listening) that prove to be creative, collaborative, and productive (see Eoyang 2003: 199-213; Human System Dynamics Institute 2006). Without coherence across these four points, useful endeavor rarely gets started; or if it does it is rarely sustained. Whatever the cause that generates an impetus, it has to matter enough to everyone concerned to stay committed, engaged, and to:

Follow through on promises. Everything in IofC comes about because someone answered their "call" and followed through. The Mountain House in Caux was bought after World War II by Swiss individuals and families to support the prevention of future wars; each program and conference starts with an individual inspiring others to collaborate in co-creation

IofC is a living paradox. The more I have engaged with it, the more I see that it is unquestionably a powerhouse force for good in the world. Yet, the focus and extent of its activities are unpredictable, as individuals move into action according to their own context and calls of conscience. People within grow the know-how (consciously or intuitively) to set the conditions for meaningful action in their part of the world. They come with what they have, trusting that in sharing their intentions, what is needed will be found. They learn to sit with ambiguity and uncertainty and to:

Turn scarcity into creativity. The practices of IofC have cultivated in its fellowship the capacity to see beyond scarcity and to source contribution in all its guises—time, effort, skills, knowledge, guidance, money, equipment, buildings, etc. The House in Baranivka[8] started out as the dream of a group of young people in Ukraine. Many thought they were mad, yet now it is a building with a community of volunteers

Action arises from need, inspiration, willingness, and passion. IofC is a germinating greenhouse, cultivating in its fellowship the capacity to see beyond scarcity and to trust that, if their purpose and passion is strong enough, whatever is needed is found. Those who have been

8 The mission of the 'House in Baranivka': a meeting place that is aimed at the harmonious development of individuals and the creation of a community of like-minded people who will work to improve society, http://www.baranivka.org/en.

lifetime volunteers are our teachers, actively playing their part in inspiring leaders for future generations.

Life-changers not movement-makers

Recovering from a life-threatening illness in 1943, Buchman had a revelation. He had been "trying to create a movement to change lives" and suddenly saw that a movement was the outcome of changed lives not the means of changing them.[9] He recalibrated, seeking instead to become a great "life-changer." He, and those who followed, co-evolved the patterns and seed behaviors experienced in IofC today.

These behaviors are in and of IofC and I, as a relative newcomer, chose to name them, making the implicit explicit. Why? Because I could. Because I felt myself to be a part of IofC. Because I believed they would support people, new and old within IofC to better articulate, share and guide others to grasp the essence of what it means to be involved. I knew this would be a mutual process of sharing, education, and clarification. I started the seed behavior experiment in 2012 and received some very encouraging feedback from a lifetime Elder.[10] In 2013, I realized that I had started something and, at that point, only I could carry it forward if it was to have any chance of benefiting IofC. Generally the seed behaviors

9   His insight was profound—in the parlance of complex adaptive systems he switched from trying to change a pattern (i.e. a movement) at the pattern level (which is not possible); to working with the agents (individuals) and on the conditions (e.g. quiet time, action guided by the Four Standards) that combined to give rise to those patterns. http://wiki.hsdinstitute.org/complex_adaptive_system, accessed 4 April 2014.

10   Keisuke Nakayama was a so-called full-time staff worker of IofC (then MRA) 1963–70. He got a job and remained in the auto industry as a staff interpreter and executive secretary in the years 1970–92, in a US–Japan joint venture. From 1992 to 2006 he served as head of Asia-Center in Odawara, originally affiliated with MRA/IofC near Tokyo. Since 2007, he has served as Director of International IofC Association of Japan. He also currently serves as one of the Elders of IofC international. He sought me out and commended the seed behaviors as the most tangible articulation of the 'spirit of Caux' he had come across—something that had never been done before. This is what spurred me on in 2013.

have been welcomed *because* they reflect reality in IofC circles. In Caux, people have experienced them in action and have been able to practice them daily. Having them written down has enabled individuals to take them "down the mountain" to use them wherever they go:

Table 20.2 Seeding the practice and spirit of Caux and IofC

Engage in "quiet time"	Care for others, our planet, and ourselves
Turn judgment into curiosity	Follow through on promises
Share and learn through honest conversation	Engage with purpose*
Serve and receive service joyfully	Turn scarcity into creativity*

If I had unilaterally "conjured up" a list based on what I thought people *should* be doing, there would have been no recognition of them or resonance within the system; and very likely there would have been significant resistance—there was not. This is a crucial point for those wanting to use seed behaviors (or simple rules[11]) to support change in their own situations. Start first with *what is actually present*. This is radically different from the usual ways in which leaders attempt to "change culture," by first naming "desired/espoused" values that often bear no relation to the dynamics actually playing within their organizations. The consequent gap between reality and desire is often too vast for the system to make the transition. The change effort fails, succeeding only in wasting time and money.

Beyond narrative and description: a systemic explanation

Every seed behavior can be seen as a part of the Four Standards, which simultaneously call forth the behaviors. The causality is non-linear. The

---

11 In identifying simple rules, the focus is on *actual* behavior and not abstracted 'values' statements. Each behavior starts with a verb, is framed in the positive, is general enough to apply across scales in the 'system' and is specific enough to be interpreted and applied to anyone in any role in that system.

seed behaviors point to conditions that together give rise to repeating patterns that manifest across all levels and scales of IofC. In the sciences that explore complex adaptive systems (CAS), such patterns are called "fractal" (Gouyet 1966). The conditions for fractal patterns are simple, repeatable, and scalable. In other words, when the same conditions are applied repeatedly in other or all parts of the particular system (e.g. individual, group, organization, community, nation), a recognizably similar pattern will emerge. This is why strangers can go from Caux to visit IofC groups in Japan, Uganda, the UK, or India and *know* they are amid the IofC fellowship. What happens at Caux plays out on a smaller scale in IofC groups, families and communities across the world.

Fractal patterns occur in any large-scale human system that has expanded and endured across geographical space and time. Take, for example, Alcoholics Anonymous, which grew from the same Buchman/Oxford Group roots. Anyone who is a member of both would recognize some similarities as well as some seemingly crucial differences. They both share the principle of small circle gatherings, sharing personal stories and struggles; and the focus for both is on personal transformation, honest exchange, and a commitment to love and empathy over judgment. There are other similarities and some fundamental differences, but both have endured over a similar time-period. Being able to see and understand the meta-principles that are at play in both—and indeed in any other large-scale human system—makes it more possible to influence the depth and spread of a movement. This is about "scale" and "replication," that is, vertical and horizontal growth. Being able to see, understand, and take systemic action from this perspective requires a paradigm shift.

Beyond Newton

Notions such as vertical and horizontal growth are predicated on Newtonian thinking, which assumes the ability to control and predict with some certainty. Such thinking often leads to misguided "solutions" that involve detailed, systematic (linear) processes or checklists/templates that define required inputs and explicit outputs. In the realms of CAS, such interventions may, under limited circumstances be a good fit; yet frequently they can be a waste of time or worse, be deeply disruptive. Every CAS is unique, with different members and contexts and an infinite number of unknowable and interdependent variables. When we accept that reality is this complex, we do not waste effort, time, or money on seeking *the* best way because we know there could be many possibilities. We understand that the best practice for any given situation is simply our best conclusion of what might be "best fit" in this moment in time. The quality of our conclusions depends on our ability to shift from "fast" to "slow" thinking, to engage in conscious[12] adaptive action (Eoyang and Holladay 2013) or, in IofC terms, to engage in quiet time.

IofC: a theory of change through new lenses

IofC has changed fundamentally, no longer being a solely Christian-based fellowship, but there are core practices that remain essentially the same. On its website[13] you will find:

> **Who we are.** Initiatives of Change (IofC) is a world-wide movement of people of diverse cultures and backgrounds, who are committed to the transformation of society through changes in human motives and behavior, starting with their own.

Their work is personal, purposeful, and practical; it is in community rather than being hierarchically organized; there is ebb and flow more than directed control; there is supported, volunteer contribution more than employment and payment for time and services. The emphasis is on contextually relevant, inner-sourced, intentional (not destinational) action and not externally commissioned, end-focused outputs. It is about "life-changers" not "movement-makers"; engagement not consultation;

---

12 In truth, every CAS is engaging in adaptive action unconsciously—unaware of itself. Human beings have the potential capacity to bring awareness into play. When we become conscious of the system and of ourselves in it, we give ourselves more options for action and need never get stuck.

13 https://www.iofc.org/iofc-international.

action not merely talking about action. In bringing together all these dimensions, a more holistic sense of IofC's change process emerges.

> **Purpose.** We work to inspire, equip and connect people to address world needs, starting with themselves, in the areas of trust building, ethical leadership and sustainable living.

Figure 20.1 is my attempt to distil the exquisite simplicity of IofC from the complexity at play. Most organizations focus only on "planning" and "taking focused action"; some actually "engage people" in co-creative dialogue. Few understand the concept and benefits of sourcing inspiration "starting with oneself"—trusting individuals to source their own work and be responsible for carrying it through. Honoring the interdependence of all three realms has enabled IofC to be effective and enduring.

Figure 20.1 Initiatives of Change: a theory of change in action

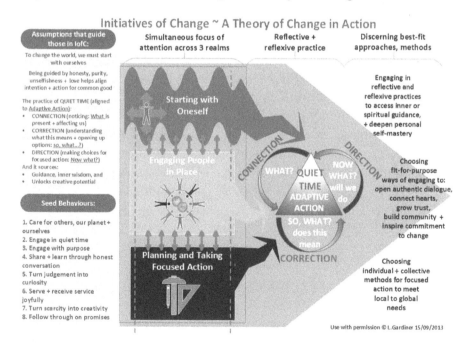

Few know the scale and scope of IofC's work in its entirety. Central control is an impossibility; the desire for it futile. The focus and extent of its activities remain unpredictable and members continue to follow their own calls of conscience. Together they are proof enough

that life-changers working together, do indeed give rise to social-change movements. IofC is not an organization, it is a self-organizing system, constantly re-creating itself.

Beyond logic, systemic magic!

That so many diverse peoples from the poorest and richest regions of the world find their way to Caux each summer is a testament to all that is clear, focused and coherent. That speakers and corporate and world leaders self-fund and then find themselves alongside ordinary citizens, washing dishes or cooking an evening meal together, defies logic. That these so-called "conferences" take place at all, when some participants pay moderate sums and only for "bed and board" while others pay nothing at all; that teams of volunteers step forward to make those summer gatherings happen again and again; that all this happens, is evidence of the monumental willingness of so many to contribute whatever they have to give to make a difference. That some volunteers travel from the furthest reaches of the world for one week to prepare Mountain House for focused service; and that more return eight weeks later to close it, is a humbling reminder of the myriad contributions of service that are needed to enable Caux to play its part in changing lives and changing the world. These are not conferences in the ways many might expect. These are life-changing community experiences—ways of living, learning, giving, and receiving that prove we can be in the world in radically different ways that enhance the lives of everyone involved.

Who leads? No one and everyone

Newcomers to IofC and Caux are puzzled and beguiled by something that appears to have no clear lines of leadership and authority. Our human tendency for needing to and believing we can control the world around us is shaken in this place. Outsiders skilled in influencing hierarchies look for lines to the seats of power—*the* person/people at the top. There is no single person in charge; no single pathway to decision-makers and for decision-making—not even the President of the International

Association (the membership body for IofC member countries). Leadership is distributed among and across multiple formal and informal bodies. Routeways to decisions depend on relational, emergent processes; and pathways and outcomes are unforeseeable. We might ask: How does anything get done? How has so much been achieved at personal, community, national, and international levels? The preceding pages, I hope, shed some light.

IofC: a complex adaptive system

In essence, I believe that those within have learned how to work with complexity and emergence—rather than succumbing to the seductive Newtonian illusion that the world, people and processes can be controlled through force and formal power. IofC has adapted and endured, supported by the simple, repeatable conditions that scale up and down the network. Everyone leads and no one leads and everyone has access to the DNA that is IofC:

DNA of IofC. Engaging in quiet time; gathering together in community, in intentional service, guided by a compass of four universal human standards (patterns)—manifesting through and in consistent behaviors, which, when illuminated and articulated, enable newcomers and old to grasp the tangible from the intangible; ultimately supporting generative[14] adaptation and ever greater coherence

The Caux laboratory: a place to convene, connect, commune, and co-create

Caux holds, in glorious magnitude, the essence of IofC. Mountain House is our global northern hemisphere home. It is the grand-scale equivalent

---

14 Generativity is another word for sustainability but it emphasizes the potential for life-enhancing expansion and change rather than keeping something (sustaining) the same.

of a community group within one of our conferences. It is the place to which we return, to be among friends, to share, to learn, to serve, and to remember together who we are and why we commit our time, energy, and attention; it is where we welcome in and seek to create new bonds with people we have yet to come to know. It is the heart and hearth of our global family, and it is in this place that we reconnect, reinvigorate, and resource ourselves to continue in current endeavors or find new inspiration.

It was, and is, ever thus. Caux is in IofC and IofC is in Caux. As one and both: ever-changing—expanding, contracting, changing shape, and reacting to local and global uncertainties; and ever the same—fundamentally maintaining an extraordinary consistency, continuity, and constancy of purpose. We are in IofC, and IofC is in us.

References and further reading

Boobbyer, P. (2013) *The Spiritual Vision of Frank Buchman* (University Park, PA: Pennsylvania State University Press).

Borton, T. (1970) *Reach, Touch and Teach* (London/New York: McGraw-Hill).

Driscoll J. (1994) "Reflective Practice for Practise," *Senior Nurse* 14.1: 47-50.

Eoyang, G.H. (ed.) (2003) *Voices from the Field: An Introduction to Human Systems Dynamics* (Circle Pines, MN: Human Systems Dynamics Institute Press).

Eoyang, G.H., and R.J. Holladay (2013) *Adaptive Action: Leveraging Uncertainty in your Organization* (Stanford, CA: Stanford Business Books).

Gouyet, J.-F. (1996) *Physics of Fractal Structures* (Heidelberg, Germany: Springer Verlag).

Human System Dynamics Institute (2006) *Be a Star: A Tool to Maintain Team Effectiveness* (Circle Pines, MN: HSD Institute, http://s3.amazonaws.com/hsd.herokuapp.com/contents/17/original/beastar.hsd.3.16.11.2_2_.pdf?1332189857, accessed 4 April 2014.

Kahneman, D. (2011) *Thinking, Fast and Slow* (London: Penguin Books).

Reynolds, C.W. (1987) "Flocks, Herds, and Schools: A Distributed Behavioral Model" in *Computer Graphics* 21.4 (SIGGRAPH '87 Conference Proceedings): 25-34.

21

A meta-collaboratory

The Globally Responsible Leadership Initiative[1]

John North
GRLI Africa, South Africa

Anders Aspling
GRLI Foundation, Belgium

In this chapter we consider the evolution of the initial definition of the collaboratory within the 50+20 community by looking at two recent and ongoing initiatives of the Globally Responsible Leadership Initiative (GRLI).

The two GRLI initiatives are both ongoing at the time of writing. The first describes how GRLI partner institutions in South Africa convened concerned stakeholders around the Western Cape wine region to develop an agenda of responsible action for that particular regional industry. The second initiative describes the convening and early activity of an innovation cohort of management educators focusing on the question of implementing 50+20 in their own institutions.

In closing, we suggest some points for consideration and investigation to further inform the initiation and development of future collaboratories.

---

1 The authors wish to thank Arnold Smit and Nick Ellerby for making valuable contributions through their review of this chapter.

Defining 50+20 collaboratories

When the wording of the 50+20 Agenda was being finalized a term was sought that could describe the central and defining feature of the vision. The blend word "collaboratory" offered an appropriate portmanteau to fuse the key elements of "collaboration" and "laboratory" without making it exclusively about the one or the other.

The term suggested that new types of laboratories of research and learning are needed within management education, and that the basic conditions and requirements of what is generally understood by "laboratory" needed to be modified through the introduction of prerequisite collaborative elements or "collaboration." A laboratory provides a safe space for experimentation where qualified professionals distil and verify truths or findings and explore their potential to enable innovation. Such an environment typically favors reductionist approaches investigating *how* something functions or exists, often by isolating and studying its component parts and ignoring mostly the question of *why* something functions or exists—purpose is mostly ignored. While the need for study, innovation and learning through experimentation in relative safety (laboratory) remains legitimate and needed, collaboration suggests that traditional scientific inquiry conducted exclusively by qualified researchers, concerned mostly with the inner workings and component parts at the expense of understanding the whole, is insufficient. The term "collaboratory" implies that scientific pursuit and the learning associated with that pursuit may not be confined to the inside of the symbolic laboratory and that research, education and innovation embedded at the coalface of the practical world, that is, societal issues, ought to be trialed. The collaboratory stretches into the space of transdisciplinarity, where scientific knowledge and method blend with real-life experience and wisdom—shared in the form of narrative. Mainstream scientific approaches and perspectives may sit less comfortably here. In the collaboratory learning is spurred when diversity of experience and knowledge is present, and the head, heart, hand, and will are engaged. Purpose and impact are fundamental to any collaboratory, and the presence of deeper emotions and sense-making is essential.

With the launch of the 50+20 Agenda during the Third Global Forum on Responsible Management Education, which took place as part of the

Rio+20 Earth Summit in 2012, the co-authoring group hosted and facilitated learning circles referred to as collaboratory meetings, collaboratory sessions or simply as collaboratories.[2] These were held in order to provide participants of the Third Global Forum a sampling of what management education for the world implies, and they also offered a tangible, visibile, and ultimately complementary action to the launch of the written 50+20 Agenda.

Box 21.1 Fishbowl sessions

Fishbowls involve a group of people seated in circle, having a conversation in full view of a larger group of listeners, and are useful for ventilating "hot topics" or sharing ideas or information from a variety of perspectives. In an "open" fishbowl chairs are open to "visitors" (i.e. members of the audience) who want to ask questions or make comments. Although largely self-organizing once the discussion gets underway, the fishbowl process usually has a facilitator or moderator.[3]

The method employed to facilitate these sessions was similar to fishbowl sessions (see Box 21.1) or Open Space gatherings (see Box 21.2) that were also in use during some of the 50+20 visioning retreats that took place in the build-up to the Rio+20 Summit. The sessions at Rio+20 were well attended, offering well over 100 management educators an opportunity to participate actively in one of three facilitated learning circles on the issues of gender equality, corruption, and poverty. The Rio+20 collaboratories were well received and attracted encouraging feedback and positive comments.

These sessions set the tone for how participants, many of whom became future champions of 50+20, understood and interpreted the central element of the 50+20 vision. The term "collaboratory" became associated very closely with the particular style and format of learning and investigation that took place in Rio de Janeiro in 2012. Subsequent to the launch several participants at the time simulated these collaboratory meetings in their own settings or institutions, simply referring to these meetings or events as "collaboratories."

2   See: http://50plus20.org/documentary.
3   See: http://www.kstoolkit.org/Fish+Bowl.

Box 21.2 Open Space (also known as Open Space Technology or OST)

OST is a method for convening groups around a specific question or task or importance and giving them responsibility for creating both their own agenda and experience. The facilitator's key task is to identify the question that brings people together, offer the simple process, then stand back and let partici-pants do the work.

The collaboratory meetings held at Rio+20 were a symbolic demonstration and enactment of the central philosophy of the vision. A fuller realization of the vision would see management educators assume their role in collaboratory development and hosting more completely. Ideally they would move beyond initiating and hosting one-off collaboratory meetings, to a future scenario where the institutions themselves become ongoing collaboratories-in-action and ultimately conveners and initiators of collaboratories.

Later described more fully by differentiating between "bolt on," "built in," and "platform" solutions (Muff 2013) using a three-order model of innovation, the positive response from management educators to the 50+20 call of developing collaboratories could range through these stages:

1. Initiate and facilitate one-off collaboratory meetings in and among traditional educational offerings. This may result in a series of collaboratory-based events that deal with a particular issue of relevance to that institution and its constituents

2. Active displacement of traditional learning and research initiatives with collaboratory-based programs of learning and research

3. A full transformation of the entire educational offering and operating model of a management education institution to become a collaboratory-in-action that shapes its work and ways of working around new and ongoing collaboratory investigations that in turn are identified and scoped through ongoing societal and environmental stakeholder engagement

The varying degrees or levels of collaboratory participation and engagement described, all satisfy (on the surface at least) the concise and ambitious original 50+20 definition of a collaboratory as "an inclusive learning environment where action learning and action research meet" (Muff *et al.* 2013). It should, however, be understood that the core ingredients identified here are about fostering active collaboration among a diversified group of stakeholders, convened around a central issue or question, and working with whole person learning, creative, and systemic approaches to foster collective problem-solving and co-creation.

Through this chapter we propose examples of collaboratories in full knowledge that the concept is evolving. The 50+20 vision is meant to describe stretch goals—an aspirational state. Optimistically, these examples may also provide a starting point for theoretic purists to supply the collaboratory ideal with its epistemological and methodological foundations.

In the years since Rio+20, many of us who have experimented with the collaboratory method have come to realize that there may be more dimensions to collaboratories that we need to explore and understand. There are also lessons to be learned from earlier initiatives such as the GRLI, which has been modeling and refining aspects of the collaboratory since 2004.

The GRLI partnership as collaboratory and container

Founded in 2004 the GRLI may be viewed as an early and continually evolving collaboratory prototype; 21 corporations and learning institutions were invited to join a one-year process of hands-on investigation into the question of what global responsibility implies from the perspective of their organizations. They had to be strategically committed, dedicated, and equipped to introduce new practices. The inquiry was facilitated on a peer-based and whole person learning basis as later articulated in *Learning for Tomorrow: Whole Person Learning for the Planetary Citizen* (Taylor 2007). The initiating GRLI partners formed what we now label a "collaboratory" with the open space meeting at INSEAD in April 2006, facilitated by Harrison Owen, kicking off GRLI as an enhanced global community of learning and action. It assembled then and still does using the circle as a setting for collective work and dialogue. What evolved since then is a more elaborate language and explicit conceptualization regarding the format of collaboratories and lots of learning and development regarding the facilitation.

Today GRLI operates as a partnership of companies, learning institutions and global organizations, working together to enable the development of individual and collective leadership and practice that is globally responsible. The strength of GRLI lies in its ability to lead the discourse on what globally responsible leadership and practice represents beyond current mainstream experience and understanding. The GRLI has a proven track record of convening organizations and individuals, across all spheres of society, committed to sustainable human progress built on recognition of the need for deep, systemic change.

Decisions about the focus and content of GRLI's work as a global partnership, and the ways in which it delivers that work, is informed by a number of guiding principles as summarized in Box 21.3. These guiding principles are reflected visibly in the 50+20 visioning process and outcome, both of which the GRLI partnership and associates actively contributed to. An earlier version of these principles was implied in the original invitation to the 21 initiators of GRLI in 2004; and voiced again explicitly in the first GRLI report (2005).

Box 21.3 The GRLI Guiding Principles

1. Everything we produce is a contribution to the global commons and is freely shared

2. What we do should create hands-on results on the ground, stand the chance of producing long-lasting, scalable effects, and is not being done better elsewhere

3. Our operating mode is built on the entrepreneurial approach of "Think big. Act small. Start now"

4. Effective change requires work at individual, organizational, and systemic levels: "I," "We," and "All of Us"

5. Making an impact at the organizational and systemic level requires committed, dedicated, and empowered individuals who are willing to bring a "whole person" approach to their work and to their lives

Through these principles the GRLI is led, or driven as it may appear, to operate as convener and host of what it calls **Communities of Responsible Action** (CoRAs). CoRAs are groups of people and organizations willing to respond to a strong call, often issued in the form of a central unanswered question, dealing with an aspect of enabling globally responsible leadership and practice. They have no formal membership or leadership structure; in fact actors and participants within a CoRA may not even recognize the term "communities of responsible action," but remain linked through a common and shared intention of addressing or working with a core question. A CoRA always requires a convening person or team to sustain and maintain its momentum and impact.

For example, the growing body of individuals and organizations identifying with, and in places actively responding to, the 50+20 call, may be thought of as a broad and inclusive CoRA. At the outset of developing the 50+20 vision, the call to critical thinkers—within and outside management education—was to ask how management education ought to be transformed in the interest of serving society and making business sustainable. This call attracted a diverse group of more than 150 people, some acting in their personal and others in their organizational or professional capacity, to collaborate on the development of a collective response. The visioning process that followed, a collaborative effort in itself, resulted in the 50+20 Agenda. The vision and inherent call articulated through the 50+20 vision continues to attract interest and spark action.

The GRLI's guiding principles, and at minimum a subset of the first three principles, are typically tabled and reaffirmed at the initiation of GRLI projects. In the case of the Western Cape wine industry group the first three guiding principles were tabled upfront and collectively agreed as relevant and foundational to any potential work the group may undertake jointly. In the case of the 50+20 Innovation Cohort the participating group agreed, using different terms or language, to operate according to these principles.

Considering GRLI as an early form of collaboratory and initiator of subsequent and similar initiatives suggests that the 50+20 collaboratory at present may be defined as an emerging methodology for initiating a multi-stakeholder inclusive discourse convened around societal issues, aimed at catalyzing systemic change through individual and collective action.

Let us look at more detail into the GRLI initiatives, starting with the wine industry group.

The Western Cape wine industry group: convening diverse stakeholders around a central issue

As leading contributor to the agricultural export economy of the Western Cape province in South Africa, and with a history dating back to 1659, the wine industry not only employs a major percentage of the local population and arable land, but also presents a microcosm of the changing role of business and industry in the region.

Towards the end of 2012 the General Assembly of the Globally Responsible Leadership Initiative was hosted by Spier Wine Estate outside Stellenbosch in partnership between GRLI, University of Stellenbosch Business School, Spier, and the Albert Luthuli Centre for Responsible Leadership at University of Pretoria. One of the learning journeys planned for the event had to be cancelled due to farmworkers in the region protesting nearby demanding increases that would see them being paid a so-called living wage. Visible news coverage of the protests, which by then had turned violent, were set against the meeting backdrop of the Spier wine estate—a champion of socially and environmentally just winemaking and food production in the region. These contrasting realities underlined the urgent need for the local wine industry to increase efforts to be responsible stewards of economic and social progress while being mindful of the impact on the natural environment.

In the months that followed, the co-hosts of the 2012 GRLI General Assembly issued an open invitation to stakeholders in the Western Cape wine industry to participate in the development of a shared and open agenda for responsible action in the region—the Western Cape Wine Collaboratory. The signatories to the letter were positioned simply as the "conversation starters" jointly calling on the collective to co-develop an agenda for responsible action.

It was proposed that existing organizations and projects concerned with ethical, responsible, and sustainable winemaking and business practice—along with other critical voices that ended up including representative from key industry bodies, several wine producers, and societal stakeholders across government, civil society (including three union representatives), and academia—join in a facilitated discussion where they might:

- Develop coherence and synergies among individual strategies for responsible action

- Identify and initiate key actions within the landscape that might accelerate and aid collective efforts to develop responsible action

- Consider approaches that might add value to the development and continuation of such a collaboratory

The full-day session was facilitated by GRLI and it employed the collaboratory methodology used at the 50+20 launch complete with a traditional knobkierrie (a South African club or stick) used as a talking stick.

The discussion and input of the circle reached a rich and personal level fairly quickly—participants sensed early on that this was a safe space within which they could share openly and directly. The discussion took a dramatic turn about three hours into the meeting shortly before lunch. One of the visible figures of the protest movement, a former unionist himself, took hold of the talking stick for the first time—until then he had only been listening to the contributions of major players and producers. The anticipation within the circle was palpable. He started by acknowledging that the carefully convened and facilitated collaboratory event created the first real opportunity, in his view, for farmworker representatives along with business owners and industry stakeholders to engage in constructive dialogue about the issues at hand. He proceeded to share how, unbeknown to the winemakers present, further strikes were being mobilized at the time—a fact that was confirmed a few days later. While this news was not entirely unexpected it could hardly prepare them for what followed. The speaker then admitted that his participation in the collaboratory, something which he experienced as a unique process of building a shared agenda, convinced him to advise the union structures not to protest against or target producers that actively participate in initiatives of ethical, responsible, and sustainable winemaking.

This was clearly a breakthrough moment and it released energy and stimulated initiatives within the group that could not have been imagined beforehand. The small group work that followed over lunch and into the afternoon resulted in a number of actions being agreed by the end of the day. Most notably it was agreed within the collaboratory that they would draft and issue a joint public declaration, signed by key industry bodies, farmworker unions, and producers to condemn unfair labor practices such as unilateral enforcement of changed working conditions and non-compliance with minimum wage legislation. The statement would also call for avoidance of potentially imminent strike action.

Although the public declaration was completed and issued it was unfortunately signed only by the sub-group to whom the action was delegated. Doing so clearly did not match the spirit and intention of the agreed guiding principles. In the view of participants interviewed after the issuance of the press release, the potential impact such a statement could have had was greatly diminished since it appeared to be coming from only one grouping within the industry. Despite this clear and obvious failure this example holds a lesson or two about convening a collaboratory and keeping the collaboratory accountable. Let us look at another example from GRLI before concluding with some suggested learning and topics for investigation.

The Innovation Cohort: responsible action through peer-learning and prototyping

In contrast to the one-off meeting of the Western Cape Wine Industry Collaboratory, the 50+20 Innovation Cohort is a work in progress rather than a work in limbo.

The launch of the 50+20 Agenda invoked positive responses worldwide and a demand for practical support in moving forward in its implementation. In response the GRLI announced a global peer-based laboratory that would enable management educators, leadership developers and organizational leaders to innovate and transform their own organizations and offerings around the key roles articulated in the 50+20 vision: educating globally responsible leaders; enabling business to become the best for the world; and engaging with societal transformation.

In May 2013 a handful of deans and directors, within a facilitated process, validated the need to bring a global network of committed peers together to prototype and pilot globally responsible change in education and business. They envisioned a shared journey and program for business school, leadership development, and corporate university leaders to jointly build on insights developed through the 50+20 project and put the vision into action.

By the end of October the first intake of the 50+20 Innovation Cohort had been recruited and was preparing for their first meeting to take place at the University of St. Gallen in Switzerland. Each of the 18 participants representing 16 institutions prepared an overview on what they would like to contribute to the cohort and also gain from participation in the cohort. It was clear from the outset that this was a group of dedicated and committed change agents who were willing to engage fully in a process of co-learning and co-creation.

The cohort operates along the same guiding principles that inform other CoRAs and indeed the GRLI itself. From the outset it was agreed that the cohort's work would answer to the key dimensions of:

- **Result orientation.** Will it deliver visible results on the ground?

- **Long-term effects.** Will it live on and continuously affect the development of globally responsible leaders and practice?

- **Uniqueness.** Will it get things done that could not be achieved elsewhere?

Along with these criteria the cohort also agreed to undertake its work being mindful of the following:

- To encourage development through innovation with others

- To mobilize collective and individual potential

- To work with learning approaches that seek to offer both safety and freedom

- To prepare the self as an instrument of change (building on the "whole person learning" concept of GRLI and the Oasis School of Human Relations)

Underlying this approach is an acknowledgement and desire to develop globally responsible leadership and practice at individual, organizational and systemic levels—or put differently, through "I," "we," and "all of us." The "I, we, all of us" phrasing and approach was first formulated by GRLI Chief Executive Mark Drewell, inspired by Don Beck's work on Spiral Dynamics. This concept also formed the basis for the three ellipses of the GRLI logo commissioned by Anders Aspling in 2006.

Within a day and half of the first cohort meeting the group self-organized into three working clusters. The clusters can be thought of as workstreams within the cohort through which participants, bringing diverse interests and strengths, may channel their energy and effort. Apart from the cohort delivering a practical or actionable output that builds on the 50+20 Agenda and vision, there are also three sub-projects driven by the clusters. The cohort also represents an explicit model of peer-based learning with all the challenges, dynamics and possibilities that such an approach shapes and demands. It is an ongoing experiment that calls for learning and development in each person, each grouping, the cohort as a whole and those facilitating the process.

Necessary phases within the effective development of the Innovation Cohort collaboratory appear to echo previous work by GRLI partners on what was termed "authentic collaboration" (Ellerby, Lockwood, Palin, Ralphs, and Taylor 2010), namely:

- Preparation and checking readiness

- Enabling authentic collaboration

- Working with the emergent challenges

- Reviewing the process

Each phase has subsets with related activities, and it is clear that while they may appear linear, it is in reality an iterative, challenging and dynamic process.

Six months after the final session the cohort will be invited to meet with the next 50+20 Innovation Cohort to support its development, to share experiences, build networks and reflect on learning and progress.

Conclusions

Informal discussions with Rio+20 collaboratory participants and participants of subsequent one-off collaboratory meetings confirmed that participation in itself was experienced as impactful or powerful and generally helped awake a sense of purpose and urgency among participants to deal with the central issue. However, many of the individual participants were left with the impression that the collaboratory refers merely to the one-off meeting and the particular style of facilitation used. Those participating in a sequence of meetings experienced raised value and learning both as individuals and for their organization—and a pronounced appetite for continued learning and development of the collaboratory.

It is important to emphasize that a meeting in itself and the facilitation style employed is only one practical and visible act of transforming management education. The ultimately goal should be to transform our institutions and the management education industry to fully emulate the collaboratory approach in all its work—individually and institutionally.

Hosting an event or participating in a collaboratory-style meeting could, and hopefully does, signify the start of an involved process of organizational and personal inquiry into a particular issue and way of working, a process that is not only issue-centered but ultimately also demands some transformation on the part of the actors involved. And perhaps this is where both the original definition and some of the current perspectives on the meaning of collaboratory ought to be elaborated on. Should we more fully acknowledge and explicitly state the need for individual and organizational transformation through the process of continued contribution in a collaboratory setting?

First-hand enactment of the vision through participation in a session has the potential to open new perspectives on the role of institutions and individuals in solving real-world issues, even beyond the immediate research and educational interest or relevance of such issues. It appears to surface and recognize an explicit ethical dimension to the purpose of research and educational activities. This suggests to many the need for some form of "internal" work at individual and institutional level. Differently put, there is work to do at the "I" level as well as the "we" level in order to affect change at the systemic "all of us" level. Sparking action and specifically responsible action at the "me" level seems to be a critical requirement for a successful collaboratory.

In hindsight the Western Cape Wine Collaboratory had no visible and agreed mechanism in place to keep the group accountable to the actions it generated. Delegating emerging actions to smaller working groups ensured a minimum amount of momentum and responsibility at the "I" and "we" level. The group as a whole did not commit to continued development of the shared agenda, or collective and continued development of their individual and organizational roles in the system, and as a result this collaboratory quickly ran out of steam.

On the positive side—the level of interest shown when the Wine Collaboratory was first announced, and the speed at which seats were confirmed, far exceeded the expectations of the conveners. The positive response was an indication that participants were drawn to the urgency and content of the call, but also to the innovative nature of the process as described. Immediate feedback on the process was that participants experienced it as unique and radically innovative. It proved in a real-world setting that it is possible to work together on common ground with individuals and organizations with a commitment beyond responsibility to themselves and serving the common good.

Since the Wine Collaboratory was not concerned with transforming management education it may be added here that the essence of the 50+20 vision appears to carry meaning and relevance beyond the immediate management education fraternity. Informal discussions with faculties of Law, Engineering, and Natural Science (to name a few from the higher education landscape) and direct participation from those areas in collaboratory events, confirmed how they equally own the urgency to respond to the 50+20 call—to develop responsible leaders, to enable organizations to serve the common good, and to engage more broadly and vigorously in transforming our societies and economies towards inclusive modes of being and operating.

At a minimum it appears that the degree of inclusivity required of the collaboratory, from an early agenda-setting phase through to eventual societal impact having materialized, needs to reach even further beyond the immediate and obvious stakeholders. A level of openness is required of individual and institutional participants alike, to the possibility and often necessity of transforming their own views and practice through active contribution in the collaboratory process.

These suggestions are based in part on early stage observations and come less than a year since the full 50+20 vision was published in book form as *Management Education for the World* (Muff *et al.* 2013). However it also draws on ten years of work done within and through the GRLI. Learnings from the GRLI and initiatives like the ones presented above, along with preliminary insights drawn from informal discussion as referred to earlier, hopefully serve to enrich and ultimately progress both our theoretical understanding and our practice of convening and hosting collaboratories.

References

GRLI (Globally Responsible Leadership Initiative) (2005) *A Call for Engagement* (Brussels: GRLI Foundation, www.grli.org).

Ellerby N., A. Lockwood, G. Palin, S. Ralphs, and B. Taylor (2010) *Working Relationships for the 21st Century: A Guide to Authentic Collaboration* (Boston Spa, UK: Oasis Press).

Muff, K. (2013) "Developing Globally Responsible Leaders in Business Schools: A Vision and Transformational Practice for the Journey Ahead," *Journal of Management Development* 32.5: 487-507.

Muff, K., D. Dyllick, M. Drewell, J. North, P. Shrivastava, and J. Haertle (2013) *Management Education for the World: A Vision for Business Schools Serving People and Planet* (Northampton, UK: Edward Elgar).

Taylor, B. (2007) *Learning for Tomorrow: Whole Person Learning for the Planetary Citizen* (Boston Spa, UK: Oasis Press).

Part 4

How to get started

Now that you have immersed yourself in Part 3 in a range of possibilities of where and how to use a collaboratory, the one question that remains is "but how do I get started?"

Chapter 22 aims to do mission impossible by providing a roadmap for how to design and co-create a collaboratory. Rather than coming up with a dry checklist, this step-by-step account makes reference to how the most recent collaboratory at the time of writing was co-designed and co-facilitated. I offer a commentary on all the things that went right and wrong in the hope that this better prepares current and aspiring social-change agents when you are planning and running your own collaboratory. Remember: no collaboratory is like another one. In this step-by-step account, I make reference to the many recommendations and insights that are dispersed like nuggets of gold throughout this book.

Chapter 23 compares the collaboratory against other group facilitation methodologies. And in an attempt to close the book with another overview, Chapter 24 provides a concluding summary of the book and looks at questions left open.

If you do have questions and would like to talk to any of us, or any of the many people who are using the collaboratory (or any other similar) methodology, please don't hesitate to contact us at

22

Designing a collaboratory

A narrative roadmap

Katrin Muff

Business School Lausanne, Switzerland

Using the example of a collaboratory that took place for two days in Norway, this chapter is an attempt to provide a step-by-step road-map of how to go about co-designing and co-creating a collaboratory.

Collaboratories can take very many different shapes and forms and need to be designed, better still, co-designed, for the occasion each and every time afresh. I am using as an example the two-day collaboratory on "Leadership in Transformation" that took place from 27 February to 2 March 2014 in Trondheim, Norway. This event is part of a European Union-sponsored project (Leadership in Transformation: LiFT) featuring five collaboratories across Europe in a period of 18 months.

The chapter is structured in a series of reflections on how to:

- Level 1: Co-design a collaboratory

- Level 2: Co-create a collaboratory

We will shift back and forth between these two levels in order to simulate a real-life occurrence of such an event. We will start with Level 1 Part 1, move to Level 2 Part 1, spiral back to Level 1 Part 2, then spiral forward to Level 2 Part 2, and spiral one level back to Level 1 Part 3.

Level 1 Part 1 → Level 2 Part 1 → Level 1 Part 2 → Level 2 Part 2 → Level 1 Part 3

I will complement each level with references to relevant chapters in the book.

Level 1: Co-designing the collaboratory event (Part 1)

Co-design starts way before the event, a few months ahead when the group of organizing participants meet to decide on the purpose of the collaboratory event. In our case, we met virtually on Skype a number of times to clarify the purpose and intention of the "workshop," who we wanted to be present, and how to go about inviting them.

As an initial framing, we had decided initially that we, as a core group would meet for four days around the issue of "Transformative leadership in changing times." The first and last days would be reserved as our own space—both to set the stage for ourselves and the group of stakeholders that would join us for the second and third days and to reflect on the collaboratory event and close the space afterwards.

We met again on Skype approximately one month before the event to discuss how the stakeholder engagement went, how this would influence the event, and if and how each of us could be engaged in the role of co-designing the event at the same time as wanting to be active participants.

One week before the actual event we connected again to finally set the skeleton agenda for the two days (see Figure 22.1). As the appointed facilitator, I presented a proposal and as a group we discussed how the agenda would enable the transformative journey we all aspired to. We decided to split the collaboratory into two separate sections: Day One afternoon, downloading–dialoguing–visioning–harvesting; Day Two morning, review harvesting–prototyping, with an option to potentially re-do another short visioning exercise to start. We sent this very rough agenda to all signed-up participants so that they could start their inner and outer journeys to the event. At that point, we knew that we could expect roughly 25–30 participants from seven countries.

Figure 22.1 The proposed skeleton agenda one week before the event

LiFT - Leadership for Transition Collaboratory 2-day session

TRANSFORMATIVE LEADERSHIP IN CHANGING TIMES

Are you aiming to lead change or make progress on complex issues? Do you find a need to translate your ideas from one domain to another? Do you and your colleagues see the issues you are facing continually becoming more complex and connecting with the needs of ever wider circles of stakeholders, who themselves also struggle to find the leverage points for change?

Friday, 28 February

9am	Check-in – purpose of the 2 days	In a large plenum
	Reflections on leadership	In small teams
	Reflective walk	In pairs
11.30	LUNCH (45 min.)	
12.15	Collaboratory 1 – downloading & visioning	Circular setting with fishbowl
	Open space	Free
16.00	Closing for the day	

Saturday, 1 March

9am	Check-in – clarification fo purpose	In a large plenum
	Collaboratory 2 – prototyoing	In groups
11.30	LUNCH (45 min.)	
12.15	Presentation of prototypes	In the plenum
	Reflective walk	In pairs
	Open space	Free
	Space for personal reflection	Individual
	Final reflection and closing	In the plenum
16.00	End of event	

The northern darkness greeted us as we arrived late at night from many different directions at Trondheim airport. Our local host very kindly picked us up and drove us to our respective hotels. The next day, ten of us met as the core group at an amazingly inspiring spot in the heart of Trondheim. We spent the morning checking in and warming up to the topic of transformative leadership. Interesting elements came up around "lazy leadership," the tension of wanting to assure impact, and the subtle inner space of lightness where change actually happens. We treated ourselves to both a lecture and a concrete application of holacracy as an emerging new organizational form that we had agreed to use as our own organizational model for the 18 months we were working together. Having a holacracy expert in our midst was too precious a gift not to explore.

Shifting into a different energy, we then stepped outside and started to prepare the space for the two-day event that would take place for the following two days with the invited stakeholders. We started first by sharing who was coming (background, perspectives, and motivations as far as was known) and then closed our eyes to open the space for the two-day workshop inviting the intentions and presence of all participants into this subtle space we would be co-responsible for holding. I am always fascinated by what happens once the "space is created" and how this enables—probably subconsciously—participants to start floating in and populating the energetic field.

We looked at the rough agenda design we had drafted a week earlier and started to fill out the details. The afternoon of Day One was the heart of the event, with a visioning exercise that would call on the emergent future to inspire us with new insights that we would then transform into prototypes on Day Two. For this it was critical to ask precisely the right question for the collaboratory theme. After much debate and word-smithing (this is critical and deserves all the time in the world) we settled on "In these coming times, what kind of a leader am I called to be?" From this central question, we worked backwards to define the preparatory stages we considered to be important for all participants to go through in order to be ready to answer this question in the afternoon of Day One. For this, we needed to define:

1. The check-in question

2. The question for the small group reflection on transformative leadership

3. The question for the reflective walk right before lunch

Not surprisingly, we spent most of the time defining what was needed to set up the space both physically and metaphorically in the opening moments. We sorted out both logistical and contextual framework information and most importantly how we wanted all stakeholders to check in. We shifted from the initial proposal of "What in your past has triggered you to accept this invitation?" or "What brings you here?" (a classic) to "What wants to move now?" This question was to be introduced with the remark that we were all moved to come here for one reason or another and that we invited everybody to share "what wants to move now?" for them. We had somebody assigned to decorate the center of the circle of the check-in by bringing a tissue and a few items of different textures to be placed on this tissue.

The other two questions (b and c above) derived from the check-in as we decided to focus all stakeholders on clarifying where they were themselves—personally and individually—in terms of transformative leadership.

For the question for the small group reflection (b), I borrowed a set of questions used by Andrew Dyckhoff: we invited the groups to first individually reflect on and then share the following questions: In terms of transformative leadership, what is (1) my remembered self? (what am I proud of?) (2) my reflected self? (what do others say about me?) (3) my current programming? (what are my beliefs and assumptions about myself?) and (4) my aspirational future self? (what kind of leader would I like to be?).

For the reflective walk questions (c), I suggested that pairs of people who had not yet worked together would further digest and develop this set of questions by looking at: What could I (1) stop doing, (2) continue doing, and (3) start to do?

The organization of the collaboratory required three preparatory actions:

1. Deciding together who the initiating "experts" in the fishbowl would be—for example, would we draw them from our core group or would we invite key participants? We decided on two of each based on the desire to have as much diversity and contrasts in the discussion right up front. We agreed on who would approach the two participants and we also had two back-up volunteers in case the two "externals" did not want to be "experts"

2. Determining the four volunteer note-takers for the harvesting after the visioning process and clarifying among them how they would smoothly take notes by defining a rotation mode

3. Writing the visioning journey. Given that we had now agreed on what we wanted to achieve in the collaboratory, I took on the task of developing the storyline for the meditative visioning journey for the group. I let this sink in for a few hours and ended up finalizing the story late that first night. As I consider developing such storylines as the most sensitive part in facilitating a collaboratory, I add here as an example the exact notes of the storyline (see Box 22.1).

The only thing left to consider was the open space after the collaboratory. Well, an open space is an open space and all I brought to that in preparation was an idea of what could be proposed. But, open spaces follow the law of two feet (we all go where the energy leads us) and so this cannot be prepared much in advance.

Related chapters

Chapter 5 Enabling the transformative journey—Bill Burck
Chapter 7 Creating collaboratories in society—Zaid Hassan
Chapter 8 Inviting stakeholders to engage—Caroline Rennie)
Chapter 9 Creating and holding a space—Janette Blainey
Chapter 11 Building cooperative capacity for generative action: Appreciate Inquiry—Ronald Fry

Level 2: Co-create the collaboratory event (Part 1)

Luckily, I had checked on the room the night before the event—everything we had asked for had been forgotten and I needed to persuade the night guard to help remove all tables, search for the four flipcharts, and find all the chairs we needed for the circle of chairs. At least I could sleep well, knowing that the next day we would find the place as we expected it.

We started at 9 a.m. sharp with the introductions as planned. What I added was an explicit description of my role as a facilitator and the disclosure that I would add "editorials" here and there during the process to offer transparency of what my moves and considerations as a facilitator were. I did this because many participants had a keen interest in further developing their own facilitation skills. I clarified my facilitator role by explaining that I was of Swiss-German origin and that our people were not gifted with a sense of humor (which of course got everybody to laugh and relax). I made this cultural reference as the large majority of the group were Scandinavians and I had no experience in how to relate to Scandinavians in terms of their cultural programming and frame of reference. I told them that the Germanic tribe was known to be very direct and straightforward and that I could be known to come across as harsh in some of my interventions. I explained that my intention in my interventions would be to differentiate between activities that held back the process and those that would help advance it, and that I would try to prevent the former and encourage the later. I also said that I was not a flawless facilitator and that I did not always manage to make this distinction correctly and that I would do my best to own up to my mistakes. I added that they could be just as harsh and direct with me, if they felt the need. The resulting effect was a great relief and sense of relaxation in the room. The rules of play were clear.

The check-in (see Figure 22.2) was amazing and took a full hour. The centerpiece arrangement with the handful of small items (a seashell, a rock, a small pig, a globe) contributed significantly as participants often related their choice of object to what they had to say. We invited everybody to share on "what wants to move now?" What was revealed was highly inspiring and revealing and set the tone for the rest of the event.

Figure 22.2 Day One check-in on "what wants to move now?"

After the check-in and the small ten-minute intervention, we were left with just one hour before lunch, which felt a bit short for the two exercises we had still planned to do. The group, however, was in a great spot and I figured that if I manage to ensure all were mindful of their time and how their actions would impact their small groups, a tight timeframe could still allow enough space for everything. Rather than 90 minutes, we had 40 minutes for the first small group exercise and 20 minutes for the reflective walk (see Phase 1 above for the related questions). We quickly established both the groups and the buddies for the pair-walk and got them to self-manage their break and the start of the group work. After half-time, the individual part was completed leaving 20 minutes for sharing. I briefed them for the pair-walk and reminded them where to find lunch and when to be back. The discussions at lunch were both animated and deep.

In the afternoon we launched right into the collaboratory (see Figure 22.3) for which I quickly explained the context (50+20) and the rules:

- The experts in the inner circle (fishbowl) would start off with their individual positions and an exchange among themselves

- Thereafter, everybody in the outer circle was encouraged to replace the experts in the inner circle by tapping on their shoulders or using the one empty chair

- The talking stick would moderate by sitting in the middle of the inner circle and whoever held the talking stick could not be interrupted for as long as he or she held the talking stick

We had an inconsistency between the PowerPoint slide, which still showed the original collaboratory purpose questions ("How does each of us (how do I) develop our transformative leadership potential?") and the flipchart, which showed the questions we had developed the previous day ("In these coming times, what kind of a leader am I called to be?"). We needed to explain that the former was meant to guide the initial discussion while the latter would be the question we wanted to answer by the end of the collaboratory. I failed to use this occasion to uncover a moment of improvisation. At that moment, I wanted to get going.

Figure 22.3 Collaboratory setting with inner circle (fishbowl)

Interestingly, our "transformative leadership in changing times" topic brought up little or no controversy and the energy in both circles was slow and quiet, to the point that two people on the outside were either meditating or had fallen asleep. I was wondering if I should intervene by drawing attention to the energy and empowering people to influence this. Not 20 seconds after my reflection, one of participants who had shown signs of impatience got up and moved into the inner circle. Within two minutes, two more high-energy participants followed shifting the energy to a productive and simulating level. Most impressive in this "downloading phase" was how the energy shifted to include the emotional level. One of the participants made a very personal and emotional statement, which another participant acknowledged and recognized. The air changed and the entire room shifted.

The visioning (see Box 22.1) and the harvesting that followed went as planned. As it turned out, the harvesting contained a lot of controversy and mixed messages (see Figure 22.4). I was confused by not being able to come up with a summary picture. Rather than taking the time to tell the story that resulted from the harvesting, I let everybody take a 15-minute break. We continued with a ten-minute personal reflection whereby I invited everybody to come up with emerging prototype ideas that people could develop for an hour in the open space. Seven ideas were put forward and there was much energy in the open space hour and around these ideas before we closed at 4 p.m.

Box 22.1 Storyline developed for the visioning process

I am now going to take you on a visioning journey and I am asking you to trust me for the five to seven minutes this journey takes. Respect the process by staying in your seat and not leaving the room. I promise I will bring you all right back here again at the end (smile).

Please put both feet on the ground and sit comfortably in your chair, putting whatever you have in your hands on the floor. It often helps to close your eyes during this process; it helps you to see better.

We have talked a lot about transformative leadership and I invite you now to connect to your body more fully. Take a deep breath and follow your breath within your body (pause).

Let's explore where in your body you connect to transformative leadership:

- Where do you feel something when you "set direction"?
- What happens in your body when you "build commitment"?
- When you "create alignment" where do you sense something in your body?
- When you "support initiatives" what moves in your body and where?
- How does your body feel when you "develop a coalition"?
- How does that feel? What happens when you interconnect all these different spots and spaces? How do you experience this sensation within you? Now, imagine that you had a volume knob that you could turn on full blast—how would that feel? Take a deep breath and let this sensation expand and grow.

Feel fully in your body grounded and connected, you as a human being the link between the earth on which you stand and which grounds you and the sky and heaven above you that is full of insight and inspiration. Imagine you could feel that connection, that you are between these spaces.

Now, imagine the world in which you live and belong, and how it is evolving:

- The increasing volatility in everything
- The increasing speed, and information flow
- The overlapping and contradicting demands

- The external forces, the cracklings of the old systems
- The sprouts of new emerging hope
- The innovative solutions, the breakthroughs
- The tensions, the confusion, the choices, the loss of orientation

(pause) Take a deep breath and reconnect to your earlier bodily sensation.

Who can you be in this world—what is calling you? What happens when you connect this inner sense of self and of what leadership feels like. In your body. How does the world react and respond to you? What images appear? What sounds? What words? How do people look at you? Interact with you? (long pause). What roles do you play? What opportunities emerge? What do you hear, see, smell, sense? (long pause).

Take a deep breath and wiggle your fingers and toes, and come back to the "Here and Now." Do it in your own time. Open your eyes. Welcome back! **Note:** obviously reading this storyline is weird—the experience of the inner journey needs to be lived and cannot be simulated by reading a dry storyline. This example is provided for those who are struggling to come up with such stories. Chapter 15 (Students leading collaboratories) shows another more readily adapted example of such a storyline.

Level 1: Co-designing the collaboratory event (Part 2)

Our core group met at the end of Day One to reflect on how to continue on Day Two. We debated whether we should start with another visioning exercise in the morning of Day Two or should simply continue with the prototypes we had already started. We ended up deciding that we wanted to keep both alternatives open and that we would choose according to where participants were in the planned check-in. There were other valuable suggestions including the idea of starting the day in silence. What we had planned was to start with a few revealing constellation questions, yet we had had no time yet to explore these. This had be done in the evening in addition to developing another visioning storyline in case we might want to have another visioning.

I further reflected on what to do with the group on Day Two and decided to be fully transparent about my confusion, having been unable summarize the results of the visioning process in a conclusive picture. I prepared a comparison with the check-in in the morning (see Figure 22.4). After a good night's sleep things were clear the next morning: we would do a check-in with everybody; I would provide my "editorial comments," highlighting process-related choices; and we would engage in another visioning exercise from which we would draw additional prototype ideas that would be combined with those that emerged in the open space.

Figure 22.4 Attempt to see shifts from check-in to visioning harvesting

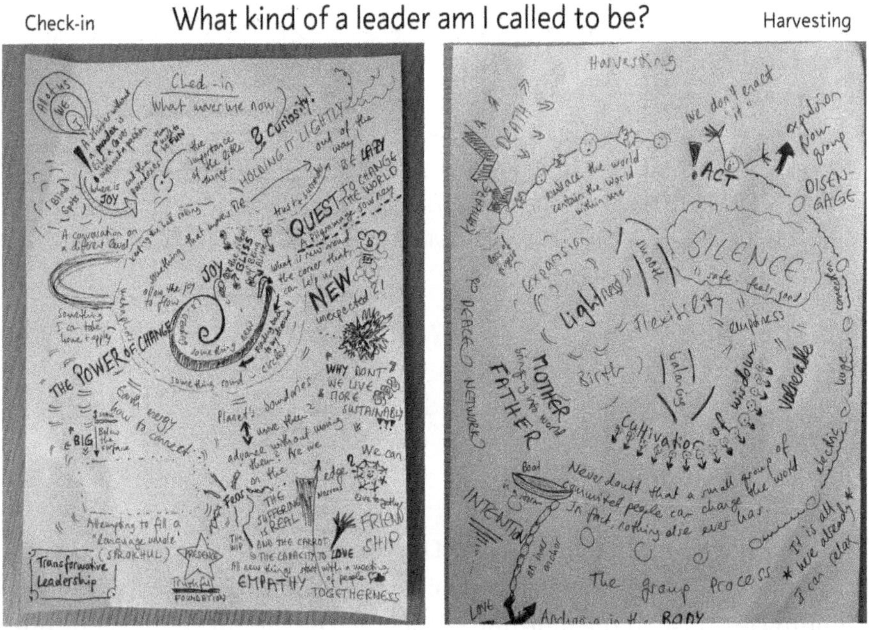

Level 2: Co-create the collaboratory event (Part 2)

The check-in and two constellation questions revealed that the large majority of the participants did not have concrete or specific expectations from the workshops—they were mostly curious. There was also broad alignment that transformative leadership combined both the individual and the collective spheres. I reflected on these notions by making the consequences of unclear expectations transparent and also by reflecting that our visioning exercise the previous day had focused on the individual dimension only ("In these coming times, what kind of a leader am I called to be?"). I built the path for us to experiment with a new visioning exercise: "Imagine a world where transformative leadership is a lived reality at all levels—the individual, organizational and societal (I—we—all of us) levels." This time, I gauged the journey on my own speed as I physically went through the experience (the visioning model I used was an adaptation of the model described in Chapter 15). The harvesting was extremely rich and resulted in a coherent and comprehensive picture of what such a world would look like (see Figure 22.5).

Figure 22.5 Harvesting result from visioning of Day Two

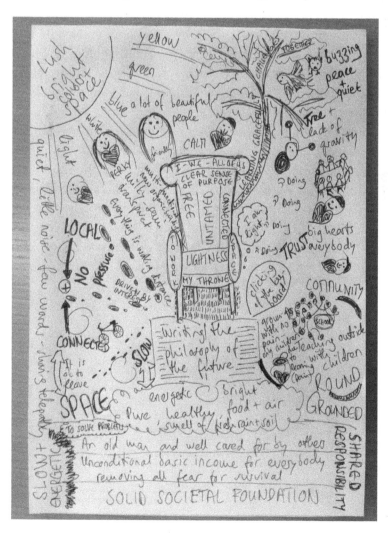

The harvesting took us through to 11 a.m. and was followed by a 30-minute free brainstorming on possible relevant prototypes that could be created now based on the inspiration of the lived experience of the future. By the (Norwegian) lunchtime of 11.30, we had a full flipchart of ten ideas that were about halfway between the ideal future and an implementable prototype.

The core team met during lunchtime to condense and rephrase the long list of brainstorm ideas and those projects developed in the open space of Day One, coming up with six concrete proposals and an open "to be defined" rebel group (see Figure 22.6). We defined the "prototyping rules" and distributed facilitator roles among us to ensure that each of the potentially seven teams would be well accompanied to come up with concrete actions to be implemented in the next one to two months together with an accountable person. After an hour and a half of intense teamwork, the results were most impressive and astounding. Most teams had developed a series of "next action" steps and even the rebel group surprised us with a very concrete and highly relevant project with clear action goals and accountabilities.

After a 30-minute reflection walk, where participants were invited to select somebody they had not yet connected with and share their personal learnings from the course, we were ready for the final debriefing and closing round. We had prepared a survey where we collected feedback of participants about the effectiveness of our proposed process and journey. And at 4 p.m. sharp we ended two intense days around transformative leadership in changing times—with still a bit of time for a long walk up to the local castle before the sun set quickly in the north of Europe.

Figure 22.6 The challenge of combining emerging brainstorming prototypes and open space projects from the previous day

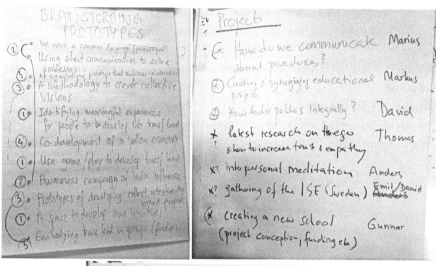

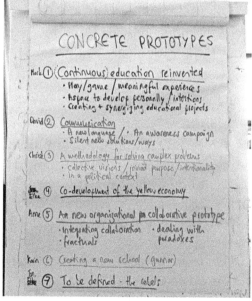

Related chapters:

Chapter 6 Facilitating a collaborative space—Bill Burck, Svenja Rüger, Patrick Frick, Aaron Williamson, and Grégoire Serikoff

Chapter 10 Whole person learning—Claire Maxwell

Chapter 11 Building cooperative capacity for generative action: Appreciate Inquiry—Ronald Fry

Chapter 12 Stepping into the emerging future: principles of Theory U—Otto Scharmer

Chapter 13 Transformative scenario planning—Adam Kahane

Chapter 15 Students leading collaboratories: University of St. Gallen—Thomas Dyllick and Katrin Muff

---

Level 1: Co-designing the collaboratory event (Part 3)

On Day Four, our core team met to review and reflect on the two-day workshop. These were the key learnings in a nutshell:

General:

- The way we ran the collaboratory meant there was too much pressure on the lead facilitator

- The topic was too generic and insufficiently specific to generate very powerful results. There are many ways we could have better dealt with this: (a) to provide that clarity upfront by being very specific about the invitation, (b) by harvesting the perspectives and expectations at the beginning of the workshop and then developing strategies addressing key challenges, (c) using the entire workshop to work out the clarity of the question and create powerful learning experiences in the process

- We were unsure if we could expect the participants to be as open as they were in future events

- Reflecting outside of the space of the workshop, for example, visiting a museum, was most useful

- The way we issued the invitation was too general and broad, leading to very divergent expectations of participants

Process and design-specific feedback:

- It would have been good to have more formal time to meet and exchange among the many participants

- There was a hunger for more formal input/inspiration/insight/resources (documentation) about the topic—in a situation where the topic is more specific this would happen naturally

- It would be interesting to have a track where the methodology and process were discussed (further developing the "editorials" introduced during the session—a very useful idea). At the same time, there was a question of to what degree it was helpful or confusing to invite participants into such a multilevel "nested" space. This issue arose because the core group wanted to understand the methodology (and was still hungry for more)

- We understood that there were different elements of the "editorials": (a) meta-level comments, (b) comments about the methodology, (c) facilitation-related comments, and (d) comments about our core team reflections about the process. It would be worth deciding which of these would be smart to share, when and how, and which of these are not necessarily constructive to share

A question we were left with was whether the collaboratory methodology was actually suitable to advance more meta-level, unspecific issues. Most successful applications of the collaboratory so far were addressing complex but concrete multi-stakeholder issues. Given that the Trondheim collaboratory workshop was one of the first events dealing with a very broad, unspecific topic such as "Transformative leadership in changing times," our core group's reflections were inconclusive. The prevailing feeling was that even though not perfect, the collaboratory did produce serious, important and relevant results. And nobody was aware of a methodology that could have produced better results. Our host finally concluded that it was very worthwhile to prototype a sequence of improvements of this methodology in the context of being delighted to have a "clumsy solution for a wicked problem."

To be experienced, lived, and enjoyed!

23

Differences from other facilitation approaches

Eddie Blass
Learning Innovations Hub, University of New England USA

Peter Hayward
Swinburne University, Australia

This chapter presents two personal reflections on the facilitation of the collaboratory process from two very different and experienced group facilitators. The differences in the process from the facilitator's viewpoint are drawn out including the challenges faced in the processes and the need for the facilitator to live with the discomfort this creates during the process itself. Both facilitators use the first part of the collaborator process only: the talking circle element. They use this as a means of deepening a group conversation rather than leading straight into a visioning process.

Reflection 1

I'm probably quite a "traditional" facilitator normally in that I tend to work with groups to help facilitate an outcome to a set agenda. Normally I have a brief of what the question is and, to a degree, what the desired answer is, and I work with the group to move them from where they are to where the organization wants them to be by asking questions, probing into answers, and scribing on a flipchart something that represents the response in words aligned to the desired outcome, and I engage in lots of checking with the group, summarizing and ensuring everyone is travelling together. It is a very managed process, arguably quite manipulative, but facilitative in terms of moving a group from one space to another. In short, I am in control, I do quite a lot of talking/feeding back, and I can do the facilitation job alone.

With the collaboratory process the facilitation is very different. First, the person facilitating the circle cannot also be the scribe. If a record is to be made of the collaborator conversation, it needs to be scribed by someone outside the circle who simply scribes and does nothing else. They do not interrupt to check understanding; they try not to paraphrase too much but record the key words as spoken; and they do not play an active role in the group. The person facilitating the circle sets the rules of the talking stone and then steps back and awaits the first contribution. They move around the circle so that they are always opposite the person speaking in order to make eye contact and reassure them. This also helps them hold the space, so to speak, as the standing facilitator acts almost as a block on the conversation leaving the circle because the facilitator is a physical barrier opposite to but distant from the speaker. The facilitator walks round the circle slowly, and this pace is important as it helps slow the conversation down and ensure active listening. Gradually the participants naturally find they wait for the facilitator to reach the opposite point before they start talking although this instruction is not given consciously. In our case, apart from holding the space, the facilitator says and does nothing until the time allocated to the circle is completed.

As a facilitator who is used to being in control of the group and the conversation, facilitating the collaborator is a very interesting experience. The discomfort of not being in control of the conversation is startling. You have no conventional means of directing the conversation, steering it, reassuring anyone, or supporting any points. What the outcome of the conversation is lies beyond the facilitators reach, and whether the conversation stays on track is for the group having the conversation to decide. In essence it is like dropping a stick from a bridge into a stream and seeing where it drifts out once it has gone under the bridge. You set a conversation in motion but then have no input on the direction, pace, tone, or pitch of the conversation. It is quite challenging to be comfortable with this—and also quite challenging to facilitate the debrief after the collaboratory conversation has ended. Often, taking a mood measure of how people are feeling or what they are thinking after the event is a good way of debriefing rather than focusing on the content that was revealed.

I now use the collaboratory process as a teaching tool as well as a management tool when I want a group to engage in deep thinking about something rather than being necessarily outcome focused. It can still feel scary to set something in motion that could end up somewhere other than where I expect, but I am learning to manage that emotion myself and use the energy it creates positively by reflecting afterwards on why I had preconceived one outcome that was so different from that of the group. To that extent, the collaboratory process is as much of a development exercise for myself as it is for the group involved, and it never ceases to amaze me how tired I am after facilitating a session compared to a more traditional, controlled facilitation.

Reflection 2

My own style of facilitation arises from the notion of creating supportive and safe places for people to explore transformation of their thinking and actions. For me facilitation is as much about being aware of the movement of energy among people as it is about the things that are being said and done. It may seem somewhat counterintuitive to hear it but I think that there is often the most happening in a group when nothing is being said or done; silence tends to magnify the energy in a group, whereas, typically, talking often takes the energy out of a process.

So when I first encountered the collaboratory process I tended to see it as a process that accumulated energy through stillness and listening and also moved the energy around in a fairly comfortable circular fashion. So the elements we added—using the talking stone to slow the conversation down and standing opposite the speaker to give witness to their testimony and to support them seemed the natural thing to do.

The standing facilitation role does sometimes have to play a governance role. At the start the standing facilitator should explain the rules of the collaboratory: only one person speaks, people are replaced by someone sitting next to them, if you are not replaced then you stay, and let the stone rest before the next person picks it up. I usually say that the conversation will start when I have all the benches full and I will wait silently for as long as I have to before it starts. I ask people already seated to be silent until the circle is complete. In my experience it is quite typical for there to be quite a bit of tension and anxiety among the group at the start of the collaboratory process. I think this is the beginning of the accumulation of the energy that builds throughout the process so as a facilitator I let it happen and actually hope it occurs.

Because there are so few rules the circles can quickly start to create their own norms—handing the stone directly to a person as if saying "it's your turn to say something" or getting up to leave the circle after they have spoken without anyone replacing them. The standing facilitator sometimes has to intervene and stop norming behavior if you think it is working against the spirit of the collaboratory. This is not a democratic process—you either intervene or you do not. Such interventions I find are best done in the moment—if the moment passes and you do not intervene then I think you have allowed the norm to stay and so it must be left alone. So act in an instant or do not ... and no regrets from whatever you do.

Finally, the collaboratory does not always create a "deep dive." Sometimes the conversation just moves around, often very politely, but the standing facilitator knows that there is no energy moving around, nothing is really happening. My advice as a facilitator is to resist closing it down too quickly; just watch and wait. It is not failing because what is happening is what the participants are making happen. As such the collaboratory is a very good mirror of group norms and behaviors. Without social norms a group of relative strangers can go to depth quite quickly whereas groups that have spent time together will have perhaps unconsciously created norming behavior that makes sure that everyone plays a part in keeping thinking just where it is. On occasions the dynamic of the collaboratory is worth debriefing with a group, especially if you think the process was revealing some unhelpful dynamics in a group of people. Sometimes people have blamed the "process" saying that it was an unhelpful way of discussing something because the conversation was directionless and just wandered all over the place. Again, the only advice I can give you is to let these statements be said and heard;

do not defend the process because that is not the point. Sometimes the conversation the group wanted happens *after* what happened, or did not happen, in the collaboratory. You just never know.

Conclusions

There are three key points we want facilitators to take away from our reflections on facilitating the collaboratory process that differ from most other facilitation processes:

1. Learn to be comfortable with the process of setting something in motion and then allowing it to go where it takes itself. This may be where you anticipated or wanted, or it may not be. Sometimes groups are not ready to deepen a conversation but simply talk at a superficial level, getting irritated by the attempt to slow the conversation. This may be a mirror of where a group is at and reflecting on that afterwards is important

2. Concluding the collaboratory process is very important. Some people use the process as a means of starting a visioning process, taking the participants into a process of creating a new shared vision out of the process. We do not conclude in this manner. We tend to reflect on the process itself and see where people are after the conversation and how they are feeling. Hence we tend to debrief on how people found the process itself rather than focusing on the content of the process. This makes the process one that deepens the group's understanding of how they operate and impact on each other, allowing greater reflection and learning about the self. The content we then revisit later

3. Design the question for discussion well. The issue you want the group to discuss needs to be phrased in such a manner that it does not have a bias, judgment or pre-set answer in its formation. It needs to be phrased in such a way that it allows multiple views and answers and there is no one correct outcome. Questions we have used in groups, for example, have included "What does globally responsible leadership look like?" (in a mixed

group of business leaders and business educators) or "Let's talk about death and dying" (in a workshop looking at organizational taboos). Sometimes you will want to run more than one cycle, with an initial question to bring people into a space, and then a supplementary question as a second cycle to deepen the conversation in one particular area. Allow enough time for a debrief as well as for the process to run its course—again, be comfortable with the lack of control this necessitates

24
Concluding summary

Katrin Muff
Business School Lausanne, Switzerland

What follows is an attempt to summarize the rich contributions of the many authors in the book by providing a high-level overview of the book and its ambition to provide a practical handbook for practitioners of transformative change. The following summary directly relates to the contents of the individual chapters and in some instances quotes directly from them.

Part 1 The collaboratory idea

The collaboratory idea stems from the visioning work of a large group initiative including scholars, artists, consultants, students, activists, and other professionals who worked together on the 50+20 vision (www.50plus20.org).

The "collaboratory" is a blend word fusing two elements: "collaboration" and "laboratory," suggesting that we are building a space where we explore collaborative innovations. The laboratory also nicely implies a notion of exploration and experimentation, thus staying clear from the notion of perfection or standardization. The philosophy of the collaboratory involves a facilitated, circular space that is open to stakeholders to meet and discuss burning societal issues. It is an open space for all stakeholders where action learning and action research join forces and students, educators, and researchers work with members of all facets of society to address current dilemmas. A collaboratory focuses on visceral real-life issues and provides solutions that are driven by issues, *not* by theory. Participants in a collaboratory employ problem-solving tools and processes that are iterative and emergent. Emerging solutions are directly tested and amended while supporting both knowledge production and diffusion, which occur in parallel.

A collaboratory is a facilitated space open to everybody and in particular to concerned stakeholders to meet on an equal basis to co-create new solutions for societal, environmental, or economic issues by drawing on the emergent future. It is a place where people can think, work, and learn together to invent their common futures.

The philosophy of the collaboratory revolves around an inclusive learning environment where action learning and action research meet and where the formal separation of knowledge production and knowledge transfer dissolves.

In our dreams, the collaboratory becomes the preferred meeting place for citizens to jointly question, discuss, and construct new ideas and approaches to resolves sustainability challenges on a local, regional, and global level.

Each collaboratory is different and needs to be carefully designed to fit the context, ambition and purpose, stakeholders, culture, setting, and anticipated duration of the space given to address an issue. For creating and holding such a space facilitation is of critical importance. As Zaid Hassan has framed so well in Chapter 7:

> A recipe or a checklist is predictive in the sense that if one combines certain ingredients under particular conditions and uses the prescribed techniques, one gets the expected outcome. However, it does not make sense to think of either being *falsifiable* in the way we would think of theory in the natural sciences. A recipe that fails in the hands of a bad cook does not mean the recipe does not work. But then how does one tell if a recipe is bad? Well, one simple answer is experience. When you cook it, it tastes bad. If a recipe corresponds to a set of instructions for producing a particular outcome, then the point of phronesis is that the only real way of learning how to cook is to cook.

If you don't try it, you won't know whether you like it!

As the Wine Collaboratory in Chapter 21 highlights, the collaboratory—as essence of the 50+20 vision—appears to

> carry meaning and relevance beyond the immediate management education fraternity. Informal discussions with faculties of Law, Engineering, and Natural Science (to name a few from the higher education landscape) and direct participation from those areas in collaboratory events, confirmed how they equally own the urgency to respond to the 50+20 call—to develop responsible leaders, to enable organizations to serve the common good, and to engage more broadly and vigorously in transforming our societies and economies towards inclusive modes of being and operating.

The book will explore exactly to what degree such broader applications of the collaboratory, as the heart of the 50+20 vision, are indeed possible.

Part 2 Dimensions of the collaboratory

There are five dimensions to co-designing, co-creating and unleashing a collaboratory. These are:

- Designing the entire process: chapters 5 and 6

- Inviting for the journey: chapters 7 and 8

- Creating the space and facilitating the event: chapters 9 and 10

- Designing and structuring the event: chapters 11 and 12

- Understanding the larger context of the transformative journey: Chapter 13

We discover that there are many different ways of co-designing and co-creating a successful collaboratory. The choice of tools, methods, and approaches depends entirely on the context of a specific transformative journey, the stakeholders involved, the cultural, societal, organizational, and individual circumstances, the duration of the collaboratory journey and sub-event, as well as the implicit and explicit expectations in terms of purpose, outcome, and future spin-off activities.

Chapter 5 Enabling the transformative journey: the DesignShop

The DesignShop (as developed by Matt and Gail Taylor in the 1980s) is a "crucible for transformation. It is not a consensus-building mechanism, nor a place where you convince people you are right." It is a place "to gather people who have a key stake in the change you are trying to make … the more the merrier." As such, the DesignShop collaboratory is different from a traditional workshop in six different ways:

1. **Fostering collaboration by engaging participants in design conversations** based on what is meaningful

2. **An intense, focused, collaborative experience** that can last from three hours to three days (or more)

3. **The iterative, non-linear process enables a group to explore the full complexity of the challenge** they are there to address before making major decisions and designing final outcomes

4. **Collaboratories that are social systems designed and facilitated in such a way that this emergence happens naturally and unavoidably.** The right conditions and feedback loops are created for the system to emerge

5. **This emergence is a form of group transformation**—the system shifting into a higher order and establishing new patterns of thought and action and new working culture

6. **The future is brought to life through stories** participants tell each other about what life will be like when they change the world. These stories evolve and integrate into a shared story

Participants spend a considerable time "creating the problem," which involves a collective vision of what the future change could be. Through a picture and through the stories they tell each other, they are able to abstract from their individual positions and reasons why they join the session to totally change their mind-set to develop a shared understanding of the future as it might be. Through modeling and storytelling, they change from defending what they think to be a right to collaboratively designing a shared future.

Chapter 6 Facilitating a collaborative space

Besides the all-important notion of playfulness, the following conditions are required to co-design an event:

1. A clear and compelling purpose

2. Engaging the right players (see also Chapter 8)

3. Structural components (schedule, place, economy)

4. The collaboratory journey

5. The right facilitation approach

6. The role of sharing—the virus of the collaboratory

Chapter 7 Creating collaboratories in society

There are a number of requirements to make a collaboratory work in society:

- Constitute a diverse team (is there a critical mass of easily influenced people who are connected to other people who are easy to influence—this will ensure an idea gets spread)

- Design an iterative process (trial, error, observation, and reflection)

- Actively create systemic spaces (beware of static spaces: "the desk is a dangerous place from which to view the world")

How do you go about starting a "social lab" (or a collaboratory):

1. Clarify intention

2. Broadcast an invitation (see Chapter 8)

3. Work your networks

4. Recruit willing people

5. Set direction

6. Design in stacks (innovation or problem-solving such as done through Theory U; information and learning; capacity-building; governance). Design each stack only when you need it; don't spend years planning!

7. Find cadence

Chapter 8 Inviting stakeholders to engage

Caroline Rennie frames the invitation as a gracious request that says "Welcome!" from the first contact until the starting moment of the event. As such "the invitation is not a summons, nor a letter alone, nor a call. It is the graciousness that reaches out to those who have a yearning to contribute and accompanies them into the event itself." Whom to invite and when to invite are two critical elements. Once clarified, the following elements need to be considered and addressed:

- Salutation

- Statement of invitation

- Possibility

- Specificity of the request

- The nature of the invitation

- Who else has been and can be invited

- Contacts for more information (and a warm invitation to do so)

- What will be done with the outcome of the event

- What they can expect before, during and after the event

- Reiteration of welcome

Chapter 9 Creating and holding a space: Learning circles

Janette Blainey explains that space to her is the "natural and build environment of place, as well as the "field" in which the circle and the learning take place." Learning in this context is used to include "knowing" in the broadest sense as well as the acquisition of knowledge and skills. Circles are not just about shape and structure but also what such a structure enables through a "wisdom-enhancing mode." Importantly, she states that the fundamental belief of "we are all one" underpins the way she has learned to create and hold space.

Important elements include: working with the circle, opening the circle, processes to enhance collaboration in circles, and closing the circle. Here is a summary of her conclusions:

- **Respect** for place, people, and participation by all

- Honor the place (do not ignore the setting in which the learning circle is to take place)

- Create a clear opening of the circle, so that all are aware of purpose and process

- Engage in a circle (do not assume that everyone present knows how to operate respectfully in a circle)

- Honor everyone's place in the circle (do not forget to share the holding of space with everyone in the circle)

- Encourage openness in mind and body and remember to laugh (do not allow people to question others while they are sharing their perspective/story/idea, and do not support people cutting others off as they offer their perspective)

- Support an ethos of learners being responsible for their learning and of "listening"

- Close the circle with a moment of gratitude to all (do not forget to close with respect)

Chapter 10 Whole person earning

Whole person learning calls for "a meeting of minds, hearts, and humanity, in all aspects of what it means to be human: feelings, senses, intuition, connection to others and to the cosmos, as well as to the familiar ground of the mind and the intellect." As the heart of whole person learning is a "commitment to working collaboratively, to encouraging the participation of others and self," including a shift of authority and power regarding the learner and the teacher (the encouragement, development, and practice of adult-to-adult relationships).

The central tenets of whole person learning are:

- **How we relate to one another.** Adults stand in relation to one another as peers (or equals) despite different roles and contributions; based on honest, open dialogue, and debate concerning the matter at hand in a clear way

- **How we view the other.** The recognition that differing perspectives all have a contribution to make allowing individuals to freely give voice to their authentic concerns

- **How we teach and how we learn.** An aware understanding of the affective dimension when working with people and a willingness to work with the immediate and emergent

- **How we structure our decision-making forums.** Enabling shared, "owned" decision-making with a commitment to stand by what one agrees to and to work with the consequences and implications of the decision

Chapter 11 Building cooperative capacity for generative action: Appreciative Inquiry (AI)

AI is a "strength-driven process and approach to human system change and development." Ronald Fry demonstrates how AI is a form of study that "selectively seeks to locate, understand, and illuminate ... the life-giving forces of any human system's existence." This positive core and the "realization of shared strengths becomes a new platform for imagining possibilities for a preferred future."

AI holds a life-centric view of organizations (e.g. as centers of vital connections and life-giving potentials) and involves a cooperative search for the best in people, their organizations, and the world around them. The key steps or phases include:

1. Discovery of the best of what is

2. Dream to imagine what could be

3. Design of what will be

4. Destiny—to enact change and improvisational learning to become what is most hoped for

The core principles behind the practice of AI are:

- **The constructionist principle.** As we talk, so we make

- **The poetic principle.** As we choose topics of inquiry, so we open new horizons of action

- **The principle of simultaneity.** As we ask positive questions, so we transform

- **The anticipatory principle.** As we imagine, so we create

- **The positive principle.** As we express hope, joy and caring, so we create new relations

- **The narrative principle.** Stories weave a connectedness that bridges the past with the future.

Chapter 12 Stepping into the emerging future: principles of Theory U

Theory U seeks to illuminate a critical blind spot related to the source dimension of effective leadership and social action. We know what leaders do and how they do it, but we know little about "the inner place, the source from which they operate." Slowing down to understand is an important practice to recognize how people interact and respond by engaging in four dimensions of listening:

- **Downloading.** Listening by reconfirming habitual judgments— "yeah, I know that already" (I-in-me)

- **Factual.** Listening by paying attention to facts and to novel or disconfirming data—"ooh, look at that!" (I-in-it)

- **Empathic.** To really feel how another feels, we have to open our hearts—"oh yes, I know exactly how you feel" (I-in-you)

- **Generative.** Listening from the emerging field of future possibility—"I can't express what I experience in words. My whole being has slowed down. I feel more quiet and present and more my real self. I am connected to something larger than myself" (I-in-now)

Based on these four listening forms, there are four different ways to take conversational, organizational and global action. To move from one to another involves a journey, a process (a "U-shaped" process) that consists of five movements:

1. **Co-initiating.** Build common intent. Stop and listen to others and to what life calls you to do

2. **Co-sensing**. Observe, observe, observe. Go to the places of most potential and listen with your mind and heart wide open

3. **Presencing.** Connect to the source of inspiration and common will. Go to the place of silence and allow the inner knowing to emerge

4. **Co-creating.** Prototype the new living examples to explore the future by doing

5. **Co-evolving.** Embody the new in ecosystems that facilitate seeing and acting from the whole

Chapter 13 Transformative scenario planning: A new way to work with the future

What are situations when it makes sense to use transformative scenario planning?

- When people see the situation they are in as unacceptable, unstable, or unsustainable

- When people cannot transform their situation on their own or by working only with their friends and colleagues.

- When people cannot transform their situation directly

What are the five steps of transformative scenario planning and how do these relate with the Theory U?

1. Convene a team from across the whole system (co-initiating)

2. Observe what is happening (co-sensing)

3. Construct stories about what could happen

4. Discover what can and must be done (co-presencing)

5. Act to transform the system (co-creating)

Having summarized the key learnings of the many dimensions of the collaboratory, let us now look at what we can derive from the many examples of the collaboratory.

Part 3 Examples of the collaboratory

There are different types of collaboratories and they can be classified into different patterns, such as:

- From sequential, educational events (chapters 14 and 15) to local and intra-institutional events (chapters 16 and 17), to regional and inter-institutional (chapters 18 and 19) to large, long-term global (chapters 20 and 21) collaboratory processes.

- Covering the educational sphere (chapters 14, 15, and 16), the corporate sphere (chapters 17 and 18), the institutional sphere (Chapter 19), and the global movement (chapters 20 and 21).

Chapter 14 The collaboratory in the classroom: Bentley University

The example offers interesting reflections and comments on how to facilitate a collaboratory:

- Is the collaboratory an intimidating place?

- How does it maximize contributions?

- Experiencing the deepening of listening within the idea of presencing

Chapter 15 Students leading collaboratories: University of St. Gallen

The example provides a detailed account of how to facilitate three parallel collaboratory sessions over a course of 12 weeks by enabling students to fully assume the facilitation role, thus offering insights into both how to facilitate a collaboratory but also how to facilitate novice facilitators. The account is enriched by concrete outcomes of one of the three collaboratories (the tap water collaboratory).

A special treat is the detailed description of the visioning journey led by the professors—probably the only such life example in the book, and the detailed overview of the learning outcomes of the master's degree students derived from their reflection papers. This is a good chapter for anybody who wants to know in every detail how to use and apply a collaboratory and how to involve others in its facilitation and preparation.

Chapter 16 Creating connection, conversations, and courage: the Exeter collaboratory

In this example the need for a place, a physical space, to connect otherwise dispersed individuals is vividly described. It shows the importance of:

- Creating a presence

- Foundational work

- Community-building

The authors use a traumatizing event to illustrate the significance of a space for different kinds of conversation and what emerged from them and draw conclusions in pursuit of permanence and recommendations for others.

Chapter 17 Transforming an organization: participatory leadership and the Art of Hosting

This excellent example of how a collaboratory can help an organization embrace a seemingly impossible change challenge shows how the "eight breaths of design" of the Art of Hosting have helped initiate the collaboratory process:

1. **Call.** Naming the issue

2. **Clarify.** Moving from need to purpose

3. **Invite.** Determine how to ensure the parts of the system you are seeking to change should be represented, and by whom. Structure the invitation.

4. **Meet.** Design the meeting to ensure you can build trust, deepen understanding and design prototypes for action.

5. **Harvest.** Make sense of what emerged in and from the meeting(s) and how that informs future action

6. **Act.** Determine how to implement the agreed actions and implement

7. **Reflect and learn.** Explore both the results and the "how did this process work for us? How did we work together? What does this tell us about how we could do this again?"

8. **The breath that holds the whole**

This set of tools helped in building rapport and trust, clarifying the situation and developing solutions, and enabling implementation, buy-in, and an assessment. The key findings outlined in this example are critically important for any other collaboratory too and are thus worth highlighting:

- A common purpose creates the call to interact

- Effective change processes need to create the conditions in which people master themselves, are open to hearing what others are saying to increase their own understanding, participate in a productive fashion, and help take care of the group. This is what participatory methods do—often by creating formal roles (e.g. guardian, scribe, timekeeper)

- The knowledge you need to change a system is already alive in the system. The people who hold it just need to be invited to discuss it together and, with common purpose, together develop the path forward

- The setting and conditions for the interactions therefore need to be designed to provide safety and minimize fear

- Respectful listening not only diminishes fear, it releases the speakers from their point of view and enables willingness to work together

- Plan not only for the event, but for the outcomes of the event and how they will be distributed, implemented, and assessed—including the more intangible assessments

- When you are unsure what to do, turn to the affected people and have them work together to design the change

- To get meaningful change you need to feel that things are a bit out of control because the most vital and generative area lies on the edge of what feels chaotic—where order and chaos meet

- Many techniques will bring you good results. A mix of techniques can help the discussion stay fresh and broaden perspectives. The Art of Hosting thus uses established techniques and practices such as World Café, Open Space Technology, the Circle Way, Appreciative Inquiry, and Pro Action Café.

Chapter 18 Regional organizational change: community-building in action

This example demonstrates beautifully the power and effectiveness of professional community-building as defined by Philip Mirvis as an "aim to increase a group's capacity to function as a single intelligence." "Dialogue, a community-building practice, has individuals speak to the "group as a whole" about matters of interest and simultaneously scan their feelings, assumptions, and reactions to the experience. As such, it also reflects ideas about the interconnection of human thought and energy."

The Foundation for Community Encouragement has defined the following key principles of community-building:

- **"I" statements.** Use the first-person singular pronoun to claim knowledge, feelings, and observations rather than ascribe them to "we" or to "everyone"

- **Moved to speak.** Follow the Quaker injunction to wait until you are personally moved to say something and, when so moved, to speak

- **Emptiness.** Share personal thoughts and feelings, especially those that prevent you from being fully present in the dialogue

- **Witnessing.** Welcome and affirm others' stories and points of view and, in the spirit of community, bridge differences with love and respect

- **Difficult issues.** Face difficult issues that arise rather than deny, disregard, or downplay them

Peck's community-building is both similar and different to other group development and group dialogue processes as it provokes a deep dive into the group consciousness beyond standard processes such as "forming-storming-norming-performing" by Tuckman.

Facilitating a community-building exercise is (speaking from experience) not a thing for the weak-hearted. It does, however, have the advantage of allowing the facilitator to become familiar with the following important concepts:

- Self-reflection

- "Letting go"

- A container

Chapter 19 Transforming collaborative institutions: Australian business schools

This example shows the application of transformative scenario planning (Chapter 13), of the Theory U (Chapter 12), and of the 50+20 collaboratory methodology (Chapter 4) including the talking stone.

Chapter 20 Long-term stakeholder engagement: Initiatives of Change in Caux

The seven-decade-long example of how Initiatives of Change (IofC) has managed to sustain its efforts is most impressive and telling. Louie Gardener delicately offers key insights and patterns that have emerged across space and time to describe a group of people worldwide who do not see themselves as "movement-makers" but as "life-changers." Key practices of IofC include:

- Serve and receive service, joyfully

- Care for others, the planet and ourselves

- Engage with purpose

- Follow through on promises

- Turn scarcity into creativity

- Turn judgment into curiosity

- Engage in quiet time (a particularly impressive daily practice of group consciousness)

- Share and learn through honest conversation

A systemic explanation of this phenomenon occurs when we explore complex adaptive systems, or in other words "fractals." "Conditions for fractal patterns are simple, repeatable, and scalable," meaning that if the same conditions are applied repeatedly in other parts of a particular system (e.g. at the individual, organizational, and societal levels) a recognizable similar pattern will emerge. IofC is a beautiful example that demonstrates how this meta-principle is at play and can influence both the depth and spread of a movement. It is about scale and replication, about vertical and horizontal development.

An important concluding thought here is that

> when we accept that reality is this complex, we do not waste effort, time, or money on seeking *the* best way because we know there could be many possibilities. We understand that the best practice for any given situation is simply our best conclusion of what might be "best fit" in this moment in time.

At IofC the quality of their conclusion depends on their ability to "shift from fast to slow thinking, to engage in conscious adaptive action," or, as they call it, to engage in "quiet time."

Chapter 21 A meta-collaboratory: the Globally Responsible Leadership Initiative (GRLI)

The GRLI example demonstrates a number of noteworthy collaboratory elements:

- It highlights the GRLI as a container for ideas and projects across time and space

- It offers insight into a number of tools, such as fishbowl and Open Space Technology

- It offers two collaboratory initiatives: the Western Cape wine industry group and the 50+20 Innovation Cohort—both still in process at the time of print

As a container, GRLI has developed strong guiding principles that enable it to serve its purpose powerfully:

1. Everything we produce is a contribution to the global commons and is freely shared

2. What we do should create hands-on results on the ground, stand the chance of producing long-lasting, scalable effects, and is not being done better elsewhere

3. Our operating mode is built on the entrepreneurial approach of "Think big. Act small. Start now"

4. Effective change requires work at individual, organizational and systemic levels—"I," "We," and "All of us"

5. Making an impact at the organizational and systemic level requires committed, dedicated, and empowered individuals who are willing to bring a "whole person" approach to their work and to their lives

All of the examples listed in Part 3 of the book are just that: examples. There are so many more in so many other fields. Please share your experience with us and please do tell us and others what you have learned and how others can improve their practice as a result.

Part 4 How to get started

Chapter 22 Designing a collaboratory: a narrative roadmap

In many ways, Chapter 22 is the capstone chapter of the book, offering a comprehensive narrative into how to co-design, and co-create a collaboratory—not in an abstract theoretical manner but reporting from the messy reality of a real-life situation. I have added drawings and pictures to illustrate this reality. It is my hope that this chapter will serve as encouragement and an important supporting tool for those ready and willing to launch into facilitating societal change. It offers a clumsy visioning journey that didn't quite work and refers to Chapter 15 for one that does. It also shows that too many cooks can spoil a meal—having had to hold a group of observing co-facilitators at the same time as holding the space for the group of participants in the collaboratory was more than I was able to manage elegantly. But that is OK: it was an important learning experience that gave me so much back in return.

Chapter 23 Differences from other facilitation approaches

The collaboratory is different from other standard group processes and workshops. Eddie Blass and Peter Hayward offer us their insights into how they experienced the differences and how—from their individual perspectives—they see the collaboratory used and applied.

There are important questions that remain open with regard to the application of the collaboratory in a variety of settings that go beyond transformational change processes that are covered in this book. Specifically, we want to look at two related applications not covered in Part 3:

- Peacemaking efforts

- Conflict resolution

We refer to Kay Pranis in Chapter 1 who offers six structural conditions for peacemaking efforts to succeed. While we have not witnessed the collaboratory approach in peacemaking, we can imagine that it could be adapted to be of great service in certain aspects of such efforts, namely when various parties are failing to recognize or identify a common vision for a future that is desirable for everybody.

With regard to conflict resolution, we need to differentiate our response in two sub-parts: "yes" and "depends":

- **Yes.** We believe the collaboratory methodology can be of service as an approach and tool to advance the process of conflict resolution by providing a clearly defined methodology of how to arrive at a mutually desirable, positive future scenario

- **Depends.** Conflict resolution requires very different facilitation skills from being able to lead a debate about a given issue. For example, non-violent communication as advocated by Marshall Rosenberg, creator of Nonviolent Communication, can be a most helpful if not essential element in conflict resolution. However, beyond the use and application of extra tools and methods, conflict resolution does require the expertise of a seasoned mediator who may—once familiar with the ins and outs of a collaboratory—choose to work within such a methodology in order to advance in setting an environment in which parties with a conflict can advance

Concluding summary

This brings us right to the end of this book, to this chapter here, which is an attempt to summarize the countless nuggets of gold that the many authors have so generously dispersed throughout this book.

What we have all realized having shared our stories these past months is that there is a very sizable and mostly scattered community of practitioners of societal change agents. If all of us lit a candle, the world would be full of twinkling light and we could easily pass on the flame of inspiration, insight, experience, and shared passion.

Many thanks to all of you out there for keeping the world lit up both inside and outside!

I can but end with my favorite quote of Margaret Mead: "Never doubt that a small group of thoughtful, committed citizens can change the world; indeed, it's the only thing that ever has."

Bibliography

Adams, P. (2011) *Grouped: How Small Groups of Friends are the Key to Influence the Social Web* (Berkeley, CA: New Riders).

Argyris, C. (1982) *Reasoning, Learning, and Action* (San Francisco: Jossey-Bass).

Arthur, W.B. (2009) *The Nature of Technology: What it is and How it Evolves* (New York: Free Press).

Baldwin, C., and A. Linnea (2010) *The Circle Way: A Leader in Every Chair* (San Francisco: Berrett-Koehler).

Bales, R.F., F.L. Strodtbeck, T.M. Mills, and M.E. Roseborough (1951) "Channels of Communication in Small Groups," *American Sociological Review* 16: 461-68.

Banerjee, A., and Duflo, E. (2012) *Poor Economics: A Radical Rethinking of the Way to Fight Global Poverty* (New York: Public Affairs).

Barrett, F.J., and R.E. Fry (2005) *Appreciative Inquiry: A Positive Approach to Building Cooperative Capacity* (Chagrin Falls, OH: Taos Institute).

Bergmann, J., and A. Sams (2012) *Flip Your Classroom: Reach Every Student in Every Class Every Day* (Washington, DC: International Society for Technology in Education).

Block, P. (2008) *Community: The Structure of Belonging* (San Francisco: Berrett-Koehler).

Bohm, D. (1989) *On Dialogue* (Ojai, CA: David Bohm Seminars).

Boobbyer, P. (2013) *The Spiritual Vision of Frank Buchman* (University Park, PA: Pennsylvania State University Press).

Borton, T. (1970) *Reach, Touch and Teach* (London/New York: McGraw-Hill).

Buono, A.F. (2009) "Consulting to Integrate Mergers and Acquisitions," in L. Greiner and F. Poulfelt (eds.), *Management Consulting Today and Tomorrow: Perspectives and Advice from 27 World Experts* (New York: Routledge): 303-29.

——, and R.S. Sisodia (2011) "A Conscious Purpose," *Global Focus* 5.2: 56-59.

Cialdini, R. (2007) *Influence: The Psychology of Persuasion* (New York: Collins Business Press).

Chin, G., Jr, and C.S. Lansing (2004) "Capturing and Supporting Contexts for Scientific Data Sharing via the Biological Sciences Collaboratory," in *Proceedings of the 2004 ACM Conference on Computer Supported Cooperative Work* (New York: ACM Press): 409-18.

Cogburn, D.L. (2003) "Human–Computer Interaction in the So-called Developing World," *Interactions*, March–April 2003: 80-87.

Cooperrider, D.L. (1999) "Positive Image, Positive Action," in S. Srivastva and D.L. Cooperrider (eds.), *Appreciative Management and Leadership* (Westlake, OH: Lakeshore, rev. edn): 91-125.

——, and S. Srivastva (1987) "Appreciative Inquiry in Organizational Life," in R.W. Woodman and W.A. Pasmore (eds.), *Research In Organizational Change And Development* (vol. 1; Stamford, CO: JAI Press): 129-69.

——, D. Whitney, and J.M. Stavros (2008) *Appreciative Inquiry Handbook* (Brunswick, OH: Crown Custom Publishing, 2nd edn).

Daly, R.E., and D. Nicoll (1997) "Accelerating a Team's Developmental Process," *OD Practitioner* 29.4.

Dewey, J. (1910) "Natural Resources in the Training of Thought," in *How We Think* (Lexington, MA: D.C. Heath): 29-44.

Driscoll J. (1994) "Reflective Practice for Practise," *Senior Nurse* 14.1: 47-50.

Dutton, J.E., and E.D. Heaphy (2003) "The Power of High-quality Connections," in K.S. Cameron, J.E. Dutton, and R.E. Quinn (eds.), *Positive Organizational Scholarship* (San Francisco: Jossey-Bass).

Ellerby N., A. Lockwood, G. Palin, S. Ralphs, and B. Taylor (2010) *Working Relationships for the 21st Century: A Guide to Authentic Collaboration* (Boston Spa, UK: Oasis Press).

Eoyang, G.H. (ed.) (2003) *Voices from the Field: An Introduction to Human Systems Dynamics* (Circle Pines, MN: Human Systems Dynamics Institute Press).

——, and R.J. Holladay (2013) *Adaptive Action: Leveraging Uncertainty in your Organization* (Stanford, CA: Stanford Business Books).

Ferdman, B. (2013) *Diversity at Work: The Practice of Inclusion* (San Francisco: Pfeiffer).

Fisher, R., W. Ury, and B. Patton (2011) *Getting to Yes: Negotiating Agreement without Giving In* (New York: Penguin Books, rev. edn.).

Fromm, E. (1956) *The Art of Loving* (New York: Harper & Row).

Gardiner, L. (2014) "Women Who Mean Business," *the3rdimagazine*, http://www.the3rdimagazine.co.uk/2014/01/women-who-mean-business/, accessed 6 April 2014.

Gergen, K.J., and M.M. Gergen (1991) "Toward Reflexive Methodologies," in F. Steier (ed.), *Research and Reflexivity* (Trowbridge, UK: Redwood Books): 76-95.

Gibson, D.R. (2003) "Participation Shifts: Order and Differentiation in Group Conversation," *Social Forces* 81.4: 1335-81.

GLRI (Globally Responsible Leadership Initiative) (2005) *A Call for Engagement* (Brussels: GRLI Foundation, www.grli.org).

Goffman, E. (1983) "The Interaction Order: 1982 Presidential Address," *American Sociological Review* 48, February: 1-17.

Goldratt, E.M., and E.F. Fox (1997) *The Race* (New York: North River Press).

Gordon, J. (2007) *The Pfeiffer Book of Successful Conflict Management Tools* (San Francisco: Pfeiffer).

Gouyet, J.-F. (1996) *Physics of Fractal Structures* (Heidelberg, Germany: Springer Verlag).

Gozdz, K. (ed.) (1996) *Community Building in Business* (San Francisco: New Leaders Press).

Hamel, G. and C.K. Prahalad (1989) "Strategic Intent," *Harvard Business Review* 67.3: 63-78.

Haslam, S.A., S.D. Reicher, and M.J. Platow (2011) *The New Psychology of Leadership* (New York: Psychology Press).

Hassan, Z. (2014) *The Social Labs Revolution: A New Approach to Solving Our Most Complex Challenges* (San Francisco: Berrett-Koehler).

Human System Dynamics Institute (2006) *Be a Star: A Tool to Maintain Team Effectiveness* (Circle Pines, MN: HSD Institute, http://s3.amazonaws.com/hsd.herokuapp .com/contents/17/original/beastar.hsd.3.16.11.2_2_.pdf?1332189857), accessed 4 April 2014.

Isaacs, W. (1999) *Dialogue and the Art of Thinking Together: A Pioneering Approach to Communicating in Business and Life* (New York: Doubleday).

James, W. (1902) *The Varieties of Religious Experience: A Study in Human Nature* (New York: Longmans, Green & Co.).

Kahane, A. (2009) *Power and Love: A Theory and Practice of Social Change* (San Francisco: Berrett-Koehler Publishers).

—— (2012) *Transformative Scenario Planning: Working Together to Change the Future* (San Francisco: Berrett-Koehler).

Kahneman, D. (2011) *Thinking, Fast and Slow* (London: Penguin Books).

Katzenbach, J.R., and D.K. Smith (2001) *The Discipline of Teams* (London: John Wiley).

Kerber, K.W., and A.F. Buono (2005) "Rethinking Organizational Change: Reframing the Challenge of Change Management," *Organization Development Journal* 23.3: 23-38.

Kofman, F., and P. Senge (1993) "Communities of Commitment: The Heart of the Learning Organization," *Organization Dynamics* 22.2: 5-22.

Lefebvre, H. (1991) *The Production of Space* (London: Wiley).

Levine, S. (2000) *Getting to Resolution: Turning Conflict into Collaboration* (San Francisco: Berrett-Koehler).

Lowitt, E. (2013) *The Collaboration Economy: How to Meet Business, Social, and Environmental Needs and Gain Competitive Advantage* (San Francisco: Jossey-Bass).

McNaughton, C. (1988) *There's an Awful Lot of Weirdos in Our Neighbourhood* (London: Walker Books).

McNiff, J., P. Lomax, and J. Whitehead (1999) *You and Your Action Research Project* (New York: Routledge).

Mackey, J., and R. Sisodia (2013) *Conscious Capitalism: Liberating the Heroic Spirit of Business* (Cambridge, MA: Harvard Business School Press).

Mirvis, P.H. (1997) "'Soul Work' in Organizations," *Organization Science* 8.2: 193-206.

—— (2002) "Community Building in Business," *Reflections* 3: 45–51.

—— (2008) "Executive Development Through Consciousness Raising Experiences," *Academy of Management Learning and Education* 7.2: 173-88.

—— (2011) "Unilever's Drive for Sustainability and CSR: Changing the Game," in S. Mohrman, A.B. Shani, and C. Worley (eds.) *Organizing for Sustainable Effectiveness* (vol. 1; London: Emerald).

——, and W.L. Gunning (2006) "Creating a Community of Leaders," *Organizational Dynamics* 35.1: 69-82.

——, K. Ayas, and G. Roth (2003) *To the Desert and Back: The Story of One of the Most Dramatic Business Transformations on Record* (San Francisco: Jossey-Bass).

Muff, K. (2012) "The 50+20 Collaboratory Methodology and Approach for Short One-time Sessions," http://50plus20.org/wp-content/uploads/2013/02/50+20-Collaboratory-Approach.pdf, accessed 6 April 2014.

—— (2013) "Developing Globally Responsible Leaders in Business Schools: A Vision and Transformational Practice for the Journey Ahead," *Journal of Management Development* 32.5: 487-507.

——, D. Dyllick, M. Drewell, J. North, P. Shrivastava, and J. Haertle (2013) *Management Education for the World: A Vision for Business Schools Serving People and Planet* (Cheltenham, UK/Northampton, MA: Edward Elgar).

Naam, R. (2013) *The Infinite Resource: The Power of Ideas on a Finite Planet* (Lebanon, NH: University Press of New England).

O'Brien, W. (2008) *Character at Work: Building Prosperity Through the Practice of Virtue* (Boston: Paulist Press).

O'Donovan, B. (2010) "The Motivations to Study of Undergraduate Students in Management: The Impact of Degree Programme and Level of Study," *International Journal of Management Education* 9.1: 11-20.

Owen, H.H. (1997) "A Brief User's Guide to Open Space Technology," http://www.openspaceworld.com/users_guide.htm, accessed 6 April 2014.

—— (2008) *Open Space Technology: A Users Guide* (San Francisco: Berrett-Koehler, 3rd edn).

Peck, M.S. (1987) *The Different Drum: Community Making and Peace* (New York: Simon & Schuster).

—— (1993) *A World Waiting to be Born: Civility Rediscovered* (New York: Doubleday).

Pranis, K. (2005) *The Little Book of Circle Processes: A New/Old Approach to Peacemaking* (Intercourse, PA: Good Books).

Reynolds, C.W. (1987) "Flocks, Herds, and Schools: A Distributed Behavioral Model," *Computer Graphics*, 21.4 (SIGGRAPH '87 Conference Proceedings): 25-34.

Robinson, K., and L. Aronica (2011) *The Element: How Finding your Passion Changes Everything* (London: Penguin).

Scharmer, C.O. (2009) *Theory U: Leading from the Future as it Emerges* (San Francisco: Berrett-Koehler).

——, and K. Kaufer (2013) *Leading from the Emerging Future: From Ego-System to Eco-System Economies* (San Francisco: Berrett-Koehler).

Schein, E.H. (2003) "On Dialogue, Culture, and Organization Learning," *Reflections* 4.4: 27-38.

Schon, D. (1983) *The Reflective Practitioner: How Professionals Think in Action* (London: Temple Smith).

Schwarz, R. (2002) *The Skilled Facilitator: A Comprehensive Resource for Consultants, Facilitators, Managers, Trainers, and Coaches* (San Francisco: Jossey-Bass, 2nd edn).

Senge, P.M. (1990) *The Fifth Discipline: The Art and Practice of the Learning Organization* (New York: Doubleday).

——, and C.O. Scharmer (2001) "Community Action Research: Learning as a Community of Practitioners, Consultants and Researchers," in P. Reason and H. Bradbury (eds.), *Handbook of Action Research: Participative Inquiry and Practice* (Thousand Oaks, CA: Sage Publications).

——, C.O. Scharmer, J. Jaworski, and B.S. Flowers (2005) *Presence: An Exploration of Profound Change in People, Organizations, and Society* (New York: Crown Books).

Shell (2008) *Scenarios: An Explorer's Guide* (The Hague: Shell International).

Sisodia, R.S. (2011) "Conscious Capitalism: A Better Way to Win," *California Management Review* 53.3: 98-108.

Sonnenwald, D.H., M.C. Whitton, and K.L. Maglaughlin (2003) "Scientific Collaboratories: Evaluating Their Potential," *Interactions* 10.4: 9-10.

Srivastva, S., and D. Cooperrider (1986) "The Emergence of the Egalitarian Organization," *Human Relations* 39.8: 683-724.

Stein, H.F. (1994) *Listening Deeply* (Boulder, CO: Westview Press).

Stookey, C.W. (2012) *Keep Your People in the Boat: Workforce Engagement Lessons from the Sea* (Halifax, Nova Scotia: ALIA Press).

Taylor, B. (2007) *Learning for Tomorrow: Whole Person Learning for the Planetary Citizen* (Boston Spa, UK: Oasis Press).

—— (2010) *Whole Person Learning in Action Manual* (Brussels: GRLI Press; Boston Spa, UK: Oasis Press).

—— (2012) *Ecology of the Soul* (Boston Spa, UK: Oasis Press, www.oasishuman relations.org.uk) .

Tuckman, B.W. (1965) "Development Sequences in Small Groups," *Psychological Bulletin* 63: 419-27.

Vis, J.K., H. Hamilton, and E. Lowitt, (2013) "Renewing the Global Food System," in E. Lowitt, *The Collaboration Economy: How to Meet Business, Social, and Environmental Needs and Gain Competitive Advantage* (San Francisco: Jossey-Bass).).

Watts, D.J., and S.H. Strogatz (1998) "Collective Dynamics of 'Small-World' Networks," *Nature* 393.6,684: 440-42.

Wenger, E. (1998) *Communities of Practice: Learning, Meaning, and Identity* (Cambridge, UK: Cambridge University Press).

Wheatley, M.J. (1993) *Leadership and the New Science: Discovering Order in a Chaotic World* (San Francisco, CA: Berrett-Koehler).

Wilson, T.P., J.M. Wimann, and D.H. Zimmerman (1984) "Models of Turn Taking in Conversational Interaction," *Journal of Language and Social Psychology* 3: 159-83.

Wulf, W. (1993) "The Collaboratory Opportunity," *Science* 261: 854-55.

Zadek, S. (2001) *The Civil Corporation: The New Economy of Corporate Citizenship* (London: Earthscan).

About the authors

 **Anders Aspling** received his master's in Economics and Business Administration and his doctorate in Business Administration at the Stockholm School of Economics. He served as President and Dean of the Swedish Institute of Management, as Dean of Vlerick Leuven Gent Management School, Belgium, Senior Vice President and member of the Executive Board of Siab/NCC, Sweden, and Senior Partner of the ForeSight Group, Sweden. He has been active as chairman, board member and senior adviser to numerous boards and organizations in Sweden and internationally, including the European Foundation for Management Development. He is also Secretary General, the Globally Responsible Leadership Initiative (GRLI), Professor at Tongji School of Economics and Management, Affiliated Professor at CENTRUM Graduate Business School and Chairman of the Advisory Board of Turku School of Economics. Anders has always been deeply engaged in issues of human development, social justice and economic and environmental sustainability with an explicit international outlook.
anders@aspling.net

 **Jacqueline Bagnall.** With an academic background in social psychology and a leadership development background centered on complexity, action learning and enquiry, Jackie enjoyed ten years based at the University of Exeter Business School. She joined the Centre for Leadership Studies at the University of Exeter in 2003 where she launched "Leadership Southwest" a regional center of excellence for leadership. This six-year project focused on developing leadership capacity in organizations across sectors such as health, education, sport, arts and commercial business. In addition to teaching and designing both postgraduate and undergraduate programs at Exeter, Jackie co-directed the One Planet MBA, joining a team of inspired colleagues all focused on changing the face of management education. She is currently based in an independent Quaker school in north Somerset in the UK, serving as Director of Peace and Global Studies.
Jacqueline.bagnall@sidcot.org.uk

Aboriginal colleagues call **Janette Blainey** their "sister" or "aunty." Many call her a "cultural interpreter." She originally studied at UNSW. Janette's passion for "learning" has been the driving force in her life and her career in education since the mid-1960s. Her work and learning experiences have taken her into families, communities and villages, into education and health institutions, bureaucracies and private- and public-sector business. She has worked with people of different ages and abilities and from different cultural backgrounds. Her work has taken her to cities, and communities in Australia, and to the Solomon Islands, Papua New Guinea, Hawaii, Fiji and Japan. She has given seminars in New Zealand and Switzerland. Janette values learning with and from native peoples and sees "respect" as the core of collaboration and the future.
janette@earthtrust.org.au

Eddie Blass is a foresight leader in higher education and an academic. She is currently Executive Director, Learning Innovations Hub at University of New England and specializes in developing new ways of working within higher education, new curriculum, and new pedagogic endeavors. She began her career in employee development and then specialized in leadership development before focusing further on the development of leaders, and the role of HE in achieving this. Eddie moved into foresight thinking when she completed her Doctorate of Education at Durham University presenting her thesis title "The Future University."
eddie.blass@gmail.com

Anthony F. Buono is Professor of Management and Sociology at Bentley University. He is also a former Chair of Bentley's Management Department and founding director of the Alliance for Ethics and Social Responsibility, which he oversaw from 2003 to 2013. Tony's primary research, teaching and consulting interests include organizational change, inter-organizational strategies, management consulting, and ethics and corporate social responsibility. He has written or edited 16 books including *The Human Side of Mergers and Acquisitions*, *A Primer on Organizational Behavior* and, most recently, *Facilitating Socio-Economic Intervention in Organizations*. His articles have appeared in numerous journals, including *Academy of Management Learning & Education*, *Across the Board*, *Administrative Science Quarterly*, *Human Relations*, *Journal of Organizational Change Management* and *Personnel Psychology*. He has a PhD in organizational sociology from Boston College.
abuono@bentley.edu

Bill Burck is a writer, collaboratory designer and facilitator who serves on the Executive Committee of The Value Web (www.thevalueweb.org). In the 1990s, he earned his MFA at Columbia College in Chicago and became a Certified Story Workshop Director. He taught writing workshops for ten years at Columbia while also working as an editor and publisher at trade associations. In 1994 he founded Kang Tai Press, which publishes books on traditional Chinese medicine. He began learning and practicing MG Taylor's DesignShop system and method for large group transformation in 1997. Today, he writes stories and designs and facilitates collaboratories that help groups change the world.
bill.burck@thevalueweb.org

Mark Drewell is thought and action leader at the global interface between business and society. He is CEO of the Globally Responsible Leadership Initiative and a senior partner of the Foresight Group. His background includes a decade on the Executive leadership team of Barloworld, chairing both Stockholm-based World's Children's Prize and Africa's largest indigenous environmental NGO, the Endangered Wildlife Trust, serving on the board of the International Association of Business Communicators and twice chairing its world conference, senior associate of the University of Cambridge Programme for Sustainability Leadership and working with the Aspen Institute to develop their Aspen Global Leaders Network. He serves on the Advisory Board of the Business School of Lausanne and is a Trustee of the Rudolph Steiner School South Devon. He was educated at Oxford University and is a fellow of the Royal Society for the Arts.
mark.drewell@grli.org

Thomas Dyllick has been a Professor of Sustainability Management and Managing Director of the Institute for Economy and the Environment at University of St. Gallen since 1994. He has published widely in the field of sustainability management and responsible management education. He served as Dean of the Management Department and as a Vice President for Teaching and Quality Development. Since 2011 he has served as University Delegate for Responsibility and Sustainability developing the broadly distributed activities in these fields. He is responsible for a core area in Sustainability Management as part of the Master in Business Management program and for an Executive Diploma in Managing Sustainable Business, jointly offered with Business School Lausanne and the World Business Council for Sustainable Development. He has been a founder and leading member of the 50+20 initiative and was directly involved in integrating Ethics, Responsibility and Sustainability into the EQUIS Standards for business school accreditation. He serves on the managing board of the Sustainable Development at Universities Programme in Switzerland.
Thomas.dyllick@unisg.ch

Patrick Frick is a member of The Value Web, an international network of designers and facilitators of collaboration focused on improving the state of the world. Patrick leads the organization's engagement with the World Economic Forum and the Forum of Young Global Leaders, bringing his expertise in design and facilitation of collaboration to their gatherings around the world, including the annual meeting in Davos. Patrick is a co-founder and partner of Social Investors (www.socialinvestors.com), a boutique philanthropy advisory and facilitation firm based in Switzerland. He works with affluent individuals and families worldwide, assisting them in maximizing the impact of their philanthropic engagements. He is a member of the Jury for the INDEX: Design Award, the world's largest design prize. Patrick has an MBA from the University of St. Gallen in Switzerland and studied politics and international relations at the Institut d'Etudes Politiques (Sciences Po) in Paris.
patrick.frick@thevalueweb.com

Ronald Fry received an M.S. and PhD in Organization Studies from MIT. He is Professor of Organizational Behavior at Case Western Reserve University where he has directed the EMBA and MPOD degree programs to national prominence. Ron's research in the areas of team development, functioning of the executive, organization change, Appreciative Inquiry, and adult development has resulted in ten books and over 50 articles and book chapters. As one of the co-creators of the Appreciative Inquiry theory and method, he works with organizations worldwide on how to engage whole systems in strategic thinking and change. His research continues to develop insights on large group dynamics, appreciative leadership, and businesses as agents for world benefit. Ron currently heads the World Inquiry for the Fowler Center for Sustainable Value, a global search for transformative innovations that create mutual benefit for business and society.
rxf5@case.edu

Louie Gardiner, MBA, joined Sheffield Council (UK) in 1984. On a six-month sabbatical, she drove across Africa raising awareness about the plight of the Black Rhino. In a multi-stakeholder team creating a ten-year blueprint for Sheffield, she led on health and community engagement. Louie pioneered a community leadership program for women, gaining best-practice accolades within UK health and sports governing bodies. As Partner Consultant in Priority Focus, she created unique frameworks for guiding systemic planning and stakeholder engagement. She led Corporate Performance Management and Development in Barnsley Council before being appointed Chief Executive of Centell (UK). In 2005 she established Potent 6. As an executive coach, facilitator and consultant partnering leaders in multinationals, public, health and third-sector bodies, she specializes in influencing change within complex human systems. She works pro bono within IofC.
louie.gardiner@potent6.co.uk

Jonas Haertle is Head of the Principles for Responsible Management Education (PRME) secretariat of the UN Global Compact Office. He provides global leadership in bringing together good practice in implementing the principles of PRME and the Global Compact. Previously, he was the coordinator of the Global Compact's Local Networks in Latin America, Africa and the Middle East. Before joining the UN, he worked as a research analyst for the German public broadcasting service Norddeutscher Rundfunk. He has written and contributed to a number of publications on corporate sustainability and responsible management education and serves on the editorial boards of the *Journal of Corporate Citizenship* and the *Sustainability Accounting, Management and Policy Journal*. He holds a master's degree in European Studies from Hamburg University. As a Fulbright scholar, he also attained an MSc in Global Affairs from Rutgers University. haertle@un.org

Zaid Hassan is the co-founder of Reos Partners, where he currently serves as Managing Partner of the Oxford office. He has over a decade of experience in developing strategic responses to complex social challenges, including aboriginal issues, climate change, child malnutrition, employment, energy, financial systems, global food systems, and security issues. He has a background in technology and communications. He left university to join the dot.com boom, setting up his own company, Anthropic, which focused on the delivery of new media and the social implications of technology. His extensive start-up experience includes two years as Chief Technology Office for smartchange, a non-profit start-up. Zaid is a strategic adviser to a number of organizations, writes for various publications and has just released a book on addressing complex challenges, *The Social Labs Revolution*. hassan@reospartners.com

Dr Peter Hayward is a foresight practitioner and academic. He specializes in helping organizations and communities act creatively with the future in mind—learning to see the world differently and find hopeful and inspiring futures. He is the Program Director of the Masters of Strategic Foresight that is offered at Swinburne University in Melbourne. That is the only postgraduate qualification in foresight that is offered in Australia. He began his career as an accountant and economist working for the Australian Taxation Office. Increasingly he became interested in how change happens and then how people create change. After studying systems thinking at the University of Western Sydney he became interested in the idea of how individuals and organizations can create positive futures. pmirv@aol.com

Stephen Hickman is an educationalist with over two decades of management experience in distribution and marketing. He holds an MBA, Diploma in Management, PG Dip Higher Education (HE) and PG Cert e-Learning. In 2011 Stephen was awarded a Senior Fellowship of the HE Academy. After several years with the University of Greenwich and a subsequent role as HE Manager with Cornwall College, Stephen joined the University of Exeter Business School as interim Director for the Exeter MBA. He led the transition to the new One Planet MBA, a collaboration with WWF, before in 2011 directing a curriculum change initiative to embed sustainability in the MSc International Management. Stephen now has a new role at Exeter: leading Business School activity in Cornwall, developing a new undergraduate provision in Sustainability and Social Innovation.
s.Hickman@exeter.ac.uk

Adam Kahane is a partner in Reos Partners. He is the author of *Solving Tough Problems: An Open Way of Talking, Listening, and Creating New Realities*; *Power and Love: A Theory and Practice of Social Change*; and *Transformative Scenario Planning*. During the early 1990s, Adam was head of Social, Political, Economic and Technological Scenarios for Royal Dutch Shell in London. He has held strategy and research positions with Pacific Gas and Electric Company (San Francisco), the OECD (Paris), the International Institute for Applied Systems Analysis (Vienna), the Institute for Energy Economics (Tokyo) and the Universities of Oxford, Toronto, British Columbia, California and the Western Cape. Adam has an MA in Energy and Resource Economics from the University of California, and an MA in Applied Behavioral Science from Bastyr University.
kahane@reospartners.com

Claire Maxwell has been a Co-Director of the Oasis School of Human Relations since 2011. She specializes in developing collaborative and creative approaches to whole organizational development. With a background in theatre and films, Claire went into social work, specializing in residential care of older people, community work and child protection. At senior management level in social services she led internal change processes and gained a master's degree focusing on approaches to change and leadership in hierarchical organizations. Also qualified as a lecturer, Claire worked as an independent consultant for ten years. She is developing innovative approaches to the teaching of Globally Responsible Practice within international MBA programs and co-facilitating a process with program directors exploring the integration of whole person learning into leadership development. She is a Fellow of the Royal Society of Arts and Chair of the Guardian Group of the GRLI Council of Partners.
claire@oasishumanrelations.org.uk

Philip Mirvis is an organizational psychologist whose studies and private practice concern large-scale organizational change, characteristics of the workforce and workplace, and business leadership in society. An adviser to companies and NGOs on five continents, he has authored 12 books including *The Cynical Americans*, *Building the Competitive Workforce*, *Joining Forces*, *To the Desert and Back* and *Beyond Good Company: Next Generation Corporate Citizenship*. He teaches in executive education programs in business schools around the world. He is a Fellow of the Global Network on Corporate Citizenship, Board Member of the PYXERA Global, a Washington, DC-based international development NGO, and formerly a Trustee of the Foundation for Community Encouragement and Society for Organization Learning. He received a career achievement award as "Distinguished Scholar-Practitioner" from the Academy of Management.
pmirv@aol.com

Katrin Muff began her career in the late 80s with Schindler Lifts in Lucerne and then in Australia. She holds an MBA and a doctoral degree from Business School Lausanne (BSL). A Swiss native, Katrin worked for nearly a decade for ALCOA in Switzerland as a Business Analyst, in the United States in Mergers & Acquisitions and in Moscow, Russia, as General Manager. After a one-year sabbatical dedicated to film making, Katrin joined IAMS as Director for Strategic Planning EMEA in the Netherlands. Back in Switzerland since 2000, she co-founded Yupango, a coaching consultancy for start-up companies. In 2004–06, she coached and facilitated three Swiss universities to create a competence center. Returning to BSL as Dean in 2008, Katrin led the school's transformation to combine sustainability, responsibility and entrepreneurship in education and applied research. As one of the initiators of 50+20, she developed the collaboratory idea for RIO+20.
katrin.muff@bsl-lausanne.ch

John North is a next-generation integrational entrepreneur, operating across the boundaries of society, business and academia. An MBA graduate, who created two online businesses during his undergraduate degree, he worked as an international strategy consultant advising Fortune 500 companies and was the founding head of Accenture's sustainability practice in Ireland. His passion to make a difference in his home country brought him back to South Africa in 2009. John and his wife Zilla are active in a number of community resilience initiatives in the Garden Route, where they live with their two daughters. John holds an international role as Head of Projects for the Brussels-based, UN-backed Globally Responsible Leadership Initiative and is also a senior adviser to the University of Pretoria's Albert Luthuli Centre for Responsible Leadership.
john.north@grli.org

Caroline Rennie founded and leads ren-new, a consultancy that focuses on helping people and organizations make sustainability profitable. Caroline was Director Communications Environment for Tetra Pak International where she reframed sustainability as a business issue and secured sustainability in its brand positioning. Prior to Tetra Pak, Caroline founded the Environmental Affairs function at Continental Can PET Division, and was Environmental Affairs Director through its expansion to become the largest PET company globally. She has also overseen development of recycling regulations as Political Advisor to the California Waste Management Board. She has a master's degree in Public Administration from the University of Pennsylvania and teaches executive students materiality, sustainability frameworks, risks and opportunities, capturing value and solving tough problems at Business School Lausanne. She works with clients such as Alstom, P&G, WWF and Unilever.
rennie@ren-new.com

Svenja Rüger is President at The Value Web, an international non-profit association focusing on multi-sector/multi-stakeholder collaboration in transformational projects for a more sustainable, equitable world. She takes on design lead and venture management roles with the World Economic Forum, UNESCO, INSEAD, Berlin Civil Society Centre, and several foundations. Svenja has brought the processes of collaborative group work to the world since 2001. Her focus is on social entrepreneurship engagements that give a voice to those who create and sustain social value. She also works as an independent facilitator and project manager applying techniques from improvisational theatre and collective group engagement. Holding a BA in International Business and Economic Studies, Svenja is also a happy mother, competitive swimmer, climber, painter, storyteller and networker connecting people around a common set of values.
svenja.rueger@thevalueweb.org

Otto Scharmer is a Senior Lecturer at MIT, and founding chair of the Presencing Institute. He chairs the MIT IDEAS program and co-founded the Global Wellbeing Lab. He also is Vice Chair of the World Economic Forum's Global Agenda Council on Leadership. In his books *Theory U* and *Presence* (the latter co-authored with Senge, Jaworski, and Flowers) he introduced the concept of "presencing"—learning from the emerging future. His new book *Leading From the Emerging Future: From Ego-system to Eco-system Economies* (2013) applies mindfulness to the transformation of business, society, and self.
www.ottoscharmer.com, www.presencing.com

Grégoire Serikoff is a strategic designer and facilitator based in Paris. He is a co-founder of The Value Web and a leading member of the Accelerated Solutions Environment network since 2000. Both are networks of professionals developing "co-design" to engage communities in complex problem-solving. In the past ten years, Greg has developed a multidisciplinary approach to facilitate innovation in systems, processes, interactions, communication, workspaces and visual design. Co-design expert for the World Economic Forum, Greg has run multiple sessions at Davos since 2005. His professional background includes journalism and working with the French Ministry for Foreign Affairs and Médecins du Monde (Doctors of the World) in Chechnya and Kosovo. Former Secretary General of Icograda (International Design Alliance), he is a regional ambassador of Index: Design to Improve Life.
gregoire.serikoff@thevalueweb.org

Paul Shrivastava is the David O'Brien Distinguished Professor and Director of the David O'Brien Centre for Sustainable Enterprise at Concordia University, Montreal. He also leads the International Chair for Arts and Sustainable Enterprise at ICN Business School, Nancy, France. He founded several private companies, non-profit organizations, and the ONE Division of the Academy of Management. He received his PhD from the University of Pittsburgh. He was tenured Associate Professor of Management at the Stern School of Business, NYU, and held the Howard I. Scott Chair in Management at Bucknell University. He has published 17 books and over 100 articles in scholarly journals, and serves on the editorial boards of numerous journals. He won a Fulbright Senior Scholar Award at Kyoto University.
paul.shri@gmail.com

Aaron Williamson. As an artist, facilitator, consultant and designer, Aaron uses the design of information to help decision-makers parse complexity and communicate their strategies, and the design of collaborative processes to enable diverse stakeholder groups to collectively solve seemingly intractable problems. A member of The Value Web, he also runs his own company, vis.uali.st, a white-label visual thinking, information design and facilitation service for consulting companies wanting to enrich their collaborative engagement with clients. A graduate of Queen's University at Kingston, Aaron's experience as a technology entrepreneur, a teacher and trainer and as a management consultant combine with his years of intensive training in Zen, ascetic training in Aikido and extensive travel to give him a nuanced perspective on learning, human dynamics and communication in all its forms.
aaron.williamson@thevalueweb.org